Guide to Social Assessment

Other Titles in This Series

Social Impact Assessment Series
C. P. Wolf, General Editor

Guide to Social Assessment:
A Framework for Assessing Social Change
Kristi Branch, Douglas A. Hooper,
James Thompson, and James Creighton

Designed to provide clear and detailed assistance in the complex process of assessing social change, this book emphasizes the development of an analytic approach and a theoretical framework that can be applied to the assessment of very diverse events--changes in the natural environment, the local economy, or the dominant technology. The guide, based on a sociological perspective that highlights the importance of community social organization in analyzing social change, focuses on the development of user skills in assessment design, research, analysis, and presentation.

The guide's theoretical basis and emphasis on the interrelationships that create social change make it valuable to those studying social change in general, as well as to those responsible for conducting or utilizing social impact assessments. Detailed "how to" information, clear writing, and careful design impart the skills necessary to identify and analyze the factors and processes leading to social change and to interpret and present research findings in an effective manner.

Kristi Branch, now with Battelle's Human Affairs Research Center, was senior social scientist at Mountain West Research, Inc., when the book was prepared. Douglas A. Hooper is assistant professor of management, Eastern Mountain College at Billings, Montana. James Thompson is president of Western Research Corporation. James Creighton is president of Creighton and Creighton, a consulting firm.

Guide to Social Assessment

A Framework for Assessing Social Change

Kristi Branch, Douglas A. Hooper,
James Thompson, and
James Creighton

Westview Press / Boulder and London

Social Impact Assessment Series

Published in 1984 in the United States of America by Westview Press, Inc.,
5500 Central Avenue, Boulder, Colorado 80301; Frederick A. Praeger, Publisher

Library of Congress Catalog Card Number: 84-50793
ISBN: 0-86531-717-8

Composition for this book was provided by the authors
Printed and bound in the United States of America

10   9   8   7   6   5   4   3   2

Contents

SECTION I: GENERAL PRINCIPLES

SECTION II: A FRAMEWORK FOR SOCIAL ASSESSMENT

Figures

LIST OF FIGURES (cont.)

Preface

Large-scale industrial or resource development projects, infrastructure development, social policy changes, the introduction of new technologies, and alteration of the economic structure all can produce considerable change in how people in the affected areas live. During the last decade, increased attention has been given to the effects of large-scale projects and rapid technological change on the natural and human environment. Efforts to anticipate and evaluate these effects have been expanded.

As with the other natural and social sciences, the characteristics and methodology of social assessment have evolved through trial and error, as sociologists, decision makers, and the affected population have struggled with the problems of forecasting and mitigating the social effects of diverse resource decisions and technological changes. The purpose of the guide is to provide assistance to those concerned with the social effects of change. The objectives of the guide are to provide an analytic framework, a theoretical model, and a method of research and analysis that will help social scientists design and conduct social assessments that are informative, defensible, and useful. Some users will be most interested in the guide for its contribution to their ability to examine and understand the dynamics of social change from a research or academic perspective. Others will be more concerned with the effectiveness of the guide in assisting them to conduct assessments that will influence decisions. It is designed to do both.

The guide was written for sociologists and other social science or planning practitioners with an interest in social change. It therefore assumes some background in one of the social sciences or planning areas, although those with training in resource management or business and an interest in social change could also use it effectively. To the extent possible, a minimum of special social science terminology has been used; logic, analytic thought, and applied research skills are emphasized. This is not to suggest that the methodology in this guide is somehow less "scientific," only that considerable effort has gone into developing a sound analytic framework which is stated as simply as possible and which emphasizes practical application.

Much of the work that went into the development of the guide was instigated by the need for social assessments that helped decision

makers by providing the social information necessary for more informed decisions. For this reason, considerable attention has been
paid to the development of procedures that produce usable information. An assessment methodology should produce documents that effectively identify the issues, analyze the information, and present
the conclusions in a manner that enables the decision makers to understand and have confidence in them, and, most importantly, to use
and apply them. Given the broader and somewhat less instrumental
interest that some readers have in analyzing or anticipating social
change, however, attention has also been paid to the development of
a generally applicable and theoretically based approach that would
enhance social science research on these topics.

For social assessment to be valued, it must be rigorous and valid, it must help people solve problems, it must be presented in
terms that have meaning to people, and it must exhibit sensitivity
to practical realities. We hope the guide can help you accomplish
these goals.

Kristi Branch, Douglas A. Hooper,
James Thompson, and James Creighton

Acknowledgments

To a very great extent, this **Guide to Social Assessment:** **A Framework for Assessing Social Change** is derived from the work conducted as part of the Bureau of Land Management's Social Effects Project (Contract No. AA851-CTO-46). This two-year project provided the opportunity to bring together a team of experienced sociologists to undertake an extensive review of the literature, conduct field work in ten rural communities, develop an analytic framework for social assessment, and prepare a guide for use by Bureau of Land Management social science staff in conducting social assessments of resource management alternatives. We would like to acknowledge the critical role this project and the BLM project coordinators -- Dr. Paul Myers and Ms. Julia Jordan -- played in the preparation of this book. We would also like to thank Bert Bresch and Judy Majewski, BLM social scientists, who had the courage and good grace to field test the draft version of the guide. Their diligence in this effort and their insightful, constructive criticism enabled us to identify and correct many problems and to improve the utility of the guide. In addition, we would like to thank the many BLM social scientists and managers who reviewed the early drafts of the guide and offered suggestions for its improvement. We would also like to thank Dr. William Freudenburg and his students for their review comments.

We also wish to acknowledge our debts to Stan Albrecht, Pamela Bergmann, Patrick Jobes, Robert Kimble, Errol Meidinger, James Moore, Steve Murdock, David Pijawka, Allan Schnaiberg, Matt Snipp, Gene Summers, Ken Wilkinson, and Gary Williams, whose knowledge, insights, and hard work on the BLM Social Effects Project provided the basis for this work and whose good humor and enthusiasm encouraged us to undertake the task of preparing this manuscript. Stan Albrecht, Gene Summers, and Ken Wilkinson deserve special recognition for their contributions to the conceptual issues addressed in the guide. We thank them all.

Many people have contributed to the preparation of this manuscript. Our thanks and appreciation are extended to Marie Tomasik, production manager, Janice von Vogt and Sharon Vaissiere, technical editors, Lauren Larson and Sue Tucker, word processing operators, and Ken Kunz, graphic artist.

K. B., D.A.H., J. T., J. C.

Section I:
General Principles

1. Introduction

1.1   Overview

Since the mid-1960s, a combination of national events and public values have caused renewed interest in communities and social change. The environmental movement, the reversal in urban-rural migration patterns, the energy crisis, new technologies for resource development, the decentralization of economic activities, and an increased concern for individual well-being and local political participation shifted attention from the processes and problems of urbanization and the major urban centers to smaller towns and rural areas. As a result, a wide variety of social scientists and public administrators have reevaluated the importance of the community and of the changes occurring in rural areas and the smaller towns of the country. The community as a functional social and administrative unit has reemerged as a central element in efforts to understand or control the processes of social change. The theoretical framework developed in the guide reflects this renewed emphasis on the community as a functional unit and the importance of community resources and social organization to the lives of their residents.

1.2   How to Use the Guide

The guide has been prepared as a reference manual that can be consulted either for general advice or for more specific direction on particular problems. For this reason, the guide includes a great deal of information. To make it easier to use, it is organized into sections so that you can refer to the material appropriate to the assessment you are conducting. In some cases, information that has been presented in one section has also been included in another. This has been done to make the guide more efficient as a reference document.

The complexity of social change precludes the development of a method for assessment that prescribes each analysis and anticipates each conclusion. The purpose of the guide is not to provide a specific answer for each of your questions, but to help you develop an approach that will lead you to ask the salient questions, obtain the pertinent information, and conduct an informed and rigorous analysis of your data. Social assessment is not a rote task; it requires conceptualization and complex analysis. It is difficult, but it is also very interesting and challenging. Much remains unknown about the mechanisms and meaning of social change. The guide has been designed to help you make optimal use of the knowledge that does exist, and to encourage research and analysis that will further our understanding of these complex processes.

1.3   Organization of the Guide

The guide is divided into three major sections: Section I, General Principles; Section II, A Framework for Social Assessment; and Section III, Research Methods and Techniques.

The first section presents an overview of the assessment process. It discusses the purposes of social assessment and the particular problems and issues involved in the social assessment process. The general approach advocated by the guide is then described, followed by presentation of the analytic and theoretical framework that underlie the methodology that is developed in Section II.

Sections II and III are more technical. Section II is a "how to" guide explaining how to design and conduct a social assessment that effectively meets the institutional and scientific goals set for it. Procedures for integrating and adapting the social assessment effort to the larger planning and decision-making process are suggested. Section III provides guidance on the use of social assessment research methods such as field trips, interviews, and surveys. Two technical appendixes, one on demographic forecasting and one on facilities/services/fiscal assessment, are included for those with an interest or responsibility in these areas.

This three section structure with appendixes has been utilized to ensure that the principal issues and analytic framework of the social assessment process are not obscured by too much technical detail and to allow those with different interests to more readily pick and choose what they need. The index has been designed to facilitate this type of reference use.

2. The Purposes of Social Assessment

2.1 Introduction

Many decision makers and managers do not have a clear understanding of the purpose and utility of social assessment. This chapter describes some of the major applications of social assessment information and discusses why this information is important to policy makers and managers as well as to social scientists.

2.2 Background

Throughout history, communities and their residents have been shaped by the interplay of forces that cause social change. The American West, for example, is sprinkled with ghost towns that stand as monuments to the power such forces can exert on communities and their residents. In the United States, such changes have traditionally been viewed as part of the natural course of things, with the outcomes interpreted as demonstration of economic forces that were beyond anyone's responsibility or control.

Recently, however, in large part as a consequence of the environmental movement, a quiet revolution has taken place in what we believe can and ought to be controlled and what must be attended to when making decisions, formulating policy, or evaluating alternatives. Although undeniably important, it is now less frequently assumed that economic justifications are the only criteria to be considered. It is now generally accepted that health and safety, environmental enhancement, mitigation of social impacts, and equitable distribution of benefits and costs, along with long-term organizational consequences, must also be taken into account.

There is continuing disagreement about just how these considerations should be incorporated into the decision-making processes of our country. There is no common agreement on just how much responsibility belongs to companies, which problems are properly the responsibility of government instead of the private sector or the individual, or on how much regulation is appropriate. There is, however, increasing agreement that it is appropriate to identify and consider this wider range of impacts, to make them visible, and to help people understand more clearly what the consequences are likely to be before decisions are made or policies are set.

Over the last two decades, this consensus has been incorporated into numerous laws and regulations that require governmental agencies and those utilizing public resources to clearly identify the economic, environmental, and social impacts of a project or policy before making a decison or taking action. This has led to the implementation of large-scale, comprehensive evaluation projects as well as to the inclusion of "social impact assessments" in the formal planning and decision-making processes of state and federal governments -- and by extension, into those of private businesses and interest groups. In addition, social scientists, planners, and government officials, all of whom have an intrinsic interest in understanding the relationships between different components of the economic, social, and political system, have continued to press for better information and greater attention to these issues in the ongoing research and policy formulaton processes.

2.3   Why Consider Social Information

There are a number of reasons to consider social information. Some -- those most influential in justifying social impact assessments or evaluation studies -- are related quite directly to decision making. Others are more generic and less closely related to decisions about specific programs or projects. Some commonly identified uses of social information are:

1) To predict the ability of a community or group to adapt to changing conditions
2) To define the problems or clarify the issues involved in a proposed change
3) To anticipate and assess impacts on the quality of life
4) To illuminate the meaning and importance of anticipated change
5) To identify mitigation opportunities or requirements
6) To fulfill or comply with regulations and policies

These are discussed briefly below.

To Predict the Ability and Willingness of a Community or Group to Adapt to Changing Conditions

One of the major problems in trying to determine or anticipate the social consequences of an action or policy is that the cause-and-effect relationships are not at all simple. Unlike chemicals or laboratory animals, people talk back. They act purposively. Different people and different communities react differently to similar events. When people obtain information about a proposed action or policy, they are likely to act differently because of that information, thus altering the sequence of events and outcomes. Social researchers are involved in providing information to decision makers and affected parties. Social assessment must therefore take into account the effect such information will have on decision makers and the various affected parties in terms of their ability and willingness to implement their plans or adapt to the changing conditions.

During the research leading to the preparation of this guide, it became clear that it was never possible to say categorically that a particular feature of a project -- such as the introduction of a large number of construction workers into a community -- would produce a particular impact. Instead, it became very clear that how the community was organized and how it responded were at least equally as important as project characteristics in determining what the impact would be. An important function of social assessment is to obtain and analyze the necessary information about community organization and likely responses to changing conditions.

To Define the Problems or Clarify the Issues

As implied by the previous discussion, social information is often critical to the identification and understanding of the problems and conflicts of a community or group. In some cases, existing conflicts or problems may dramatically affect the ability or willingness of a community or group to respond effectively to change. In some circumstances, aggravating existing problems or conflicts, or creating new ones, can affect the community's ability to cope with other issues that were previously manageable. It can also affect the quality of life in the community. Frequently, opposition to or support of a proposed action can be understood and addressed only when underlying issues, vested interests, or misperceptions are identified and analyzed. Social information is the basis for this analysis.

To Anticipate and Assess Impacts on the Quality of Life

It is abundantly clear that there are many important qualities of life that are not captured in reports on the gross national product or distribution of personal income or wealth. Often these qualities are called "intangibles" because they are subjective and difficult to quantify. But at a personal level, they are a very real part of what makes life pleasurable and worth living. Among other things, these factors can include feeling a part of the community where you live; knowing where you stand in relationship to other people; having a sense that you and people in your community have control over the decisions that affect your future; knowing that your government strives to act in ways that benefit everyone equitably, rather than benefiting just a privileged few; living without undue fear of crime, personal attack, or environmental hazard; and feeling confident that your children will get a fair start in life.

All of these concerns are social, and while they may be hard to quantify, their absence can contribute to behaviors that are indeed quantifiable, such as suicide, divorce, health problems, delinquency, crime, mental illness, alcoholism, and other socially and

personally destructive actions. Of course, for many individuals, a
change in these factors doesn't result in anything this dramatic.
It simply results in people not feeling good about themselves, their
community, and their lives.

Behaviors for which there are clear consequences (such as suicide or alcoholism, for example) can be translated at least partial-
ly into economic terms by considering the economic costs of dealing
with these problems. Such figures, however, even if they could be
calculated accurately, would not tell the full story. The personal
and organizational consequences of these behaviors must also be considered to give a true accounting. We still lack valid methods of
quantification and a reliable scale by which these types of effects
can be compared. In real world situations, it is still only possible to describe, not to quantify, the probable impacts of a proposed action upon those factors which we lump together and call "the
quality of life." Judgments about the relative importance of these
impacts, and the actions they warrant, are, however, informed and
improved by social information.

To Illuminate the Meaning and Importance of Anticipated Change

In advising decision makers or assisting in the formulation of
policy, it is not enough to know what changes an action will cause.
It is also necessary to know what those changes will mean to the
people who will be affected by them. If you know, for example, that
an increase in population will result in people losing the feeling
of knowing and being known by everybody in town, you must also be
prepared to ask whether this matters. Is it significant? Is it
important enough that it could cause a decline in people's sense of
well-being or the ability or willingness of the community to respond? The obvious answer is that such a change would be very important to some people and relatively unimportant to others. In
other words, the meaning of a change is determined substantially by
people's reaction to it.

One important objective of social research is to determine what
meaning a probable impact would have for a community and its residents. Would this impact be seen as very significant or unimportant? Positive or negative? Could the project materially affect
something that people consider an important aspect of their way of
life, of their culture? This kind of information is extremely important when weighing the importance of social impacts in relation
to the other types of impacts that might occur.

To Identify Mitigation Opportunities or Requirements

Another important use of social information is to determine how
those initiating an action or policy can design it to cause the
least adverse and most beneficial impacts, and to identify responses
from the community and affected persons that will encourage favorable outcomes. With the advent of the Environmental Impact Statement, the word "mitigation" has become a regular part of assessment
terminology. The term simply means actions taken to alter the

consequences of a project by minimizing or eliminating negative impacts and maximizing positive ones. Social assessment information can be crucial in determining what mitigation is necessary, what mitigation alternatives exist, and which mitigation strategies are most likely to work. As stated before, different communities will react differently, and understanding the social organization of a particular community -- and project sponsoring agency -- is very important in determining which strategies will work in a particular situation.

To Fulfill or Comply with Regulations and Policies

The value of social assessment to the decision maker and the public has been formally recognized in legislation, and a number of legal and policy requirements for social assessment have been established. Principal among these are (1) the National Environmental Policy Act of 1969 (NEPA), which established a national policy requiring comprehensive, systematic evaluation of the effects on the natural and human environment of major federal actions, and (2) the rules and regulations established by the Council on Environmental Quality (CEQ) to implement this policy. Section 102 of NEPA states:

> The Congress authorizes and directs that, to the fullest extent possible ... agencies of the federal government shall ... utilize a systematic interdisciplinary approach which will ensure the integrated use of the natural and social sciences and the environmental design arts in planning and in decision making which may have an impact on man's environment ...

The activities of individual federal agencies are further governed by additional legislation and many states have passed laws requiring similar action by their agencies. Existing regulations and policies make clear that the social effects of major federal or state actions, or actions utilizing federal or state resources, must be identified and considered in the decision-making process. This legislation, as well as grass-roots pressure from affected citizens, has provided the impetus for greatly increased attention to these issues and for improved methods of social assessment.

2.4 Summary

Important applications of social information are found in the evaluation of intentional, planned decisions such as the formulation of social policies, resource management decisions, and project or program implementation. Efforts to hold government more accountable to its mandate of acting in "the public good" have resulted in specific regulations such as NEPA and have increased the allocation of resources for the development and application of specialized techniques for "impact assessment" -- whose fundamental purpose is to determine what difference a particular action or decision will make. But social change does not come about only through planned or intentional actions. Social assessment is also pertinent to the examination of change due to less coherent factors such as techno-logical innovations and demographic trends.

Inherent in the assessment process is a comparison between what will happen if particular actions are taken or a particular set of decisions are made, and what will happen if they are not. This comparative focus, and the increasing utilization of social information in policy formulation and management decisions has highlighted the need for social scientists to clarify the cause-and-effect relationships that underly their analyses; to utilize an analytic framework that focuses the research effort on pertinent issues; and to present their findings clearly, with a decision-making orientation. Since the purposes and techniques of impact assessment and the application of social information in this context may not yet be clear, the next chapter discusses more fully the assessment process and the role of social assessment in the project evaluation and resource management decision-making process.

3. Decision Making and the Assessment Process

3.1 Introduction

This chapter presents an overview of the decision-making context in which many social assessments are conducted. It outlines the major steps involved in an impact assessment, and discusses the special features of the social assessment process. The relationship between social assessment and the other components of a typical environmental impact assessment are described to illustrate the role of social assessment in one of its common applications and to provide a background for the discussions in Section II.

3.2 Overview of the Assessment Process

General Principles

Throughout the guide, social assessment is presented as an analytic process. Social assessment is a series of research and analytic activities that have different objectives at different stages of the particular decision-making process being implemented. Limiting the use of the assessment to only one aspect of this process divorces it from the way decisions are made (no matter what the proposed action) and almost guarantees that the assessment will be of limited value.

The focus and content of an assessment depends greatly upon the type of actions proposed and the type of decisions to be made. Each assessment is unique. Learning to design a social assessment that is appropriate to the type of action being proposed, the particular decision being made, or the specific research questions being asked is the first major social assessment activity. The ability to evaluate the context of the assessment and design an effective approach is critical to the ability to conduct a good social assessment. Practical experience with social assessment and other applied social research reveals two general principles that should be kept in mind when preparing to do a social assessment:

1) **Different assessment activities are appropriate at different stages of the decision-making or research process.**

11

Social assessment, like most applied social research, evolves through stages. Assessment activities should vary by decision level, stage in the decision-making process, type of proposed action, and extent of existing information. The assessment activities of each new stage must be formulated in light of what has been learned during the preceding stages, reframing and reshaping the questions being addressed and the type of information being collected.

2) **The social assessment must be well integrated with the decision-making process at all levels, and must either be integrated with or subsume the public involvement responsibilities.** If the social assessment loses touch with the decision process, it may research the wrong questions, expend its resources on noncritical issues, or alienate key personnel. This increases the danger that the assessment will be ignored by the decision makers because the information is not useful, its utility is not clear, or its significance is discovered too late to be effectively incorporated into the decision-making process. Because of its subject matter and methods, social assessment involves much public contact and depends upon knowledge of public attitudes and actions. Those conducting a social assessment must therefore be attuned to the positions of various special interest groups and well acquainted with the public involvement program. In some cases they may assume public involvement tasks. If this sensitivity to others with an interest in the assessment is not maintained, the entire assessment effort will suffer.

The Decision-Making Process

A simple five-step process describes the decision-making context of many social assessments. These five steps are common to most resource management decision-making processes, especially those affected by NEPA regulations, although the particular terminology may differ. An important feature of this sequence is that it provides a systematic method for identifying the problem, evaluating the alternatives, and reaching a decision.

1) **Problem Identification and Scoping.** The purpose of this step is to establish the nature of the decision to be made and to identify the major issues and problems that need to be addressed. Social assessment can contribute to this effort by identifying the nature of the social consequences that might need to be considered; by providing information about the general magnitude of possible social effects; and by noting aspects of the implementing agency, organization, or decision-making process that affect the scope of the assessment or the manner in which it will proceed.

2) **Formulation of Alternatives.** The purpose of this step is to establish the range of alternatives to be considered and

to identify or formulate the alternatives that fall within that range. Although the latitude participants have in formulating alternatives varies widely from one instance to another, this step is often divided into two parts: (1) formulation of broad, conceptual alternatives; and (2) formulation of specific proposals. The person responsible for the social assessment can contribute to this effort by ensuring that alternatives suggested by others, especially the affected public, are presented for consideration; by identifying new alternatives that would be desirable to the various stakeholder groups in the affected area; and by identifying specific aspects of proposed alternatives that make them unacceptable, infeasible, or particularly advantageous. The positions of organizations and local groups toward the various alternatives can often be clarified. In addition, social assessment techniques can provide preliminary information about the nature, magnitude, and meaning of the social effects likely to result from the types of alternatives being developed.

3) **Evaluation of Alternatives.** A central feature of the decision-making process is the evaluation of the various alternatives. In this step, the impacts likely to be caused by each alternative are identified, evaluated, and compared to those of the other alternatives being considered. Social assessment not only provides the evaluation of the social impacts of the proposed alternatives but frequently also helps assess the meaning and relative importance of the changes forecast in other areas as well (for example, wildlife and recreation).

4) **Formulation of Mitigation Measures and Evaluation of Mitigated Alternatives.** The purpose of this step is to identify measures that could be used to mitigate the adverse and enhance the positive effects of the proposed alternatives, to evaluate the effects of the alternatives when mitigation measures have been applied, and to select a preferred alternative. Social assessment contributes to this task by identifying ways to mitigate or enhance the social effects of the alternatives; by helping evaluate the feasibility and acceptability of various mitigation measures; and by forecasting, evaluating, and comparing the social impacts likely to be caused by the mitigated alternatives.

5) **Design of an Implementation Plan and Monitoring Program.** The objectives of this step are (1) to design a plan for implementing the preferred alternative that incorporates the designated mitigation measures and (2) to develop a monitoring program that will document the consequences of project implementation. In many cases, social science research, organizational analysis, and program evaluation skills are needed in the design and implementation of the implementation plan and monitoring program.

3.3   The Social Assessment Process
The Generic Approach

The Basic Steps

Social assessment, as an analytic process, can be applied to each of the five decision-making steps described above. In designing an assessment that meets its research objectives and the needs of the decision maker, the level and scope of the social assessment must be adapted to the particular context in which it is being undertaken. The social assessment process is based on the premises that (1) change occurs through a process of cause-and-effect relationships; (2) these relationships can be analyzed; and (3) this analytic process can be used effectively to forecast social change, within the limitations imposed by the complexity and emergent nature of human response and social organization.

The need for a rigorously analytic approach is stressed throughout the guide. Projected impacts must be tied to the proposed action through a logical and theoretically sound analytic process. It is by identifying the important cause-and-effect relationships, analyzing their interactions, and weighing their relative dominance that judgments about social impacts can be made and defended.

Within this basic analytic framework, the impact assessment process is typically organized in a manner similar to that shown in Figure 3-1. The fundamental purpose of an assessment is to determine what difference a particular "proposed action" -- a decision, project, or event such as a technological innovation or institutional change -- will make. The assessment process therefore requires careful distinction between changes caused by the proposed action and changes caused by other, unrelated factors. Inherent in the assessment process, as shown in Figure 3-1, is a comparison between what will happen if a proposed action occurs and what will happen if it does not.

Users of the guide are likely to be concerned about proposed actions which have the potential to cause effects on the natural and human environment for an extended period of time, often months or years. Indeed, one of the major concerns of an assessment is to determine whether the effects will be transitory or long-lasting. The need to analyze project effects over time introduces a difficult analytic complication since neither the natural nor the human environment is static. Both are undergoing continual change, even in the absence of any specific proposed action. Determining the difference a proposed action will make (its impacts) thus requires the comparison of two forecasts. The first, called the **baseline projection**, describes future conditions as they would be without the proposed action. The second, called the **with-project forecast**, describes future conditions as they would be with the proposed action. Critical to the assessment process is the fact that project effects cannot be determined by simply comparing the future -- with the proposed action -- to the present. Such comparisons are invalid because they do not take into account the changes that would occur between the present and future even without the proposed action. Valid estimation of project effects requires that future conditions

Figure 3-1

Steps in the Impact Assessment Process

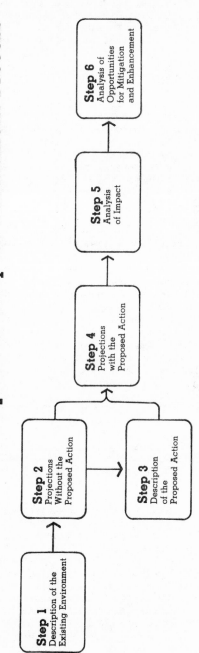

without the proposed actions also be forecast. It is this "baseline" forecast that must serve as the basis of comparison for
identifying project-related impacts. Forecasting baseline social
conditions is difficult. In many cases, it is this step that requires the greatest effort of the entire assessment process.

Direct Project Inputs

Throughout the guide, it is assumed that social assessment has
specific objectives that comprise only a portion of the analyses
needed to address the socioeconomic effects of a proposed action.
Although social assessment has an interest in and can contribute to
other aspects of the analysis, the principal objectives of the social assessment are to determine the effects of the proposed action
on social organization and well-being. Others on the assessment
team are assumed to have primary responsibility for determining the
economic, demographic, land use, facilities, services, and fiscal
effects of the proposed action. To a large extent, the results of
their analyses serve as inputs to the social assesssment. This has
numerous implications for social assessment and for the approach
developed in the guide.

Of particular importance is the allocation of responsibility for
analyzing the relationship between project characteristics (work
force characteristics and schedules, assessed valuation, production
levels, etc.) and the changes that the project will cause for each
community in terms of people, jobs, income, resources, organizations
and regulations, and public health and safety. As discussed at
length in economic/demographic and facilities/services/fiscal manuals, these analyses involve calculation of both the direct and induced effects of the project, and require careful consideration of
the interaction between the project characteristics and regional and
local economic, demographic, facilities, services, fiscal, and social conditions. Primary responsibility for much of this analysis
seldom falls upon the social assessor. For this reason, the guide
has assumed that other members of the team will have primary responsibility for translating project characteristics into the
economic/demographic and facilities/services effects for each
community, with some assistance by the social assessor.

As discussed at greater length in Chapter 4, a project's social
effects are caused by the overall (direct and induced) changes in
people, jobs, income, resources, organizations and regulations, and
public health and safety due to the project, in conjunction with
people's expectations, perceptions, and responses to those changes.
Social assessment thus utilizes the results of the economic, demographic, facilities, services, and fiscal analyses as one of the
principal starting points for forecasting the social effects of the
project. Because primary responsibility for these analyses lies
outside the social assessment component, the guide does not address
these analytic processes in detail. Rather, it defines as direct
project inputs the changes in people, jobs, income, resources, organizations and regulations, and health and safety effects due to
the project in each study area or commmunity, both direct and induced, and utilizes them as one of the principal components in the

analytic framework for assessing social change. It is important
that you understand the term direct project inputs and its counter-
part for the baseline scenario, baseline inputs, because they are
used throughout the guide. As discussed in detail in later sections, the delineation of baseline and direct project inputs is an
iterative process that requires close collaboration between the members of the entire socioeconomic team. In most cases, preliminary
estimates of baseline and direct project inputs are made to initiate
the assessment process and to help focus the research, with the
clear understanding that the estimates will be revised as additional
information is obtained.

The Social Assessment Process

Steps in the Process

The social assessment process, outlined in greater detail in
Figure 3-2, is designed to develop these two forecasts, analyze the
differences between them, and then describe and evaluate the importance and meaning of the effects that can be attributed to the
project. It is also designed to identify necessary or desirable
mitigation/enhancement measures and to evaluate their effectiveness. This approach is applicable to both highly structured impact
analyses and to research on community change since it provides an
effective framework for analyzing social change of many types.

As shown in Figure 3-2, the social assessment process can be
divided into three major activities -- scoping, assessment, and
mitigation and monitoring. The scoping activity begins with a
determination of the decision-making context of the assessment.
This is followed by (1) preliminary identification of the baseline
and direct project inputs (called "inputs" in the figure), the main
factors that could cause social change, and (2) estimation of the
variation in these inputs across alternatives. The scoping activities include collection of initial information about the existing
social environment and determination of the appropriate geographic
and topical focus of the assessment effort. The formulation of
possible alternatives based on these initial data may also be included as part of the scoping activities.

If a scoping process shows the need for a social assessment, the
assessment stage begins with an in-depth examination of the pertinent characteristics of the existing social environment. This may
be preceded or followed by participation in the formulation of alternatives, where the scoping information and description of the
existing environment are used to identify the alternatives that will
be retained for further consideration.

Once specific alternatives are developed, estimates are made of
the direct inputs for the baseline and each of the proposed alternatives. These two sets of information -- one about existing social
conditions and one about the forces for social change -- are then
combined to yield forecasts of social conditions for the baseline
and each of the alternatives. The baseline and with-project forecasts must be stated in similar terms so that the comparison between
the forecasts for the baseline and all alternatives can be made.

18

Figure 3-2

The Social Assessment Process

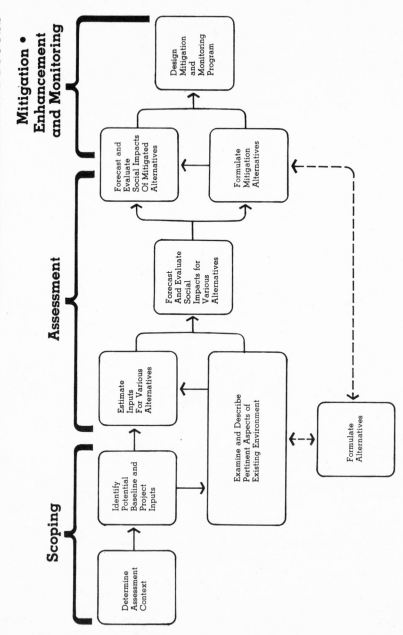

Scoping • Assessment • Mitigation • Enhancement and Monitoring

Determine Assessment Context → Identify Potential Baseline and Project Inputs → Estimate Inputs For Various Alternatives

Examine and Describe Pertinent Aspects of Existing Environment

Formulate Alternatives

Forecast And Evaluate Social Impacts for Various Alternatives

Forecast and Evaluate Social Impacts Of Mitigated Alternatives

Formulate Mitigation Alternatives

Design Mitigation and Monitoring Program

This identifies the project effects. Once the effects attributable
to the project have been identified, their importance and meaning
are evaluated. This is the major goal of social impact assessment.
Those using the guide for research on community change may be more
concerned with the accurate description of changes that have already
occurred as a result of some project or with the delineation of the
mechanisms of social change. The approach developed in the guide is
also effective for these types of research problems.

In impact assessment, the next step is to examine the impacts to
determine whether they can be mitigated or enhanced. Mitigation or
enhancement measures are then formulated for each alternative, and
the mitigated alternatives are then reanalyzed to identify the
social effects that would remain after mitigation. Any necessary
mitigation and monitoring programs are then designed and prepared
for implementation.

Each of these steps in the assessment process is addressed in
detail in Section II. There, specific guidance is provided on how
to design and carry out each step and how to present the pertinent
information in an effective manner.

The Relationship of Social Assessment to Other Components of the Impact Assessment Process

A comprehensive environmental impact assessment generally addresses the effects of a proposed action on both the natural and
human environment. Although there are a variety of ways an environmental impact assessment can be organized, social assessment is
generally included in the "socioeconomic" section of the human environment component.

There are close interrelationships among the various topics (social, economic, demographic, facilities/services, fiscal, housing,
and land use, for example) that generally comprise the socioeconomic
analysis. This is particularly true for the social assessment
since, in most cases, many of the social consequences of a proposed
action result from changes in other aspects of the socioeconomic
environment. For these reasons, the general practice is to conduct
the socioeconomic assessment as a team effort.

The causal and organizational links between the different components of the assessment make it essential that those responsible
for the social assessment understand the entire assessment process
and their role in it. Indeed, this is so essential to the successful design and implementation of a social assessment that further
guidance on defining the context of the assessment is provided in
Chapter 5. At this point, however, it is useful to clarify the
relationship between social assessment and the economic/demographic
analysis, the facilities/services/fiscal analysis, the public involvement effort, and the assessment of the physical environment.

Social Assessment and Economic/Demographic Analysis

Social assessment and economic/demographic analysis are closely
linked for two reasons. First, the major forces for social change

from many of the proposed actions being addressed by social assessment are economic and/or demographic -- changes in the number or type of jobs, in income distribution, in the number or type of enterprises, in the number or characteristics of the population. Many of the proposed actions being assessed are likely to be projects whose primary social effects result from the new jobs, income, and people they introduce. For this reason, the social assessment can hardly progress effectively without information about these economic and demographic changes. Second, in the typical organizational arrangement, economic/demographic analysts are the members of the socioeconomic team responsible for preparing most of the forecasts of baseline and with-project changes in these major driving factors -- the baseline and direct project inputs -- that provide the starting point for the social analysis. They are also generally responsible for preparing the description of existing economic and demographic conditions that provide essential information about the social environment.

This does not mean that the final figures used in the assessment come solely from the economic/demographic analyst. Because of the interrelationships between different aspects of the socioeconomic environment, the best procedure is unquestionably one which promotes close communication and collaboration among team members. For many types of proposed actions, particularly those involving large changes in people, jobs, or income, the economic/demographic analysis is complex and information about social conditions is critical to accurate results. For this reason, it is advantageous for those conducting a social assessment to understand the basic relationships involved in the analysis of economic and demographic change. Indeed, in some cases, no separate economic/demographic assessment is done and responsibility for this information falls on the person doing the social assessment. (To provide for this contingency, guidance on demographic assessment is provided in Appendix A, which also includes references to some economic/demographic assessment manuals that might be helpful.) As with other "discipline specific" analyses, collaboration among informed team members helps ensure that (1) all necessary information is being developed, (2) it is presented in a usable form, and (3) it is made available to those who need it.

Although those conducting the social and the economic/demographic analyses have many common interests, there are significant differences between economic/demographic and social assessment that can result in misunderstandings if not addressed early in the assessment process. The most important differences include:

1) **Distributional effects.** Although changing, economic/demographic analyses have usually focused on a project's aggregate economic effects, sometimes disaggregated to a community level. Social assessment is concerned with the distribution of these economic effects within a community or among individuals. An important function of the social assessment is to look at questions such as: Will everyone in the community share equally in the economic benefits, or will some groups clearly benefit more than others? Will all groups share equally in the economic costs of the project,

or will these costs fall more heavily upon some particular sector of the population? If benefits and costs àre unevenly distributed, are those who gain the least benefits also those who bear the highest costs?

2) **Values context.** All projections, including economic/ demographic projections, rest on assumptions about future conditions and behaviors. In many cases, assumptions must be made about factors that can be significantly altered by the organizational characteristics of local communities or through purposive action by their residents. The assumptions that are used in projections need to be reviewed in light of social values, which may require the involvement of local officials or community leaders. Both social assessment and public involvement concern themselves with evaluating public values. An understanding of local community values can add considerably to the accuracy and appropriateness of the economic and demographic assumptions and to an understanding of the "meaning" of the projections to the community. This is an area where economic/demographic analysis may be dependent upon social assessment and public involvement information. An understanding of local values and social organization reduces the chance that inappropriate assumptions that could invalidate the economic/demographic forecasts will be made.

One problem that occurs occasionally is that the economic/demographic forecasts are made before the social assessment is initiated. In the course of the social assessment, it may be discovered that some of the economic/ demographic assumptions are inappropriate. If this happens, it is useful (and perhaps necessary) to review the projections with those responsible for the economic/demographic analysis and determine whether revised forecasts need to be developed.

3) **Interaction effects.** Communities interact with the initial changes caused by a proposed action to produce a complex set of changes that can subsequently affect project characteristics and its inputs to the community. Adaptations are made over time as the community responds. For example, controversy over a proposed project has the potential to generate strong interactional effects that influence both project characteristics and outcome. One of the principal tasks of social assessment is to identify and evaluate these interactions. Without an understanding of these interactions, it is unlikely that projections about effects will be very accurate. Social assessment can refine both the baseline and with-project economic/demographic forecasts by examining the unique way in which a particular community is likely to interact with changing economic conditions or with a particular project.

Above all, given the importance of information sharing between the social and economic/demographic analysts, those responsible for the social assessment should ensure that they are conversant with the terminology used by the economists and demographers and that they are well enough informed about the economic/demographic analysis to identify their needs and explain them cogently.

Social Assessment and Facilities/Services/Fiscal Analysis

Social assessment and facilities/services/fiscal analysis are also closely linked. In fact, the overlap in information requirements and analysis is often sufficient to have one person be responsible for both. (For this reason, additional guidance on facilities/services analysis is provided in Appendix B.) If they are not combined, many of the aggregate figures used in the social analysis are provided by the facilities/services/fiscal component. As with information about the economic/demographic characteristics, information about recent trends and existing conditions in facility and service provision, regulations, taxation, and governmental structure and operation is critical to the description of the existing social environment. Although the specific questions may be different and data requirements vary, those conducting the social assessment frequently obtain some of their most important information from the same government officials and service providers who supply the bulk of the facilities/services/fiscal information. This commonality of information sources alone is reason enough for the social and facility/service/fiscal analysts to collaborate in collecting and analyzing their data.

Also important, however, is the contribution facility/service and fiscal information makes to the development of accurate assumptions about the direct effects of the proposed action on the population size and well-being of community residents. Workers cannot live in a community if there is no housing for them. The type of housing and the quality of community services available (such as schools, recreational facilities, medical care) influence not only the number, but also the characteristics of the population that will move into an area in reponse to expanded job opportunities. Information about recent trends, current conditions, and future plans for community facilities/services and governmental structure is essential for evaluating a community's ability and willingness to address and solve the local problems that can mean the difference between controlled and uncontrolled growth.

As with the interface with the economic/demographic component, smooth coordination between the social and facilities/services/ fiscal analyses is desirable. As discussed before, friction is likely to be reduced and efficiency increased if a common understanding of the objectives and constraints of each component is established among all team members. For this reason, it is particularly helpful if an assessment process can be developed that ensures clear definition of the responsibilities and requirements for each component and that encourages a good working relationship among the economic/demographic, facilities/services, and social assessment staff. The same need for collaboration holds true for team research efforts.

Social Assessment and Public Involvement

The relationship between social assessment and public involvement is also very close, since social assessment and public involvement are both concerned with:

1) The public's values
2) The public's attitudes toward the proposed project
3) The distribution of political power in the community
4) Issues of justice or equity

While both social assessment and public involvement look at some
of the same information, their interest in that information is somewhat different. Public involvement is primarily concerned with the
process of decision making. It considers public attitudes, values,
and political structure as they contribute to the decision of
whether or not (and in what manner) to proceed with a proposed action. The purpose of social assessment is analytic. Its major
focus is on predicting what will happen after the decision is made
and providing that information for use in making an informed decision. Community opinions, values, and political and social structure all interact with the proposed action to produce social
effects. It is these interactions and the effects that are produced
that interest the social assessor. Social assessment and public
involvement are intertwined because the information produced by the
public involvement activities informs the social assessment, and the
information provided by the social assessment can influence the
decision process.

As a result of the difference in emphasis, there are some additional differences as well:

1) Public involvement usually deals more with those people who
   are actively interested in an issue, while social assessment
   tries to assess impacts on the entire community.
2) Social assessment relies more on an analysis which synthe-
   sizes and evaluates information about the community, while
   public involvement is a more political process.
3) Public involvement activities often have high visibility
   (public meetings, media coverage, etc.), while social
   assessment is often less visible, involving one-on-one interviews, reviews of newspapers and secondary sources, and
   small group meetings.

Actually, it is not clear to what extent these differences are
inherent or simply reflect the state of both fields at the present
time. Certainly distinctions between the techniques used by social
assessment and public involvement are becoming less pronounced. In
the past, public involvement relied heavily on meetings, workshops,
and advisory committees to obtain information, while social assessment relied on field surveys and key informant interviews combined
with the use of secondary sources. But there is increased use of

interviews as a means of getting public involvement information, and many social assessors are using workshops as an effective method for gathering social assessment information.

Because of this strong complementarity, it is important for the social assessor and public involvement staff to communicate regularly. Among the possible ways in which the two can work together are the following:

1) . Social assessment interviews can be designed to ask questions that are important to the public involvement program.
2) Workshops held by public involvement staff may be structured in such a way that they also gather social information.
3) An advisory committee may be used to help interpret the social information.

Public involvement excels at providing the decision maker with information about the opinions of politically active or powerful groups or individuals, while social assessment has the additional responsibility of providing information about opinions in the broader community.

Social Assessment and the Assessment of the Physical Environment

Although there are fewer direct analytic or methodological connections between social assessment and the assessment of the physical environment, there is one primary area in which social assessment can make a contribution to the assessment of changes in the physical environment. That is in the interpretation of the meaning and importance those changes will have. It is not enough to know that a project will impact 1,500 acres of rangeland, two burial sites, and fifty acres of riparian habitat. It is also necessary to know whether that is significant or important and to whom. This significance is partly determined by technical evaluation, but inevitably a judgment about significance has to do with values. Both social assessment and public involvement can help clarify the significance and meaning the projected impacts on the physical environment will have for various sectors of the public.

<u>Summary</u>

It is important to recognize the summarizing role of social assessment. It is social assessment which has the final responsibility for analyzing and interpreting the importance of the changes forecast to occur as a result of the proposed action. For this reason, it is particularly important that the social assessment is conducted with a conceptual framework that incorporates the analytic ties among the various components and in a manner that encourages collaboration on these common analytic problems. The next chapter presents the conceptual framework of the guide and discusses the role of community in social change and social assessment.

4. The Role of the Community in Social Change

4.1 Introduction

This chapter is particularly important since it presents the
overall conceptual framework that is the basis for the assessment
process developed in the guide. The role of the community in social
change and the reasons for using the community as the unit of analysis for social assessment are discussed. The social organization
model, developed as the analytic framework for the social assessment
process, is introduced and each component of the model is described.

4.2 The Conceptual Framework

Ultimately, the goal of social assessment is to estimate the
effects of a proposed action on the social organization of the
community and on the well-being of people over both the short- and
long-term. In some situations -- the assessment of grazing decisions or transmission line sitings, for example -- the social consequences may be limited. In these types of situations, the proposed
action may have little potential to affect the resources or social
organization of the community directly, and the principal effects
may be upon the well-being of a relatively few individuals. Unless
these changes in well-being are sufficient to trigger a public response that could alter community resources or social organization,
the assessment can focus on the magnitude and duration of the effects on individual or group well-being with little need to conduct
an extensive analysis of study area communities. In other situations -- the assessment of large-scale programs or projects, or the
cumulative effects of multiple resource management, or technological
selection decisions -- the most significant social consequences stem
from the effects of the proposed action on the resources and social
organization of the affected communities. Changes in the resources
and social organization of the community have important effects on
individuals and families. These situations therefore require an
assessment framework that takes into account not only the direct
effects of the proposed action on community resources, social organization, and individual well-being, but the indirect consequences of
these initial changes on the community and individuals as well. The

linkages between community resources, social organization, and well-being and the important role communities play as administrative and participatory units make it essential that social assessments utilize an analytic framework that effectively focuses attention on the community, when appropriate, and that provides guidance for addressing the most comprehensive problems likely to be encountered.

Based on extensive analysis of resource-based actions and the social effects they have caused in communities, a model (shown in Figure 4-1) was developed to illustrate the analytic framework recommended by the guide (Thompson, et al. 1982, Thompson and Branch 1980). This model is based on the concept of community as both a social and political unit, as discussed by Warren (1978). A basic premise of this model is that an appropriate understanding of social effects cannot be attained without considering how this higher order unit of social organization, the community, will be affected. Indeed, demonstration that community resources and social organization will not be appreciably affected by a proposed action provides a great deal of information about the magnitude and scope of project effects. It should be noted here that the approach presented in the guide is only one of many that could be used, but it is one that has been found effective and applicable to a variety of assessment problems.

The analytic framework identifies four major topics to consider in assessing the social effects of a proposed action. These are represented by the four components of the model and the analytic framework that is used throughout the guide:

1) **Direct project inputs.** These are the changes in people, jobs, income, resources, organizations and regulations, and health and public safety that occur as a result of the proposed action. For the social assessor, a critical feature of this component is that it does not address the characteristics of the entire project or proposed action per se. Rather it utilizes information obtained from an analysis of the changes in these elements (people, jobs, etc.) that would result from the proposed action. The following example illustrates how this would apply at the community level. A project which would directly employ 600 people is expected to result in the influx of 1,000 new persons to the study area, 800 of whom would reside in community A and 200 of whom would reside in community B. In this case, the direct project inputs of people to community A would be 800 people. The changes in these elements that would occur in the absence of the proposed action also need to be estimated in order to construct the baseline or "no-action" alternative.

In some cases, despite an absence of projected project inputs, public perceptions or uncertainty about them results in controversy and concern. Since social assessment (along with public involvement) is generally responsible for identifying and analyzing public issues, it is important to be alert to these perceptions and the possibility that they

Figure 4-1

The Social Organization Model

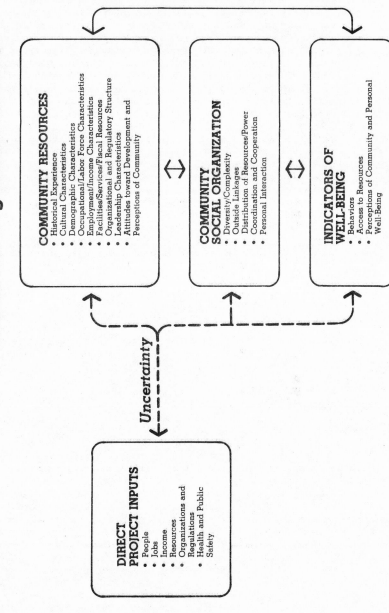

COMMUNITY RESOURCES
- Historical Experience
- Cultural Characteristics
- Demographic Characteristics
- Occupational/Labor Force Characteristics
- Employment/Income Characteristics
- Facilities/Services/Fiscal Resources
- Organizational and Regulatory Structure
- Leadership Characteristics
- Attitudes toward Development and Perceptions of Community

COMMUNITY SOCIAL ORGANIZATION
- Diversity/Complexity
- Outside Linkages
- Distribution of Resources/Power
- Coordination and Cooperation
- Personal Interaction

INDICATORS OF WELL-BEING
- Behaviors
- Access to Resources
- Perceptions of Community and Personal Well-Being

Uncertainty

DIRECT PROJECT INPUTS
- People
- Jobs
- Income
- Resources
- Organizations and Regulations
- Health and Public Safety

will be sufficient to cause social effects and/or affect
project implementation.

2) **Community resources.** This component is part of the description of community characteristics and the resources
available to the community. A number of resource characteristics have been identified as particularly important in
determining (1) the community's ability to respond and (2)
to the access its residents will have to resources. These
are shown in Figure 4-1. In many cases, the resources
available in the community will change as the community is
affected by the proposed action and other factors.

3) **Community social organization.** This component addresses
social organization, another aspect of community characteristics. Five major processes that organize and give structure to life in a community have been found particularly
important in analyzing how communities will respond to an
action and how residents will evaluate the changes that will
occur. These five processes are diversity/complexity, outside linkages, distribution of resources and power, coordination and collaboration, and personal interaction. These
five processes are subsets of the more generic social processes of diversification, external linkages, stratification, and integration that have been found to be critical
aspects in the organization of social life.

4) **Indicators of well-being.** This component integrates the
information contained in the preceding two components. The
purpose of this component is to organize and present information that summarizes or indicates the well-being of community residents. Three major topics are included among the
indicators: behaviors, access to resources, and perceptions
of community and personal well-being.

Each of these components is discussed further in the next section of
this chapter.

Direct Project Inputs

In the most direct sense, a proposed action can cause social
effects in a community by changing the characteristics of the people, jobs and technology, income, material resources, organizations
and regulations, and sometimes, the factors which affect health and
safety. A change in any of these factors has the potential to cause
change in community resources, social organization, and the well-
being of community residents. Research on past social change has
shown that it is not only what is changed that is important, but
also when and how it is changed and the degree of uncertainty that
is created in the process. For example, whether a company or agency
follows a policy of providing accurate, up-to-date information or
remains secretive about its plans can make a major difference in the
amount and kind of social change that results.

What needs to be known about a proposed action in order to assess its social effects includes the following:[1]

1) The number and demographic characteristics of the people who would enter or leave the community as a result of the proposed action, with particular attention to schedules and temporary residence

2) The number and type of jobs created, eliminated, or modified by the proposed action and their general distribution among longtime residents and newcomers

3) The amount and general distribution of income brought to or removed from the community or affected individuals as a result of the proposed action

4) The magnitude and type of material resources brought to or removed from a community or affected individuals by the proposed action (including tax revenues)

5) The number and type of organizations and regulations created or eliminated as a result of the proposed action

6) Changes in health and public safety caused by the proposed action

For large projects, substantial analysis is required to determine the magnitude, schedule, and certainty of the direct project inputs to each study area community. If this analysis is done in the course of the economic/demographic and facilities/services/fiscal assessment of the project, the social assessor will be provided with much of this information without extensive effort. Nevertheless, it is important to understand and participate in this analysis as much as possible.

One of the unique characteristics of social assessment is that the things being assessed -- the project inputs into the community and their effects -- may be altered just by informing the community about them as well as by people's uninformed speculations about them. People may start moving into the area in anticipation of jobs. People who are barely getting by economically may remain in the community in anticipation of jobs. Store owners may decide to expand their operations. School boards may start to consider what to do about future increases in the number of students. Other people may move out of the area in order to avoid anticipated impacts. Real estate prices may go up or down in anticipation. Because it is dealing with people, social assessment information can itself be a source of social change. For this reason, social assessors frequently find it necessary (or useful for the decision makers) to try to distinguish between impacts attributable to the objective changes

---

[1]To assess the no-action alternative or to establish baseline conditions, the same model and process is employed, with the changes that would occur in people, jobs, income, resources, organizations and regulations, and public health and safety under baseline conditions substituted for the direct project inputs.

caused by the project and those related more closely to the people's anticipations, expectations, or reactions. In many cases this is not an easy task.

Community Resources

The resources available to the community during its response are an important determinant of how the community and its residents will be affected by the project inputs. The importance of some of these resources is relatively obvious, such as the availability of facilities and services (e.g., enough schools, hospitals, homes, etc.). However, a part of a community's resources is what it knows and how it feels about dealing with major projects. As a result, the community's experience with development or other major community changes as well as residents' attitudes towards development need to be understood.

The community resources found to be most influential in determining how the community will react to and be impacted by a project are the following:

1) The community's previous experience with similar or related developments
2) The cultural characteristics and social groupings of the community, particularly the presence of unique populations such as American Indians
3) The demographic characteristics of the community
4) The occupational (livelihood) and labor force characteristics of the community
5) The employment and income characteristics of the community
6) The existing or planned facilities, services, and fiscal resources in the community
7) The organizational and regulatory structure of the community
8) The leadership characteristics of the community
9) The community residents' attitudes toward development and their perceptions of the community

Some of the information about both existing resources and expected changes will frequently be prepared by the economic/demographic or the facilities/services analyst, particularly in formal impact assessment efforts. Under these circumstances, coordination among team members is essential to ensure that effort is not duplicated and that the necessary information is available when it is needed.

Community Social Organization

Community social organization refers to the structures and processes that organize how people in a community relate to one another. Culture, the shared ideas and expectations which regulate behavior, is the organizing principle underlying social organization. In an earlier age, different communities had very distinct cultures. Now, in a country where almost everyone is linked by

newspaper, radio, or television coverage of events both in the
United States and around the world, much of this distinctiveness has
been lost. The proliferation of national associations and interest
groups, as well as the expanded role of federal and state government, have also played a role in reducing cultural differences.
However, the presence of a sizable number of people from a unique
cultural group, such as American Indians, or a religious group, such
as Mormons, may cause a particular community to be culturally distinct.

But social organization is not based solely on ethnic and religious ties or distinctions. There are a number of other patterns or
forms of interaction that are highly significant. There are five
characteristics of how people organize themselves in communities
which show up in social research as particularly significant in
determining what social change occurs in a community. These five
characteristics are the following:

1) Diversity/complexity
2) Outside ties
3) Distribution of resources/power
4) Coordination and cooperation among people in the community
5) Patterns of personal interaction

Diversity/Complexity (An Aspect of Differentiation)

Diversity/complexity refers to the range of values and interests
within a community. Research indicates that as a community grows
the diversity of values and groups increases, and the ways people
have to interact to get things done becomes more complex and formalized. Economic growth, particularly if associated with new kinds
of economic activities, will result in increased diversity in technology and in the kinds of occupations and sources of income within
the community. Not only will there be an increase in economic
diversity, but the accompanying increase in population will usually
also increase ethnic and cultural diversity as well as the diversity
of personal experience and background. This can be a source of both
stimulation and conflict for a community. Different groups of people in the community will have different needs, place different
demands for services on the community, and because of differences in
cultural norms, exhibit differences in social behavior. As the
diversity of the population increases, the differences in their
needs, their demands and expectations for community services, and
(because of differences in cultural norms) their social behavior
will also increase.

Social science research indicates that increased diversity/
complexity is an inevitable consequence of population growth. One
consequence of this increased diversity/complexity is increased in-
terdependence. This has advantages, but it can also increase the
effort required to keep the diverse elements operating together effectively and increase the need for more formal procedures, for
example, more explicit and comprehensive rules and regulations.

One important reason for assessing a community's complexity/
diversity before the project begins is that the amount of social

change which will occur depends on whether or not the community is
already relatively specialized and diverse. If a community is relatively homogenous, then the changes required to adapt to the introduction of new people, activities, or technology will be relatively
great and may seem more significant to the residents.

Outside Linkages

Outside linkages refers to the extent that local residents, institutions, economic resources, and decision makers are influenced
by people outside the community and the extent that the community
has the ability to call upon outside resources for support and aid.
In some towns, usually the smaller ones, people may relate primarily
to each other in providing services, selling goods, forming judgments, and making decisions. In others, there may be a greater
orientation and attention to outside markets, activities, and
trends. Some communities have established comparatively few ties
with outsiders who control resources or information that could be
useful to the community, while others have a well-established and
effective network of such ties.

As projects are introduced from the outside, particularly those
which result in a large in-migration of new residents or which radi-
cally alter the economic structure of the community, these characteristics can change dramatically. In addition to the project
developer, which is likely to have its headquarters outside the
study region, the community may become large and wealthy enough to
attract national chain stores. Sources of loans and credit other
than the local bank may become available. Local decision makers may
have to work with numerous state and federal agencies. Major decisions concerning employment may be made by the management of a company with headquarters hundreds of miles away. Newcomers arrive
bringing with them new ideas, practices, and commitments from the
larger society. Frequently, with projects that are introduced from
the outside, the products produced by community labor are shipped
out of the community to markets which have little to do with local
conditions. Such changes may substantially increase the opportunities for some people in the community. They may also lead community
residents to feel that they have less control over their future.
The ability of the community to handle or control its future may
depend upon its ability to draw on resources outside the community,
such as political power, money, or knowledge, through the establishment or utilization of outside ties.

Distribution of Resources and Power (An Aspect of Stratification)

In every community, there are some differences in access to community resources and services. These differences are linked to
people's education, occupation, financial position, family ties,
ethnicity, land ownership, political power, and so forth. The particular patterns of differential access and the factors influencing
the distribution of resources and power can vary substantially from
one community to another.

The issue of how resources are distributed in a community becomes important in assessing social impacts because it is not enough
to know that a project will introduce new resources into a community
-- for example, a certain number of dollars. It also is necessary
to know how those dollars will be distributed. Will they be distributed in a way that increases equity, or will only the rich get
richer? Will the position of powerful groups be threatened? If
only some people will benefit or if only some people will be harmed,
this may help explain attitudes towards the project and may also
explain the willingness (or unwillingness) of the community to provide support for the project.

Many assessments are conducted to evaluate the effects of new
projects or activities. Generally speaking, an increased flow of
resources into a community results in increased opportunities to
accumulate resources. Shifts in the economic structure or in population size can create problems for some people in the community
while it creates opportunities for others. People on fixed incomes
or people who are chronically unemployed, for example, may not be in
a position to benefit from the expansion of economic activities.
Consequently, as others obtain secure or high-paying jobs, they may
suffer a comparative decline in economic status.

If there is an economic or political elite in a community, it
may find itself in competition for the new resources and may be
faced with a new elite created by the changing conditions. When
change occurs slowly, membership into elite status can be extended
gradually. But a major long-term project, for example, may introduce into the community a significant number of well-paid and well-
educated people who expect to be able to "transfer" their membership
in the elite group to the new community and who therefore press for
access to resources and services that is commensurate with their
income and education. This may pose a challenge to the old elite
and generate conflict.

With rapid change in the size or composition of the local economy, economic power may be shifted from one sector of the economy to
another. This tends to cause the relative status of some groups to
decrease at the same time that it is increasing for others. In particular, economic power is likely to increase for those who are able
to organize and control resources in the community and for those who
have the best links to the outside world.

Coordination and Cooperation (Aspects of Integration)

Coordination is a term used for the process of organizing and
focusing the activities of the various elements of the community.
Cooperation is the process by which different people work together
to get something done. As mentioned earlier, increased diversity/
complexity may require an increased effort to keep things coordinated and to promote cooperative effort. Generally speaking, the
more equity there is in the distribution of resources, the more
likely it is that interconnections have been formed with all parts
of the community and that mechanisms for cooperation are established
and functioning.

Large scale projects can challenge a community's ability to take action and manage change. Existing patterns of cooperation and methods of coordination may be too limited to allow effective response, or may be disrupted by the changes brought by the proposed action. Decision making that involves outside agencies or company management can create demands that previous community decision-making processes did not have to accommodate. Leaders face a particular challenge under these circumstances as research has shown that communities without effective coordination and cooperation processes are more likely to experience adverse impacts.

In small communities, resources may simply be inadequate to support the formal processes for managing change, such as in a town that can't afford a paid planner. On the other hand, small communities may utilize informal control processes that are effective (for example, the town banker doesn't issue a loan for development that the city fathers don't think is in the community interest). The problem is that these informal processes tend to break down when resources come in from the outside and therefore may become ineffective or counterproductive just at the point where control is most needed. The banker's unwillingness to loan money would have little meaning to a major energy company. To maintain control, community leaders are likely to supplement or replace these informal processes with more formal procedures. This change can affect the complexity of the community as well as the established patterns of personal interaction.

Personal Interaction

In every community, patterns of personal relationships are established as residents interact with one another. In small communities, people frequently share a common background and often relate to one another on the basis of knowing and being known by virtually everybody in town. People in small communities tend to know each other's family background, approximate financial condition, and personal characteristics. There is little need for formal procedure because everybody is so well known. Patterns of social standing and access to resources tend to be well-established and to have become personalized through the patterns of interaction. People know who is on their social level and who is not. The political and social elite, if there is one, know how to get things done. As a community gets larger and there is an influx of people into the community, there is a tendency for patterns of interaction to become more complex and for more formal procedural norms to be established. People have to deal with a higher proportion of complete or relative strangers. Residents and newcomers alike are asked to validate their identification with official documents. The local developer who used to handle permit problems with the county commissioner now must submit formal plans, deal with a planning staff, and appear at public hearings. As sectors of the community become specialized, people may lose contact with others in the community with whom they have had regular contact in the past, or remain unacquainted with an increasing proportion of the community residents.

A proposed action or its effects may elicit a strong response by community residents that can change the patterns of personal interaction in the community. Residents may become united in their support of or opposition to the project, or they may become polarized into opposing factions. If intense and/or widespread, such changes in personal interaction patterns can affect the entire tenor of community and affect other aspects of social organization, such as the processes of coordination and cooperation.

In many ways, "personal interaction" is a summing up of the other four processes above. Changes in any of the other four will usually result in changes in patterns of personal interaction.

Social Well-being

The final major topic which the social assessment must address is social well-being. Ideally, this topic deals directly with the characteristics of and impacts upon the individual. However, most of the available indicators of well-being are actually community or county figures (for example, the crime rate in the community) upon which interpretations of individual well-being are based.

One of the problems with social well-being is that it is an inherently subjective concept. Well-being is as much a feeling one has about one's life as an objective state. Among other things, well-being is defined in relative terms, as a comparison with one's expectations of the conditions that should prevail in one's life. Somehow the assessment must attempt to objectively assess the extent to which the social well-being of various groups in the community will be affected by the project. This guide recommends an approach that combines both objective and subjective measures. The three basic measures that social science research has indicated to be most applicable to social assessment are the following:

1) Rates of behaviors
2) Access to resources
3) Perceptions of community and individual well-being

Rates of Behaviors

There are a number of behaviors that have been used as objective, aggregate indicators of social well-being for which some theoretical base and empirical data have been developed. The most useful of those for which data are generally available to an assessment appear to be patterns or rates of behavior within the community that indicate social, family, or personal problems such as crime, family violence, delinquency, divorce, and so on.

Access to Resources

Here the assessment examines the aggregate and per capita measures of resources, concentrating on changes in the pattern of

resource availability in the community. Particular attention is
given to those groups whose access is likely to be changed as a result of a proposed project. Because this analysis relies heavily on
the economic and demographic and facilities and services analyses,
there needs to be close coordination between the social assessor and
those conducting these other components of the socioeconomic analysis. The data used as indicators in this analysis has often already
been collected for the examination of community social organization.

Perceptions of the Community and Individual Social Well-being

Information concerning perceptions is essential to the forecasting and interpretation of community response to a proposed project.
As indicated earlier, residents' perceptions often do not correspond
exactly with objective changes, but perceptions can have a powerful
influence on individual and social action. If people perceive that
they do not have access to resources, for example, they can be as
closed off from the resources as if a formal system blocked their
availability. If newcomers believe that they will not be accepted,
they may never extend themselves to the old-time residents and may
never ask to join existing organizations. The behaviors and attitudes resulting from these perceptions can thus produce very real
social impacts. In addition, given the inherently individualized
nature of perceptions, measurement of residents' perceptions of
well-being prior to the proposed action is an essential element in
determining and evaluating changes in social well-being that might
be caused if a proposed action is taken.

4.3   The Social Organization Model

As guidance to the assessment process, the four basic elements
described above are organized into the social organization model
shown in Figure 4-1. The arrows between components indicate that
elements in these components interact with each other. The people
introduced by the proposed action (one element of the direct project
inputs) place demands on community resources, while the resources
introduced by the proposed action can act to mitigate these impacts. Consequently, modification of project inputs can alter the
effects on resources. For example, the work hours for construction
workers can be designed to avoid traffic peaks. The hiring of workers can be managed so that there is a steady increase of construction workers, not a sudden rush. Taxes can be prepaid. Assistance
can be provided to the community to take care of increased demand
for emergency services.

When the project inputs interact with the community social organization, there are reciprocal effects. The community may develop
new processes for dealing with the project inputs, thus changing
both the social organization and the impact of subsequent project
inputs. Of course, there is interaction between social well-being,
community resources, and community social organization. If social
well-being is lowered by the changes caused by the proposed action,
longtime residents may leave the area, or turnover among the

newcomers may be high. This in turn will affect community resources and organization.

The model also shows that the project inputs' direct effects on individuals may not be the only cause of project-related changes in social well-being. The inputs may be sufficient to cause changes in community resources and social organization that in turn will affect individual well-being. It is the job of the person conducting the assessment to examine the relationships indicated in the model, make judgments about probable impacts, and present them so that the basis for making these projections is clear to the decision maker and to others interested in the results. The next chapters provide explicit guidance on conducting such an assessment.

4.4 References

There are a number of excellent sources that discuss the role of the community in social change. To prevent duplication, these references have been consolidated into Section 8.5 at the end of Chapter 8. Those seeking additional information about the topics discussed in this chapter or the information obtained from the literature review and case study of ten communities conducted for the Bureau of Land Management Social Effects Project are encouraged to refer to these sources.

Section II:
A Framework for Social Assessment

5. Defining the Context of the Assessment

5.1 Introduction

Although the overall assessment process described in Chapter 3 has become relatively well established in environmental impact assessments, assessments vary greatly in their purpose and in the way they are organized. Before starting the actual assessment effort, it is important to take some time to make sure that you understand the particular assessment you are to work on, including: (1) why the assessment is being conducted and how it fits into the organization responsible for doing the assessment; (2) what types of decisions are to be made, by whom, and when; (3) the procedures that are to be followed, since these determine how the work is to be done, what the individual responsibilities are, and how the results are to be presented; and (4) the relationships and organizational links between the assessment team, the assessment team leaders, the decision makers, the project sponsors, and the interested public. These relationships define many aspects of your job, and it is often up to you to determine what they are and how they can be used.

This chapter discusses the questions about purpose, organization, and procedures that should be answered before you begin the assessment effort. You may already have many of the answers, either from previous experience or from previous organizational information and meetings. Nevertheless, reviewing the topics presented in this chapter before starting the assessment will help you organize this information and ensure that no recent changes have been made that will affect the design and implementation of your work.

The procedure recommended in this chapter has three benefits. First, it helps ensure that no important organizational questions that could lead you to make poor assessment or organizational decisions go unanswered. Second, it prompts you to think through the assessment process from the perspective of the organization and the decision makers responsible for the assessment. This improves your ability to focus the assessment and the presentation of results. Third, it provides an outline of the information that should be made available to the assessment team and reviewed with them before the technical assessment effort begins. This can be especially helpful to those who are responsible for directing the assessment effort or supervising other workers.

41

Two general topics are covered in this chapter:

1) **The decision-making context,** or what the assessment is to do and when
2) **The procedural context,** or how the work is to be done and the results are to be presented

5.2   The Decision-Making Context

In order to plan a responsive and effective social assessment, it is important to understand the organizational and decision-making context in which the assessment is to occur. A good starting point is to define the objectives of the proposed action and the purpose and scope of the assessment.

Define the Assessment Task

Assessment information is used to inform a wide variety of decisions. To determine what type of assessment effort is appropriate, the overall purpose of the proposed action and of the assessment and planning or decision-making process to which it applies must be understood. In some cases, the purposes are clearly specified. In others, they may not yet have been clearly defined and still require additional evaluation and discussion. Frequently, assessments are expected to serve multiple purposes, so it is important to make sure that all the objectives for the assessment are clear.

In this stage of the assessment it is useful to clarify the principal objectives of the proposed action. The objectives of the assessment and the interests of the decision makers will be quite different if the primary purpose of the project, for example, is to generate an economic return for the project sponsor than if its primary purpose is to promote social change. For projects with a primary economic or environmental protection motivation, the greatest concern is likely to be demonstration that the project will not cause significant social change. (Examples of these types of projects include coal mining, power plant development, and nuclear waste disposal). Conversely, for projects whose primary motivation is social change (for example urban renewal, VISTA) and/or economic development, the greatest concern is likely to be demonstration that the desired social change will actually occur.

If care is not taken, these differences in focus can bias the conclusions of the assessment by consistently placing the burden of proof on one side or the other of the social change analysis. Consequently, although it is important to focus the assessment on the questions pertinent to the decision makers, it is also important to guard against this bias throughout the analytic process and to be aware of the consequences of stating the questions in a particular way.

Another aspect that greatly influences the purpose and design of an assessment (as well as the assessment team's role within its organization) is the relationship between the organization conducting the assessment and the organization(s) that would implement the actions being assessed. Four types of relationships are common. Each has characteristics which have implications for the type of analysis that is feasible or appropriate and for the type of information that is needed from the assessment by the decision makers. Each is described briefly below:

1) The organization conducting the assessment has design and scheduling (including cancellation) authority over the proposed action. In these cases, the assessment is usually part of an internal decision-making process for the design and evaluation of projects that the organization itself will implement. Examples of this type of relationship within federal agencies include the assessment of a management framework or resource management plan by the Bureau of Land Management and the assessment of a weapons deployment project by the Department of Defense. Examples within the private sector include a corporate assessment of the development alternatives for their real estate or mineral holdings or the relocation of corporate headquarters.

   These assessments often provide the greatest opportunity for the assessors to work closely with the decision makers from the formulation of alternatives through to the design of implementation plans and monitoring programs because the organization conducting the assessment controls the important project design decisions. Detailed information about the proposed alternatives is likely to be available, and decision makers are likely to be interested in specific and detailed analyses.

2) The organization conducting the assessment has authority to make resource management or policy decisions that could lead to (or prevent) multiple, presently unspecified actions by other organizations. Examples of this type of assessment include (1) the evaluation of leasing decisions for minerals, timber, or grassland (for example) where the decision to lease is a prerequisite for resource development projects and (2) the evaluation of policies establishing the criteria for hazardous waste disposal siting.

   These assessments frequently involve comparison of numerous alternatives about which only limited information is available. Because of the indirect relationship between the organization conducting the assessment and the project implementors (who are often not specified at the time of the assessment), project characteristics are frequently sketchy and information about implementation plans and implementor-community relationships is often lacking. The focus of these assessments is typically on delineating the range of impacts that could result from each of the decision alternatives. This type of assessment often has many similarities to the formulation of alternatives process discussed in Chapter 7.

3) The organization conducting the assessment has regulatory authority or approval power over an action proposed, designed, and to be implemented by another organization. Examples include (1) federal or state agencies assessing a

permit application for a major facility over which they have jurisdiction (coal mines, for example) and (2) private corporations assessing a project being proposed by a subsidiary. In these assessments, detailed information about the proposed action should be available, but it may be difficult to obtain (since it has not been developed by the organization conducting the assessment) and may be subject to unanticipated revisions that can affect the assessment process. The assessment team is likely to have minimal participation in the formulation of alternatives, and an arms length, potentially adversarial relationship with the project implementor in preparing decisions and making implementation and monitoring recommendations.

4) **The organization conducting the assessment has no direct authority over the proposed action, but wishes to evaluate it.** Examples include (1) interest groups wishing to assure themselves about the validity of the assessment results and/or to provide a basis for political action and (2) assessments conducted by social scientists as part of applied research on social change (for example, a natural disaster, technological innovation, etc.)

In these cases, information concerning the proposed action may be difficult to obtain, either because it has been developed by another organization which has little incentive to release it or because no information has been developed. The latter often occurs when the assessment is addressing an event that does not have a single specified sponsor -- for example a technological innovation.

Realistic evaluation of the purposes of the assessment from the perspective of the organization conducting it is the first step in planning an effective assessment. It may well raise strategic questions about the organization of the assessment effort and the assessment's role in the decision-making process.

In many cases, the particular assessment being undertaken is part of a decision-making and planning process that involves a series of interrelated assessment and decision-making steps. In order to proceed efficiently, it is important to determine what has already been done, and what will be done following the current assessment. An important part of this task is to determine what decisions have already been made and what information has already been collected and presented to the decision makers. This information serves several functions: (1) it prevents wasting effort on alternatives or decisions that have been discarded or already addressed, (2) it provides useful evidence about the type of information that has already been gathered and about how the information was used by the decision maker, and (3) it helps to further delineate the purpose and scope of the assessment as well as the range of alternatives to be evaluated.

Sometimes you will need to obtain and review the work conducted for social assessments that occurred earlier in the decision sequence. Usually, you will review information obtained from other aspects of the planning and decision-making process. At this stage, it is not necessary to review this material in detail, but merely to

determine what is available and scan it for a general understanding
of its contents.

Understanding how the current assessment effort fits into the
overall decision-making process requires looking forward as well as
back. The purpose of the assessment, and hence the appropriate level of detail and analysis, are affected by the effort's position in
the overall decision-making process. Consequently, it is important
to establish the expectations for this assessment and to keep in
mind that not everything that should be addressed must be covered at
the same level of detail in each assessment.

Determine How the Overall Assessment Effort Is Organized

Once the overall purpose of the assessment effort and its relationship to the actions/decisions of the various organizations involved have been defined, the next step is to determine how the
assessment effort is to be organized and how it fits into the overall structure of the organization. Some common arrangements include
the following:

1) **Formation of a special assessment team.** For some assessments, special teams are formed that have a particular
   structure and relationship to the organization. In this
   case, it is important to include the team leader among the
   decision makers whose schedule and objectives should be understood.
2) **Utilization of staff in their normal positions.** In some
   cases, no special team is formed, and the assessment is conducted by staff members as part of their normal assignments.
3) **Supervision of a third party.** In still other cases, the
   actual assessment is conducted by another organization
   (e.g., a contractor), although responsibility for supervision and/or review is maintained by the sponsoring agency.

Whatever the arrangement, it is important that the organization
of the overall assessment effort and its relationship to the decision makers be clearly understood. This requires that the following
points be clarified:

1) **Authority structure.** Who is responsible and authorized to
   do what?
2) **Decision-making structure.** Who will be making which decisions regarding the proposed alternatives and the assessment
   effort?
3) **Information flow/communications.** How is information to be
   obtained and disseminated? Who will have access to what
   information and when? What other organizations are involved? How are these relationships structured?

Because these arrangements vary so greatly, no effort is made
here to describe all the alternatives that might be encountered.
However, it should be noted that assessments are often conducted in
short time frames and are subject to intense public scrutiny,

political pressure, and frequent changes in organization and procedures. It is your responsibility to ask those questions that will
enable you to perform your work efficiently and with as little organizational friction as possible. It is important to remember that
your ability to "read" the organization, to figure out how things
work, and to work within the structure will often be interpreted as
an indication of both your ability to understand the communities in
the impacted area and your skill in obtaining information about organizational and interpersonal relationships in a diplomatic and
efficient manner. Consequently, it pays substantial dividends to
attend to this problem and to approach the definition of the assessment's organizational context with care and tact.

It cannot be emphasized enough that the assessment process is
inherently political. Numerous factors representing a variety of
perspectives and vested interests will be interested in, and trying
to influence the assessment and the decision-making process. In
order to perform a valid, professional assessment while protecting
one's organization, the social assessor cannot afford to be naive
about the political nature of the assessment process. This certainly does not mean that the scientific integrity of the assessment
should be compromised, but that the political contest must be analyzed and skillfully addressed. For some helpful discussions of this
feature of assessment work, see:

Weiss, Carol
    1975 Evaluation Research in the Political Context. In Hand-
          book of Evaluation Research, Vol 1. E.L. Struening and
          M. Guttentag, eds., pp 13-26. Beverly Hills, Calif.:
          Sage.

Stufflebeam, Daniel L. and William Webster
    1981 An Analysis of Alternative Approaches to Evaluation. In
          Evaluation Studies Annual Review, Vol 6. H.E. Freeman
          and M.A. Soloman, eds., pp 70-85. Beverly Hills,
          Calif.: Sage.

Identify the Decision-Making Criteria

An underlying objective of all of the previous questions has
been to determine the criteria that will be used in decision making. In some cases, formal, specific criteria are developed to
guide the decision makers. These criteria may be established at the
beginning of the assessment effort or at some point in the process.
If such criteria are developed, it is obviously important to conduct
the assessment and present results in a manner that conforms to
these criteria. More commonly, such criteria are not formally established. In these cases, an additional part of the assessment
team's task is to determine the criteria that will be important to
the decision maker and that also adequately represent the assessment's findings.

Determine the Overall Decision Schedule

Frequently, a number of interim decisions and/or actions are made during the planning or decision-making process. In order to respond in a timely fashion, the assessment team needs to understand not only the sequence but also the proposed schedule of the decisions to be made. The decision schedule is always important for planning the assessment effort, but it is particularly important if there are to be interim decisions, such as finalizing baseline assumptions, establishing decision criteria, or finalizing the alternatives to be included that will affect subsequent assessment efforts.

Since assessments generally deal with proposed future actions, changes and delays in decisions and the availability of information are common. It is also common for the final deadlines to remain fixed while internal deadlines slip. Therefore, it is very useful to make a practice of (1) knowing the decision timetable and schedule for information availability, (2) monitoring the decision-making schedule and the alternatives under consideration, (3) evaluating whether any interim decisions would affect your assessment, (4) being prepared to reorganize the assessment to work on the areas least affected by the uncertainty of interim decisions, or to concentrate on new areas identified by interim decisions or changes in decisions, and (5) documenting the reasons for delays in your work due to lack of information or changes in information.

5.3   The Procedural Context

This section focuses on some organizational procedures of particular importance to social assessment effort. There will undoubtedly be other organizational procedures that must be followed to maintain efficiency and good working relationships. As indicated previously, your skill in effectively "reading" and working in the organization is often interpreted as an indication of your professional ability. Therefore, paying attention to procedures and being able to fit into the organization is important and can yield many benefits.

Define the Structure of the Assessment Effort and Its Budget

The organization of the assessment effort is generally determined by the type of decision to be made and the budget available for the work. Ideally, the thing to do at this stage is to sit down with the assessment manager or team leader (and, if possible, the decision maker) and review the task at hand, discussing the types of decisions being considered, the specific decision-making or planning process, the budget, and the assessment procedures and schedule to be followed. As part of this discussion, agreement about the role, responsibilities, and resources available to the social assessor

should be reached. If the social assessment will have its own budget, it is important to determine how much money is available or to
work through the steps described in Chapter 5 to develop a budget
estimate for the work that needs to be done. If you are the project
manager for the assessment, you can facilitate project start-up by
calling a meeting of the project team, including the decision makers
if possible, to clarify these issues and answer questions about the
scope and organization of the assessment effort.

Composition of the assessment team will vary according to the
type of action being proposed, and the distribution of responsibilities among team members can vary widely. Consequently, as part of
the discussion with the assessment team be sure that the areas to be
covered by the social assessment component are clearly defined. In
some cases, demographic, facilities/services, and fiscal analyses
are included as part of the social assessor's responsibilities. If
this is the case and you need assistance in these areas, guidance
for conducting an assessment in these two areas is provided in
appendixes A and B. References to other sources of assistance in
socioeconomic assessment are also included in these appendixes.

Define Your Schedule and Coordination Procedures

Now it is time to become specific about schedules. Find out
when information and directives will be provided and when information and reports have to be prepared and/or presented in formal/in-
formal meetings. Because the social assessment requires information
from other components (particularly the economic, demographic,
facilities/services, and fiscal analyses) and ideally would involve
working with those responsible for this information, the schedule
and coordination procedures in these areas are particularly important for planning the assessment effort. In some cases, the
schedules, responsibilities, and coordination procedures will have
already been established and will be available in the form of memos
or directives. In others, you will have the opportunity to participate in their development. Recognize that your role in this process
may vary from one occasion to the next.

Identify Issues Pertinent to the Decision

As part of the review of available information and decisions
that have already been made, you should identify any issues that
have developed, especially those which have affected earlier components of the decision or the decision maker. Once such issues have
emerged, care must be taken to address them systematically, clearly
documenting that they were examined and why they were dismissed or
carried forward into the analysis. As discussed further in chapters
6, 7, and 8, the social assessment, along with the public involvement program, are usually responsible for identifying the public's
attitudes toward the proposed action and interpreting the political
and sociological importance of those attitudes for the decision
makers. Identification of issues that have already surfaced is an
important aspect of this task.

In addition to identifying issues that have already emerged, the social assessment process is also responsible for identifying issues that may emerge. Sometimes these issues have not previously been noted by the decision makers. One important function of the social assessment is to identify such issues and to prepare a short, to-the-point memorandum or issue paper about impending problems. As with other interorganizational communications, it is important to keep in mind organizational objectives, communication protocol, and procedures when preparing and presenting such memoranda.

Establish the Assessment Approach

Once the assessment effort is launched and responsibilities for technical areas are being assigned, it is important to make sure that you understand how the assessment is actually to be done, what is to be included, and (equally important) what is to be excluded from the assessment. Useful questions to ask include the following:

1) **What is the scope of the assessment?** Now is the time to make absolutely clear what the purposes of this specific assessment effort are.

2) **What is the study area?** If the study area has already been established, make sure that its location and boundaries are clear. If the study area has not yet been identified, find out how and when this will be done. In some cases, the study area boundaries will be affected or determined by the location of social effects. In some cases, different study areas will be appropriate for different disciplines. If so, find out how these decisions are to be made and coordinated.

3) **What unit of analysis is to be used by the different components in their analysis and in the reports?** It is important to know whether the unit of analysis and data forecasts will be at a community, county, or regional level. It is also important to know whether the analysis will be conducted at one level (for example, communities or individuals), but the results will be presented at another level (for example, counties or region).

4) **How are the effects to be evaluated? Is there a scheme for weighting or comparing effects?** In some assessments, the effects must be summarized according to established criteria, such as duration (long- vs. short-term), extent (local vs. regional vs. national), magnitude (larger vs. smaller), or valence (positive vs. adverse). Obviously, it is useful to know if your results must be translated into such a scheme.

5) **How are other actions proposed for the study area to be addressed?** This is also known as the "cumulative effects" question. As discussed in Chapter 3, impact assessment is based on a comparison between the conditions that would occur without the proposed action (the baseline) and the conditions that would occur with the proposed action. In many cases, however, problems have developed about how to define the baseline or without-project conditions in areas where a

number of projects have been proposed but have not yet begun to be implemented. A similar problem arises when assessing multiple actions proposed for the same area. Figure 5-1 illustrates this situation.

In order to address this cumulative effects question, you must know:

-- What is to be included in the baseline forecasts, and how this is to be determined.

-- How the "cumulative" effects will be allocated among the different proposed actions. For example, is the particular proposed action to be addressed as the final increment or as a percentage of the total change? This distinction not only affects the manner of discussion, but it may also affect the allocation of impacts.

The answers to these questions often depend upon the type of decision to be made. At a preliminary stage (e.g., evaluation of multiple projects that have no specific causal relationships to one another), it may be more efficient and useful to consider the effects of each project first, and then to evaluate the likely combinations.

In most cases, the decision about what to include and how to attribute the effects will not be yours to make. However, it is very important that you clearly understand what you are to include as part of the baseline and how the effects are to be attributed to different projects.

6) **How are the attitudes and perceptions of area residents and other stakeholder groups to be addressed?** One of the responsibilities shared by social assessors and the public involvement staff is to identify and analyze public/stakeholder group attitudes, perceptions, and expectations about the assessment, the proposed action, and the project impacts that could affect (1) the implementability of the project or the assessment, and (2) the socioeconomic consequences of the project by affecting public/stakeholder response.

This can be particularly important if issues exist or are expected to emerge regarding projects that the assessment team (and decision makers) feels have little potential to cause significant objective effects. In these cases, the social assessor, the team or project manager, and the decision maker must decide how much effort should be devoted to attitude assessment and public involvement and how to interpret and respond to these attitudes, perspectives, and expectations.

7) **How is the assessment to be documented?** Obviously, before work can commence you must determine what the assessment is to produce, what reports are required, and when they are required. In order to plan your time, it is important to establish a clear understanding about the reports that you are to prepare, including their expected length, schedule, and format. A variety of reports may be required, including:

Figure 5-1

Possible Baseline and With-action Conditions

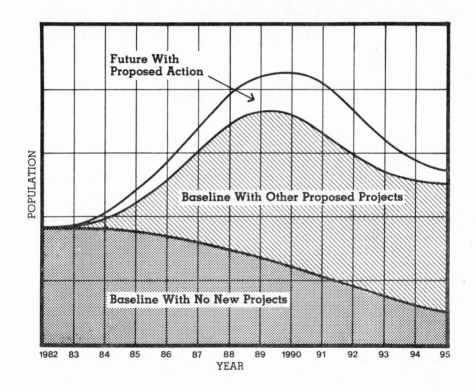

-- A work plan, laying out what you plan to do and your
   schedule
-- Progress reports, summarizing what you have accomplished
   and how you are proceeding on your work plan
-- Issue papers, highlighting topics of particular importance to decision makers
-- Technical reports, describing methods and results in
   some detail; and
-- Impact statements/environmental reports, presenting your
   methods and results in specific ER/EIS format

Early in the process, it is also very useful to determine what procedures and formats are to be followed to document and reference personal communications, secondary
sources, methods, and assumptions and whether there are particular rules regarding report organization or format, use
and format of tables, and style. Although these often seem
like minor administrative details, it can save considerable
inconvenience and frustration if you follow the procedures
from the beginning.

Initiate a Literature Review

Now is also the time to start an aggressive literature review to
inform yourself about the research that has been conducted on topics
pertinent to the assessment. An assessment is only as good as the
information upon which it is based and the rigor with which that information is applied. Familiarity with current theories and with
empirical findings is the cornerstone for conducting a valid assessment. Because every assessment problem is unique and involves very
complex relationships, research findings much be utilized judiciously, but they serve as important evidence that must be considered if
a thorough, defensible assessment is to be performed.

Even previous studies that may not include directly usable information can be invaluable in suggesting questions to be addressed,
data gathering techniques, and methods of analysis and presentation. Since it often takes several weeks to obtain requested
material, this review must be initiated early in the assessment
process. The list of references at the end of Chapter 8 may provide
some help in starting on the literature review.

6. Scoping the Social Assessment Effort

6.1   Introduction

Chapter 5 described how to determine the purpose, organizational context, and procedures for the assessment. This chapter discusses how to determine the potential scope of the assessment -- the geographical area of concern, the social phenomena which are most likely to need in-depth analysis, the units of analysis that should be addressed, and the appropriate level of detail for the assessment effort.

This preliminary assessment or scoping is important because it helps you make effective use of available resources. By considering the general type and magnitude of the potential change agents, the types of social changes they could cause, and the degree of controversy likely to be generated over the assessment or the proposed action as well as the time and budget available for the assessment effort, the assessment can be focused more effectively. Costly mistakes and false starts can thus be avoided. It is useful to complete the process described in this chapter whether or not it is required by the organization. An important function of these initial screening steps is to help you think through the task you are undertaking and develop an efficient plan for its completion.

The screening process will help you focus your attention, both geographically and topically, by using a documented and defensible process. The major steps in this process include:

1) Determine what the potential inputs from the proposed alternatives or types of alternatives are (i.e., people, jobs, income, resources, regulatory changes, organizational factors, changes in health and public safety). They differ considerably among the types of actions you may need to assess. Identify the public issues that are likely to emerge.

2) Locate readily available secondary data and information about the proposed actions and the social environment in the study area.

3) Review available information and estimate the social impacts that may occur. The social organizational model can be used to estimate how community resources, social organization

processes, and community or individual well-being might be changed by the potential inputs. It can also serve as a guide to a systematic consideration of the types of issues that may emerge (or have already emerged).

4) Estimate changes in people, jobs, income, resources, organizations, and public safety that are likely to occur without the proposed action (baseline) for the areas or communities potentially affected by the proposed action.

5) Conduct a short field trip to check your estimates of changes that might occur and to familiarize yourself with the study area.

6) If necessary, reestimate potential changes based on observations from the field trip.

7) Prepare a detailed work plan for the assessment.

6.2   Determine Potential Inputs

The first step of the screening process is to determine the proposed action's potential to cause social effects. The purpose of this step is to focus attention on the important issues and to help determine whether the impacts could be sufficient to affect the social organization of the communities in the study area. This is done by estimating the potential of the proposed action to cause real or perceived changes in any or all of the following:

1) The number and characteristics of people in the affected area

2) The number or types of jobs

3) The level or distribution of income

4) Direct changes (not those resulting from population change) in the resources of:
   -- The private sector (e.g., housing, commercial resources, recreational resources)
   -- Local or state government (e.g., revenues, facilities)
   -- The general public (e.g., land, air water, wildlife, and recreation resources)

5) Organizational and regulatory context (e.g., changes in regulatory control, change in public or private sectors, or changes in policy)

6) Public health and safety (e.g., floods, landslides, disease, etc.)

Some proposed actions (such as the establishment of wilderness areas) would restrict or prevent development in an area, creating conditions in which the baseline inputs would frequently exceed project inputs, and the with-project forecasts would be more similar to current conditions than the baseline forecasts would be. In such cases, it is appropriate to consider the project's ability tc prevent change in each input category when determining potential project inputs. It may also be helpful to note that proposals which would place restrictions on local response or development alternatives are likely to evoke concerns and issues that are somewhat different from those caused by growth-promoting proposals. The importance of these concerns and issues to decision makers may necessitate special efforts in public involvement, attitude assessment, and issue analysis.

The purpose of this step is to focus attention on the important analytic problems and to help determine the appropriate units of analysis for the study.[1] If the assessment task is to formulate and evaluate broad alternatives or to participate in an overall scoping process, the scoping should probably be done in general terms, identifying only the nature, general magnitude, and approximate geographic location of the inputs. If the assessment task is to prepare a detailed assessment of specific alternatives, this general scoping may have already been done and can be utilized to determine the potential inputs more specifically and at a disaggregated (possibly community) level. It will be useful from the onset to determine the general pattern of the potential change in these factors. Is it likely to be gradual and steady? Rapid and erratic? Rising to a peak, then dropping sharply? These patterns, and the degree of uncertainty associated with them, also affect the social consequences that will result. Attention should be given to the anticipation of change and the potential for the proposed action to generate controversy. In most cases, this will result from perception or apprehension of change in one or more of the inputs identified above. It should be kept in mind throughout that most assessments have political as well as scientific purposes, and that they have many audiences. For this reason, it is sometimes necessary to extend the assessment into areas where little project effect is expected in order to demonstrate the absence of effects.

People

One cause of social impacts is change in the number or characteristics of people living in a community. This can occur through the introduction of new jobs (as with large-scale resource development activities), through the removal of residents (as sometimes occurs with water projects, urban renewal, or plant closures), or by the retention of residents who would otherwise have left the area. Figure 6-1, included in Section 6.5, provides a format for documenting the analysis of potential change in the number or characteristics of people.

For a large study area, it may be helpful to first conduct this process for the entire area, in order to determine which portions are likely to receive most of the change, and then to repeat it in more detail for those portions. Much of the necessary information should be available either from the description of the proposed

---

[1]For example, if the assessment deals with grazing regulations, it is likely that the major project inputs would be changes in the level or distribution of income, changes in resources, and changes in the organizational and regulatory context. The focus of the assessment would therefore be directed to the effect these changes would have on the well-being of affected individuals after confirming that the changes would not be sufficient to affect the social organization of the communities in the study area.

action, through discussions with the economic/demographic analyst,
by studying areas with similar projects, or from other reports or
studies. A discussion of the factors that may influence the number
and characteristics of people that will in-migrate, move, or remain
is included in chapters 8 and 9 and in Appendix A (Demographic Forecasting and Analysis).

Jobs/Occupations

The number and type of jobs available in a community or area can
strongly influence lifestyle, economic opportunity, and perceptions
of the area. Consequently, the potential to affect the number or
type of jobs, technology, and the occupational structure of an area
(such as through introduction of large numbers of mining or profes-
sional/service sector jobs in an agricultural area) indicates a
potential for social effects that should be examined. First, it is
necessary to determine the probable magnitude of change, given the
baseline characteristics of the study area.[1] Figure 6-2 in
Section 6.5 provides a format for documenting this step of the
screening process.

Although the economists conducting impact assessments are usually more attuned to changes in employment by industrial sector and
income than to occupation, in most cases, describing employment implications will be the primary responsibility of the economist.
Therefore, the economist should have information about the employment characteristics of the existing environment and will be forecasting employment by industrial sector (e.g., mining, construction,
services, manufacturing) for both the baseline and the with-action
conditions, if the changes that would be introduced by the proposed
action warrant such effort. A change in job characteristics is
often a major issue in rural communities. At this stage, the most
efficient approach would be to meet with the economist to discuss
the magnitude of change that could occur. If you are responsible
for the economic analysis, reference to some of the economic/demo-
graphic assessment handbooks mentioned in Appendix A might be useful.

Income

A third, related factor that can result in social impacts is a
change in income level or in the distribution of income among area
residents. Again, the principal responsibility for forecasting
baseline and with-action income levels is usually the economist's,
but it is possible that the economic/demographic analysis will pay
little attention to the distributive effects of income without some
prompting from you. Changes in income levels, such as those resulting from grazing regulations or from the introduction of many new

---

[1]It is worth noting that changes in jobs (and income) are
frequently related to changes in population, especially for large-
scale development projects. However, this is not necessarily true;
hence, the separation of the factors in the screening process.

unionized jobs, can be important to the social assessment. They can affect the economic and material resources available to residents and thereby affect lifestyle, material well-being, and other behaviors which determine an area's social environment. Change in income distribution can generate conflict and affect the social organization of the area. The question to resolve is whether the proposed action has a significant potential for changing income levels or distribution and whether those changes would be sufficient to alter the social organization of the communities. Precise quantification and analysis of that change comes later. At this point, the object is to determine potential sources of social impact in order to target the assessment effort more effectively. A sequence for including income change in the scoping process is presented in Figure 6-3 in Section 6.5.

Resources

Analyzing resource availability and cost is very complex. At this stage of the screening process, the analysis is limited to consideration of potential changes in material resources that would result directly from the proposed action. This input category includes changes in the fiscal, facility, or natural resources available to an area that would result from the proposed action. Property tax payments, agency or company-provided housing or equipment, removal of recreational facilities or areas, and land use changes, are examples of resource changes that would fall into this category. Unless a specific project is being assessed, it is likely that an accurate estimate of the change in resources will not be possible. However, it should be possible to identify the general type and magnitude of the changes that could occur. Forecasts of the resource inputs and how they would affect the cost and availability of facilities and services in the community are generally made by the economist (as part of the fiscal analysis) and the facilities/services analyst. Because resource effects are among those most easily changed (for example, by decisions to prepay taxes or to construct housing), they are often of particular interest to decision makers and community residents and the focus of mitigation efforts. At this point, the object is to identify sources of social effects, not to determine the social effects themselves. Questions which can be asked about the proposed action for this factor are shown in Figure 6-4 in Section 6.5.

Organizations and Regulations

A proposed action can introduce new organizations into an area (such as new companies and businesses or new regulatory agencies). It can also introduce new regulations or modify existing ones, thereby affecting the residents of the local area. When national firms or federal or state government are involved in a proposed action, concern about the effect such involvement will have on local autonomy frequently emerges. Figure 6-5 in Section 6.5 shows

possible questions for determining whether this input is likely to
be an important factor in the assessment.

Health and Public Safety

The final factor suggested for consideration in the screening is
the proposed action's potential to affect health and public safety.
As with the other factors, the principal intent is to consider the
direct effects of the proposed action on public health and safety,
with less concern at this point on the interactive effects of population increase and service availability. That step comes later.
To illustrate, a proposed dam construction can potentially affect
public safety by reducing the chance of floods. Although the social assessment generally is not responsible for determining the
public safety effects of the proposed action, it is appropriate to
include such changes as part of the social assessment screening
process since personal and public safety (and perceptions of safety)
are important to perceptions of personal and community well-being.
Figure 6-6 in Section 6.5 presents the screening format for this
factor.

It may be helpful to work through the screening process twice,
focusing the first time on the potential for actual changes in each
factor and the second time on the potential for concern or controversy over each factor. Here, previous experience in the study
area, an understanding of the public's response to similar proposed
actions, and familiarity with the pertinent literature will be
extremely useful.

6.3 Determine Which Aspects of the Existing Social Environment Need to be Described to Complete the Scoping Process

The previous steps have identified the potential mechanisms by
which the proposed action could cause social impacts. These analyses can now be used to determine which communities or geographic
areas warrant examination in greater detail. The analysis of direct
project inputs can help focus the assessment both geographically and
topically, as discussed below.

Geographic Focus

Social effects result from the interaction between the changes
introduced by the proposed action (i.e., people, jobs, income,
resources, organizational/regulatory context, and public health and
safety) and the existing social conditions in the community. Consequently, the purpose of this step in the screening process is to
identify the communities or area that may be most affected by the
proposed action and to establish the geographic priorities of the
assessment. In some cases, the geographic focus of the various
assessment components will vary substantially. It is important that
the assessment effort be focused on those communities or areas that
will be affected by the proposed action.

If the social assessment is part of a preliminary scoping or formulation of alternatives effort for which the potential inputs have been determined at an aggregate study area level, the next step is to examine maps of the study area. The maps are used to determine where the communities or settlements are located relative to the site of the proposed action and to identify those communities or individuals that could be affected by the changes identified in the previous steps. Although it is premature to completely eliminate communities or areas from the assessment process based on this preliminary screening, this simple process can be effective in determining the number and geographic location of the study area communities that will require most of your effort. If the potential inputs have already been estimated at a community level, this step can probably be completed in the screening process described in Section 6.2. Nevertheless, it is always wise to make sure that the geographic relationship between the site of the proposed action and the affected communities is understood.

Using the information about potential inputs it should be possible to compile a list of potentially affected communities ranked in order of the magnitude of the effects they will experience from the proposed action. Using the most recent population data available for each community (generally from the U.S. Census or state estimates), other readily available general descriptions of the communities, other studies, visits to the area, and advice from other team members who are knowledgeable about the study area, the remaining steps on the screening forms (figures 6-1 through 6-6 in Section 6.5) can be completed.

The principal purpose of this process is to compare the magnitude of the potential action-related change with the characteristics of the communities and area residents and to determine where the relative magnitude of the action-related change could be sufficient to noticeably change conditions in any community. This step calls for judgment. If in doubt, it is generally best to carry a community or area into the next phase of the assessment, with the knowledge that it could require relatively limited effort.

Topical Focus

Based on this review, it should be possible to delineate, for either the entire assessment or particular communities, the major sources of potential social impact and to determine whether it is necessary to address the community as a unit of analysis. The information from this review can be used to focus the assessment on topics that need to be addressed and to help determine what information about the existing environment would be pertinent to the assessment. Different types of resource management decisions will require assessments with different topical focuses.

It is important to remember that both the screening and the assessment are analytic, not descriptive, processes. Therefore, throughout the assessment, a continuing effort must be made to identify what information is pertinent to the analysis of the proposed action's social consequences and to avoid extensive reporting of information that is merely background and has little or no direct

bearing on the assessment. However, remember that it is important
to document this process of refinement and focusing to provide a
defensible, readily available record of the assessment process.
This is useful not only for the organization, but also for your own
use. It is frequently useful to be able to review your decisions
when preparing reports. Also, if specifications of the proposed
action or baseline conditions are modified in the middle of the
assessment (as is often the case), such documentation will make it
easier for you to incorporate the modifications. A work sheet to
summarize the results of screening each of the six factors is presented in figures 6-7 and 6-8 in Section 6.5.

6.4 Obtain Preliminary Information About the Potentially Affected Communities

Using the screening information that has been developed, you now
have a better idea of what information you need about which communities or areas. It is at this point that a more detailed literature
review and coordination with other members of the assessment team,
particularly those involved with the socioeconomic assessment,
becomes especially important to avoid duplication of effort, contra-
dictory assumptions, and inefficient or inappropriate use of community contacts.

Depending upon the type of decision-making process, the extent
of previous studies or planning activities, the nature of the assessment, and the geographic area, considerable information about
the proposed action, the communities, and area residents' attitudes
and perceptions relating to the potential changes may already have
been compiled and be readily available from secondary sources.
These sources should be identified and examined, to the extent that
they are pertinent, before additional primary data are collected.
Examples of such data sources include the following:

1) Previous research or studies on similar types of actions or
   similar communities
2) Census data, including special censuses
3) County comprehensive plans
4) Clippings from local newspapers
5) Employment data, from either the U.S. Bureau of Economic
   Analysis or state employment offices
6) Records of public meetings about the proposed action, such
   as scoping meetings, official public meetings, and hearings
7) Records of public response to the proposed action or similar
   proposals

In addition, other members of the team are frequently excellent
sources of information.

6.5 Work Through the Screening Process

The next step is to work through the screening process illu-
strated on the following pages in figures 6-1 through 6-8. This

Figure 6-1

People

Could the proposed action:

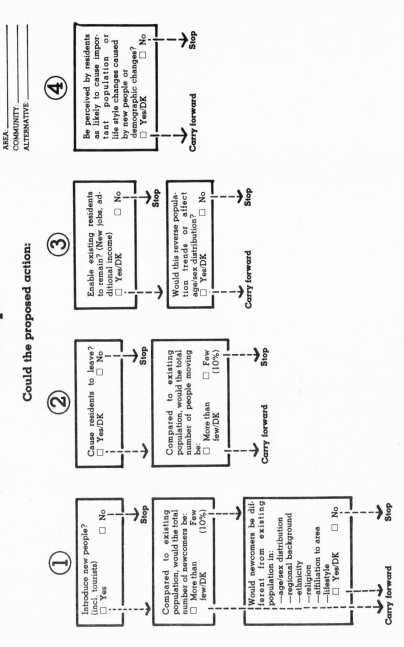

AREA: _____
COMMUNITY: _____
ALTERNATIVE: _____

④ Be perceived by residents as likely to cause important population or life style changes caused by new people or demographic changes?
☐ Yes/DK → Carry forward
☐ No → Stop

③ Enable existing residents to remain? (New jobs, additional income)
☐ Yes/DK
☐ No → Stop

Would this reverse population trends or affect age/sex distribution?
☐ Yes/DK → Carry forward
☐ No → Stop

② Cause residents to leave?
☐ Yes/DK
☐ No → Stop

Compared to existing population, would the total number of people moving be:
☐ More than few/DK → Carry forward
☐ Few (10%) → Stop

① Introduce new people? (incl. tourists)
☐ Yes
☐ No → Stop

Compared to existing population, would the total number of newcomers be:
☐ More than Few (10%)
few/DK

Would newcomers be different from existing population in:
—age/sex distribution
—regional background
—ethnicity
—religion
—affiliation to area
—lifestyle
☐ Yes/DK → Carry forward
☐ No → Stop

62

Figure 6-2

Jobs

Would the proposed action:

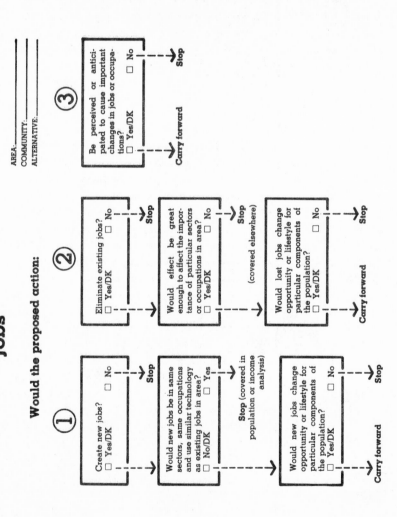

AREA:
COMMUNITY:
ALTERNATIVE:

① Create new jobs?
☐ Yes/DK   ☐ No ----→ Stop

Would new jobs be in same sectors, same occupations and use similar technology as existing jobs in area?
☐ No/DK   ☐ Yes ----→ Stop (covered in population or income analysis)

Would new jobs change opportunity or lifestyle for particular components of the population?
☐ Yes/DK   ☐ No ----→ Stop

Carry forward

② Eliminate existing jobs?
☐ Yes/DK   ☐ No ----→ Stop

Would effect be great enough to affect the importance of particular sectors or occupations in area?
☐ Yes/DK   ☐ No ----→ Stop (covered elsewhere)

Would lost jobs change opportunity or lifestyle for particular components of the population?
☐ Yes/DK   ☐ No ----→ Stop

Carry forward

③ Be perceived or anticipated to cause important changes in jobs or occupations?
☐ Yes/DK   ☐ No ----→ Stop

Carry forward

Figure 6-3

Income

Could the proposed action:

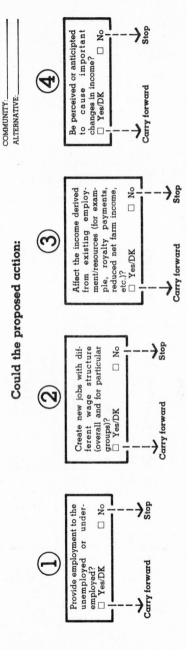

AREA: _____
COMMUNITY: _____
ALTERNATIVE: _____

① Provide employment to the unemployed or under-employed?
☐ Yes/DK   ☐ No ----→ Stop
----→ Carry forward

② Create new jobs with different wage structure (overall and for particular groups)?
☐ Yes/DK   ☐ No ----→ Stop
----→ Carry forward

③ Affect the income derived from existing employment/resources (for example, royalty payments, reduced net farm income, etc.)?
☐ Yes/DK   ☐ No ----→ Stop
----→ Carry forward

④ Be perceived or anticipated to cause important changes in income?
☐ Yes/DK   ☐ No ----→ Stop
----→ Carry forward

64

Figure 6-4

Resource Availability or Cost

Could the proposed action add or remove:

AREA: _____
COMMUNITY: _____
ALTERNATIVE: _____

① Private sector resources (e.g., recreational facilities, housing (through actions like construction camps, confiscation, condemnation)?
☐ Yes/DK   ☐ No

Carry forward →   Stop →

② Local or state government resources (e.g., revenues, access to land)?
☐ Yes/DK   ☐ No

Carry forward →   Stop →

③ Federal government resources (consider commodity resources as well as natural environment resources)?
☐ Yes/DK   ☐ No

Carry forward →   Stop →

④ Resources causing change that the population is likely to perceive or anticipate as important?
☐ Yes/DK   ☐ No

Carry forward →   Stop →

Figure 6-5

Organizations and Regulations

Could the proposed action:

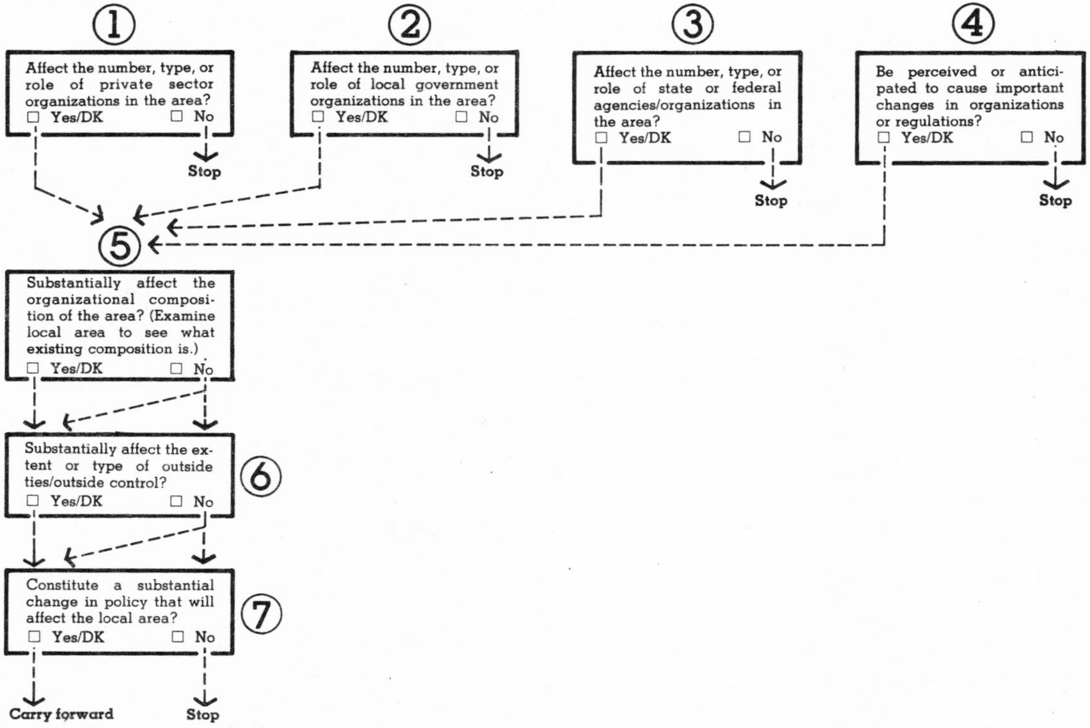

AREA: _____
COMMUNITY: _____
ALTERNATIVE: _____

① Affect the number, type, or role of private sector organizations in the area?
☐ Yes/DK ☐ No → Stop

② Affect the number, type, or role of local government organizations in the area?
☐ Yes/DK ☐ No → Stop

③ Affect the number, type, or role of state or federal agencies/organizations in the area?
☐ Yes/DK ☐ No → Stop

④ Be perceived or anticipated to cause important changes in organizations or regulations?
☐ Yes/DK ☐ No → Stop

⑤

Substantially affect the organizational composition of the area? (Examine local area to see what existing composition is.)
☐ Yes/DK ☐ No

⑥ Substantially affect the extent or type of outside ties/outside control?
☐ Yes/DK ☐ No

⑦ Constitute a substantial change in policy that will affect the local area?
☐ Yes/DK ☐ No → Stop

Carry forward

Figure 6-6

Health and Public Safety

AREA: _____
COMMUNITY: _____
ALTERNATIVE: _____

① Could health and public safety be affected or perceived to be affected by the proposed action?

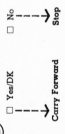

☐ Yes/DK   ☐ No

Carry Forward   Stop

67

Figure 6-7

Summary

AREA: _____
COMMUNITY: _____
ALTERNATIVE: _____

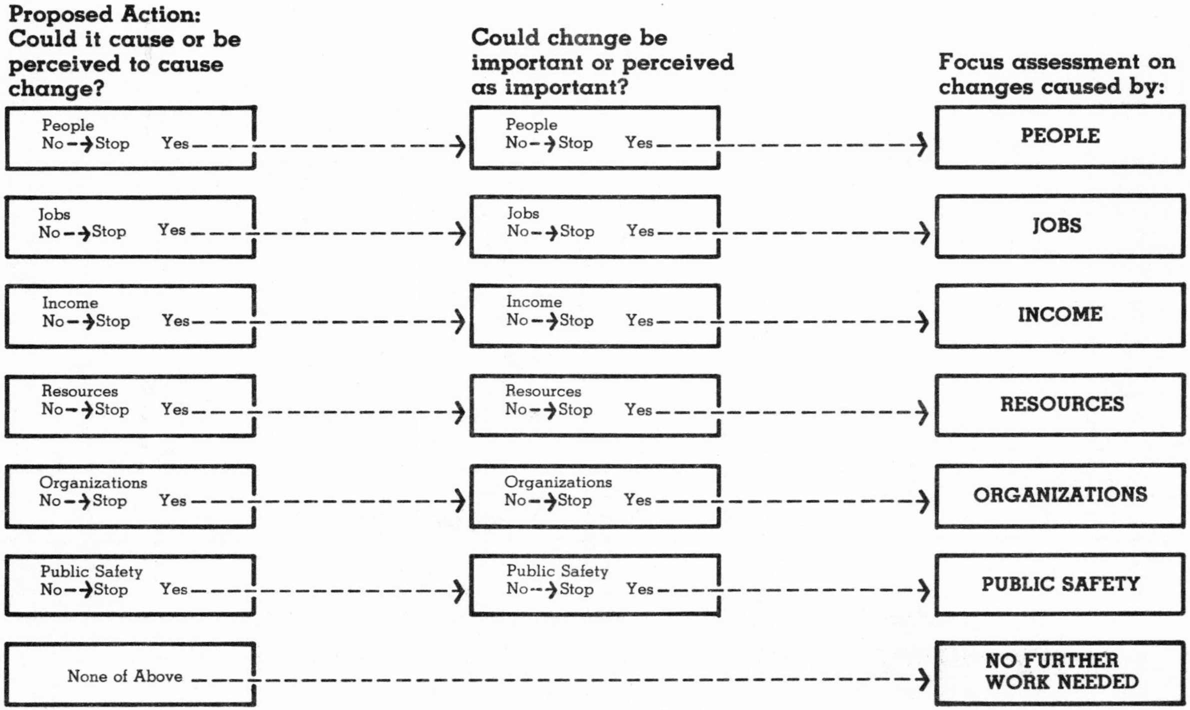

Proposed Action:
Could it cause or be
perceived to cause
change?

Could change be
important or perceived
as important?

Focus assessment on
changes caused by:

People
No →Stop Yes

People
No →Stop Yes

PEOPLE

Jobs
No →Stop Yes

Jobs
No →Stop Yes

JOBS

Income
No →Stop Yes

Income
No →Stop Yes

INCOME

Resources
No →Stop Yes

Resources
No →Stop Yes

RESOURCES

Organizations
No →Stop Yes

Organizations
No →Stop Yes

ORGANIZATIONS

Public Safety
No →Stop Yes

Public Safety
No →Stop Yes

PUBLIC SAFETY

None of Above

NO FURTHER
WORK NEEDED

Figure 6-8

Summary: Estimated Range of Inputs Across All Alternatives by Community or Area

RANGE OF INPUTS ACROSS ALTERNATIVES

Communities	People	Jobs	Income	Resources	Organizations/ Regulations	Health/ Safety
1.						
2.						
3.						
4.						
5.						
6.						
7.						
8.						

process can be completed at either the study area or community level, or both, as appropriate for the particular assessment. If the proposed action will restrict the development of an area (for example, wilderness designation), the questions may be more clear if stated in terms of preventing or restricting change.

6.6 Plan and Conduct a Field Trip

Unless precluded by budgetary or schedule constraints, it is very useful at this time to make a preliminary field trip through the study area. Nothing provides quite the same information as actually seeing a community, traveling through an area, and talking to area residents. Guidance on organizing and conducting a field trip is provided in Chapter 12 in Section III.

The purpose of this step is to obtain sufficient information about likely baseline conditions, perceptions about anticipated effects, and the potential interaction between the proposed action and the communities to enable you to focus your effort and develop a work plan for the social assessment component or to document that no further assessment work is required. This field trip provides an introduction to the project area, it is not expected to serve as the major research component of the assessment.

6.7 Determine Expected Changes in the Input Categories for Baseline Conditions

Especially in areas where other development activities are underway or planned, it is important to forecast the changes in each of the input categories -- people, jobs, income, resources, organizations, and health and public safety -- that would occur even without the proposed action (baseline conditions). As with the potential project inputs, most of this information will be collected and provided to you by those responsible for the economic/demographic and facilities/services components, since they will be forecasting these factors as part of the baseline conditions for their analyses.

The purposes of this step are (1) to determine whether the changes in the baseline conditions could either diminish (and make less important) or amplify (and make more important) the changes caused by the proposed action and (2) to help prepare for the forecasting of baseline conditions. The extent of change expected under baseline conditions will affect the design of the assessment effort. Large changes in baseline conditions are likely to complicate the decision-making and assessment process in several ways. First, decisions will have to be made about what changes should and should not be assumed to occur in the baseline forecast. This may require a complex public involvement process. Second, information about each project or event that is included in the baseline must be compiled and analyzed. Third, large baseline changes frequently indicate unsettled times and heightened uncertainty. This increases the difficulty of each step in the assessment process, and often makes it more difficult to separate residents' attitudes and perceptions

about the proposed action from those about the baseline changes.
Finally, large baseline changes make attribution of project effects
more problemmatic and require even more careful coordination among
team members in the establishment of assessment procedures and the
communication of information.

6.8 Reevaluate the Screening Results

Based on your review of the secondary data and field trip (if
one was made), you should reevaluate the screening decisions and
make your determination of the geographic and topical focus of the
assessment. If the secondary data review or field trip identify any
new issues or public attitudes that are potentially significant for
the assessment or the decision maker, it may be useful to prepare a
brief (two- to three-page) summary of your findings and conclusions
and to review it with the assessment team leader and possibly the
decision maker. It is important to make this summary succinct and
to the point.

6.9 Develop a Work Plan

You should now be in a position to develop a work plan for your
assessment or to document that no further assessment work is required. Developing a work plan is particularly useful because it
forces you to think through the entire assessment effort and figure
out how you will allocate your time and budget among literature review, secondary data analysis, field work (including primary data
collection and analysis), impact analysis, and report preparation
activities. Matching your level of effort to the schedule of the
assessment often requires you to make trade-offs in terms of geographic or topical focus or level of detail. It is important that
these trade-offs are based on (1) a clear understanding of the purpose of the assessment and the level of detail required and (2) a
careful analysis of the questions raised in the screening process.
If you are in doubt about the relative importance of different aspects of the assessment, it may be wise to discuss them with the
team leader or your supervisor.

In some cases you will be responsible for developing a detailed
budget for your component of the assessment. The screening process
provides a basis for estimating the effort that will be required for
each step of the assessment. If you are unfamiliar with budgeting,
you should seek assistance from the project manager/team leader and
colleagues who can help you make realistic estimates of the time and
expense involved in each step of your assessment and develop a
budget that conforms with your organization's specifications.

6.10 Conclusions

After working through the steps described in this chapter, you
should be in a position to work through the social organization
model shown in Figure 4-1 to determine where your attention should

be focused. For some resource management decisions, attention will
focus on the relationship between direct project inputs and individuals' well-being, after documenting that the type of inputs from the
proposed alternatives will not affect community resources or social
organization. In these cases the assessment effort is likely to be
more limited and to depend heavily upon economic and/or land use
analyses and the attitudes and perceptions of the affected population. For other types of alternatives, it will be necessary to
address all components of the model, although the level of detail
will vary according to the particular purpose of the assessment being conducted. In some cases, the major emphasis will be on describing and interpreting public attitudes and concerns about the
project. Whatever the results, the conclusions reached from the
scoping process should be used in the remainder of the assessment,
including selection of the appropriate aspects of the guide.

7. Formulating Alternatives

7.1 Introduction

In this chapter, the objectives and procedures usually followed in formulating alternatives are described, and guidance is provided about the use of social information in this process. Although there is great variance in the extent to which alternative formulation occurs as an explicit, formal process, there are many similarities in the use and application of social information in formulating alternatives and in assessing their effects. An additional purpose of the chapter is to illustrate the complementarity between alternative formulation, the assessment of proposed alternatives, and the development of mitigation and enhancement measures.

As discussed in the guide, the formulation of alternatives is the process by which the relatively undefined needs and/or opportunities of a project sponsor or project initiator are defined, made more explicit, and developed into a set of proposed alternatives that are considered both desirable and viable. These alternatives then become the proposed actions that are the subject of the complete assessment process.

7.2 The Formulation of Alternatives Process

Decisions made during the initial phases of project/program development have a profound effect on the final project characteristics and upon the subsequent opportunities available for shaping or redefining the project. It is during the early stages of project formulation that the basic scope and extent of the project and the principal objectives of the project are established. These are generally first developed in broad, conceptual terms that are specified more clearly and defined more precisely as the process of alternative formulation proceeds. In the course of this process, some alternatives are discarded and many characteristics of the final alternatives are set. For these reasons, participation in the formulation of alternatives process can be very influential with the result that intense competition often develops for access to these early stages of project development.

The objectives of formulating alternatives is to develop a set
of alternatives that are well enough defined and sufficiently
limited in number that comprehensive assessment of each can be conducted. The assessment process, which is the focus of Chapters 8
through 10, evaluates and compares the effects of each alternative
to provide decision makers with the information they need to select
the one that best meets the decision criteria. In the simplist
case, only two alternatives are developed -- a no-action (baseline)
alternative and a with-action (proposed action) alternative. Frequently, however, more than one with-action alternative is developed
(for example, alternative routes for a transmission line, alternative sites for a power plant, alternative construction schedules
for a proposed dam), with the result that more than two alternatives
are presented to the assessment team for evaluation and comparison.

To a certain extent, the formulation of alternatives functions
as a preliminary impact assessment and is subject to similar political pressures and demands. The process of formulating alternatives
-- who is involved, when it occurs, the establishment and/or application of criteria for accepting or rejecting alternatives -- varies
considerably from one case to the next. In some cases, the alternatives to be evaluated are formulated by the project sponsor with
little or no participation by the assessment team. In others, the
assessment team may be called upon to participate from the earliest
project identification/needs assessment stage. The process may be
conducted with or without the active participation of the general
public or key stakeholder groups.

An invitation to participate in the formulation of alternatives
is generally viewed as an excellent opportunity to anticipate the
social and environmental consequences of various project characteristics or project alternatives and to influence the decisions which
shape the final proposals. However, effective participation in this
process requires an ability to conduct mini-social assessments, often with little opportunity to collect extensive information about
the affected community or population, and with very sketchy information about key project characteristics. If you lack experience with
social assessment and have not had the opportunity to work through
chapters 8-11 of the guide, you may find it difficult to perform
this task with confidence. You may want to obtain some assistance
in addition to reviewing the later chapters of the guide before undertaking this task.

The principal steps in a full-scale formulation of alternatives
process are:

1) To identify the full range of alternatives that should be
   considered before decisions are made to concentrate on the
   development of particular alternatives
2) To utilize the team's knowledge about environmental and
   socioeconomic impacts to work with project engineers/
   technical specialists and executives to formulate a set of
   alternatives that are implementable and that best meet the
   objectives of the various stakeholder groups (including the
   project or program sponsor) while causing the least possible
   adverse effects

In many cases, the process will yield more than one alternative (in addition to the no-action alternative) since conflicting criteria, different stakeholder objectives, or complex interactions frequently prevent clear identification of a single "preferred" alternative on the basis of this process alone. In these cases, a more rigorous evaluation of the alternatives developed in this initial process is required; this becomes the assessment of alternatives described in chapters 8 through 11.

The formulation of alternatives process should ideally be conducted to prevent situations in which (1) alternatives that could have been discarded in a preliminary screening are carried forward through the assessment process, thus increasing cost and prolonging uncertainty; (2) the full range of alternatives does not get considered either because of a failure to be innovative in identifying options or because alternatives are incorrectly assumed to be infeasible; or (3) features are included with or excluded from alternatives which unnecessarily reduce their acceptablity or positive effects.

The formulation of alternatives process may include a substantial public involvement component or it may be an internal activity, with little or no public involvement.

7.3   The Social Assessor's Role in Formulating Alternatives

The formulation of alternatives is generally a team effort. The organization of the team and the particular objectives of the process will vary from one case to the next, so it is important that you determine early-on how the team is organized, what the particular objectives are, and what procedures are to be followed.

The formulation of alternatives usually includes the following overall objectives:

1) Identifying the alternatives considered desirable or viable by stakeholder groups (including the group formulating the alternatives and/or the project sponsors) so far as they are known
2) Identifying, at a general level, the major environmental and socioeconomic effects, both positive and negative, which might occur for each alternative
3) Estimating the magnitude of these effects
4) Identifying any major implementation problems or issues due to resource constraints, engineering problems, institutional barriers, or scheduling
5) Assessing the probable acceptability of the alternatives to the various stakeholder groups

Thus, in considering the various alternatives, a thumbnail assessment of each alternative is required. This can be done verbally, as in a meeting, or in short written reports to decision makers. The ways in which the social assessor can contribute to each of these objectives are discussed below.

Identify and Consider All Alternatives

An important aspect of the social assessor's job is to identify the various stakeholder groups, talk with their representatives, and understand their positions and issues. Along with the public involvement staff, the social assessor is in the best position to receive suggestions from such groups about alternatives they consider desirable or acceptable. If the plans to develop a project have become public knowledge and you have already completed the work described in chapters 5 and 6 (or are in a position to do so in preparation for participating in the formulation of alternatives) you will normally have identified a number of alternative approaches that are supported by different members of the affected public in the course of this work. In most cases, however, the information that you have already obtained will not be sufficient for you to identify and describe the alternatives that represent stakeholders views and it will be necessary to follow up by phone or mail or even to make another field trip to clarify the interests and perspectives of the various stakeholder groups.

After making sure that you understand the type of alternatives to be considered and that you are familiar with the general characteristics of the study area (as discussed in chapters 6 and 8), it may be helpful to develop a list of the major stakeholder groups in the area and to summarize the preferences or proposals of each group. This may require considerable effort, and may involve public meetings or other formal public involvement activities. The social assessor can often create an opportunity to present the preferences of the major stakeholder groups and to explain their perspectives on important issues to the team. It may be most effective and efficient to hold public meetings to allow the stakeholders to state their own positions and to participate in the early project defining activities. This can be very effective in establishing a perception of objectivity in the process. There is no quicker way to discredit a study's objectivity than to fail to consider the proposals of some groups with an interest in the project. The social assessor may be in a position to help convey or clarify community viewpoints to the other members of the team and to work with the public involvement staff to encourage consideration of stakeholder interests and concerns.

In this process, there is frequently a tendency for the team or the decision makers to be too quick to dismiss alternatives on the grounds that they are not viable. It is important to remember that there is a considerable difference between something being nonviable and something being undesirable. Desirability is always defined by the values and role of the particular agency, company, or stakeholder group. Since different groups have different values and roles, it is inevitable that what is desirable to one group may not seem desirable to others.

Agencies are just as likely as sponsors and stakeholder groups to use their values and needs in defining a plan's viability. This can lead to the discarding of alternatives which should be considered at this early stage if the process is to be credible. One of your responsibilities can be to raise these issues and try to ensure that alternatives ruled out as nonviable are actually nonviable, rather than simply undesirable from some important stake-holder's perspective. Care must be taken, however, not to proceed in a manner which encroaches upon the prerogatives of the decision makers.

A number of public involvement manuals are available which discuss these issues in some detail. See, for example:

Creighton, James
    1980 The Public Involvement Manual. Denver, Colo.: U.S.
    Bureau of Reclamation.

Identify and Consider Major Environmental and Socioeconomic Effects

The next step in the process is to identify at a general level, the major environmental and socioeconomic changes that would be caused by various formulations of the types of alternatives being considered. (To prepare for this, you may want to read chapters 8 through 11.) If you are not already familiar with the study area, a field trip can be very useful.

When the task is to formulate broad and conceptual alternatives, it is sometimes difficult to obtain much detailed information about their potential to cause changes in the six factors identified in Chapter 6 -- the number or type of people, jobs, income, resources, organizational/regulatory context, and public safety. Typically, approximations are adequate to allow effective application of the scoping process and to lead the formulation process in the right direction. A major responsibility of each team member is to ask the right questions -- for example, Do we know whether or not all the new people will come in at once or whether there will be a gradual buildup? How do the alternatives differ in the taxes they would generate in terms of jurisdiction and timing? Questions like this will help to clarify the areas which need to be evaluated during the formulation of detailed alternatives. When considering the potential changes that could be introduced by modifying different aspects of the alternatives being developed, questions need to be asked about (1) direct project inputs, (2) community resources, (3) community social organization, and (4) social well-being. The questions about direct project inputs have generally been covered in Chapter 6. The latter three aspects are discussed briefly here, and in more detail in Chapter 8.

Community Resources

The following questions will help you identify an alternative's potential to affect a community's resources and assist in formulating the best possible alternatives:

1) **Historical analysis.** What has been the history of similar projects in the past or previous, related efforts?
2) **Cultural analysis.** Are there major cultural conflicts which would be restimulated by any of the plans, such as

disturbance of Indian sacred lands, opposition by a dominant religious group, or a threat to the existing economic base of the community?

3) **Demographic characteristics.** Would any of the plans produce a significant change in the demographic makeup of any community?

4) **Facilities and services.** Would there be major impacts on facilities and services in any community? Would mitigation of these impacts make the project economically unfeasible?

5) **Institutions and organizations.** Are there major institutions, organizations, or coalitions which would prefer particular alternatives or act to oppose a particular alternative? Are there gaps or conflicts in the institutional structure which would prevent effective response or guarantee conflict?

6) **Economic resources.** Do the economic resources needed to complete the project or project-related development exist within the community?

7) **Leadership.** Would the leaders of the affected communities be able and willing to organize the necessary response?

8) **Attitudes towards development.** Are community attitudes generally supportive of the kind of development which is being proposed, or has there been consistent opposition to this type of development? Is the opposition to the nature of the development or to its schedule or other specific characterisitics?

Community Social Organization

The following questions will help you identify potential effects on a community's social organization and therefore help identify mechanisms for designing more desirable alternatives:

1) **Diversity/complexity.** Would any of the plans produce major changes in the diversity or complexity of any community, or would little change occur either because the community has already lost its homogeneity or because the changes introduced by the project would be insignificant? In what ways could the alternatives be formulated to alter this outcome? Could the project be designed to broaden the economic base of the community rather than making it very dependent upon a single or a few industries?

2) **Outside ties.** Would any of the alternatives greatly change the organizational or regulatory context in the area? Of particular importance, would any increase the degree to which important decisions about the community are made by people outside the community? Could the community marshall the outside support and assistance it would need? How could the alternatives be formulated to ensure optimal results?

3) **Distribution of resources and power.** What aspects of the plans would serve to increase or decrease the equity of

distribution and costs and benefits within the area or the community? Would implementation of any plan strengthen or threaten an existing political or economic elite? How could the alternatives be formulated to ensure that vulnerable populations are not adversely affected and that they gain access to project benefits?

4) **Coordination.** Would any of the plans tax the coordinative mechanisms or processes within the community? How could they be designed to be most easily implemented?

5) **Personal Interaction.** Would the proposed action introduce enough new people or cause sufficient controversy that the major interaction patterns among community residents would be substantially changed? Could project implementation be designed to encourage community residents to participate in decisions affecting the community and their relationships with one another? What actions or procedures by the project implementor could reduce the extent of the changes in personal interaction patterns?

Social Well-being Indicators

The purpose for considering project inputs, community resources, community social organization, and social well-being indicators when formulating alternatives is to ensure that adequate effort has been made to avoid the creation of conditions that adversely affect well-being while enhancing conditions that improve well-being. Areas to investigate and consider in terms of well-being indicators include:

1) **Behavior indicators.** Can the alternatives be formulated to avoid introducing populations with patterns of behavior (in terms of crime, alcohol or drug use, or family violence) that would adversely affect residents' sense of community and personal security? Can the alternatives be designed or implemented in ways that would discourage/reduce undesirable behaviors?

2) **Material well-being.** Can the alternatives be designed to introduce sufficient income or resources to improve the material well-being of community residents? Can mechanisms be developed to ensure that disadvantaged groups receive a fair share of the benefits?

3) **Perceptions of community.** Can the alternatives be formulated so that the changes in characteristics and/or social organization are either viewed positively or are insufficient to affect resident's perceptions of the community?

When contemplating the potential for various alternatives to cause major environmental and socioeconomic effects, it is important to make sure that you are taking into account other activities occurring in the area. If several activities occur simultaneously, the area will experience the cumulative effect of all of them, not only the effects of the alternative under consideration. The findings of this type of review can be summarized quite briefly, or they can be presented in a longer discussion that highlights the major

trade-offs and issues discussed during the process. Which of these
approaches is selected will depend upon the needs of the formulation
team and project management.

Estimate the Magnitude of the Effects

When developing or comparing alternatives, it is often not sufficient to merely identify that an effect will occur. It is also
necessary to estimate the effect's magnitude and to assess its importance. In this process, the social assessor is called upon to
make judgments about which social effects are important. For this
reason, the discussion of social effects needs to include an estimation of their intensity and significance. Some social researchers
find this task uncomfortable because it requires them to make value
judgments. Keep in mind that the social assessor is the person on
the team who is best qualified to make a judgment about which social
effects are most important. What the social assessor is not in a
position to do alone is judge whether a particular social effect is
more important than an environmental or economic effect. This
judgment belongs to the team and, later, to the decision maker in
consultation with the public. Again, reference to the public involvement manuals which discuss these value judgments and decision
processes in some detail may be helpful. Review of chapters 8
through 11 is also recommended.

Identify Implementation Problems

After analyzing the environmental and socioeconomic effects of
each alternative, it should be possible to point out major problems
that could prevent or hinder their implementation. In addition to
public acceptability, which is discussed below, the principal concerns for the social assessor are likely to be in the institutional
and legal areas. For example, major problems could occur if an alternative requires the creation of institutions which currently do
not exist, if it requires changes in existing laws or jurisdictional
boundaries, if local taxing districts do not have sufficient authority to cover the probable demands for services and facilities, or if
it conflicts with major cultural practices.

Assess Public Acceptability of the Alternatives

Along with the public involvement staff and the decision makers,
the social assessor is responsible for identifying whether any of the
alternatives are particularly likely to gain broad public support or
if they are likely to generate continued opposition. Frequently the
information available at this stage is limited, so this assessment
should not be considered definite and is most useful in identifying
serious and long-standing opposition.

7.4 Conclusion

Although the formulation of alternatives is the first step in the definition and evaluation of a proposed action, in itself it is a mini-social assessment. The time available to formulate alternatives is generally short, with alternatives often being selected almost on an ad hoc basis. In addition, in many cases, the specific design of the final project will undergo continual modification as more complete or detailed information becomes available. A frequent frustration for those involved in the assessment of large-scale projects is continual change in the project description/schedule. Another frequent frustration is the inability to effect changes that could substantially improve the social consequences of the project. As discussed earlier, many factors influence the flexibility of the organizations proposing the action as well as those evaluating it, and many additional factors affect the degree of participation and influence of the social assessor in this process.

Careful and realistic understanding of the constraints and perspectives of those responsible for the development of alternatives, project implementation, and project assessment will help you to be more effective and less frustrated in your work. As mentioned before, it is important to focus your sociological analyses not only upon the proposed action but also upon the assessment process itself and your role and position in the organization that is conducting it.

8. Description of the Existing Environment

8.1 Introduction

This chapter presents a method for identifying and describing the characteristics of the existing environment. The purpose of examining the existing environment is analytic; information about existing social organization and attitudes forms the basis for analyzing the likely social consequences of the proposed action and interpreting their importance. For this reason, both the research you conduct and the description of the existing environment that you write up should be tailored to the particular assessment task -- it should fit the purpose of the assessment and the characteristics of the proposed action.

This chapter provides guidance sufficient for highly detailed or comprehensive assessments. If the assessment you are conducting does not require such detail, we suggest that you read the chapter carefully and then use the screening and scoping information from Chapter 6 to design a research and reporting plan that is appropriate to your particular task. Be wary of wasting effort by trying to address the problem in too much detail -- it will be frustrating and will lead to the development of a document that is less than optimal for its purposes. One simple way to get an indication of the level of detail desired is to work out page estimates for the technical report (if there is to be one) and the final report or EIS. Page limitations are often severe, and dictate the degree to which the results of your work must be condensed and summarized. Another consideration in establishing the level of detail is the budget and time allocated to the task. It is very important to match your work plan to your budget and schedule.

It should be noted that economic, demographic, and facilities/services characteristics receive relatively heavy emphasis in this analysis. The reason for this is that many of the projects likely to be assessed involve economic development or resource management activities that cause social effects primarily by changing the economic, demographic, and facilities/services characteristics of communities. This becomes quite clear in the scoping process described in Chapter 6. Four of the six project-related changes that have the potential to cause social effects are economic, demographic, or resource factors (people, jobs, income, resources). Even the remaining two factors (organizational and regulatory contexts; public health and safety) have strong economic aspects. Consequently, to determine the social consequences of most of the proposed actions likely to be assessed with this guide, it is important to understand how these economic, demographic, and facilities/services effects occur and how they cause social consequences, even though you may not be responsible for forecasting these effects yourself.

This chapter is organized into four major components. The first explains the purpose of the description of the existing environment. The second describes the steps involved in developing and documenting a description of the existing environment. The third provides a detailed discussion of how to identify the important characteristics of the existing social environment and the information needed for your assessment. The fourth provides a list of additional references.

8.2 The Purpose of the Description of the Existing Environment

The purpose of the description of the existing environment is twofold. First, it provides the primary basis for forecasting the consequences of the introduction of a project or policy into a particular locale. As discussed throughout the guide, social effects occur through a complex interaction between the project and the study area or community. It is only through a clear understanding of the history and contemporary characteristics of a community or area that one can anticipate how it will respond to and interact with a particular project. Second, the description of the existing environment, along with the forecasts of baseline social characteristics, provides the basis for measuring and evaluating the changes that are likely to occur as a result of the proposed project. The description of the existing environment is thus a key element in the entire assessment process, serving a highly analytic as well as descriptive function. Consequently, one of the major problems facing a social assessor is to determine what he or she needs to know about the existing environment in order to conduct a quality assessment.

8.3 Steps in the Process

Overview

There are four principal steps in the process of developing a useful description of the existing environment:

1) Establishing the purpose, scope, and level of detail of the assessment
2) Determining what the important characteristics of the existing environment are and what type of information is needed to describe them
3) Deciding how to obtain the necessary information and conducting the necessary research

4) Analyzing the information, documenting your work, and preparing the necessary reports

In this section, each of these four steps is addressed. However, because the second step in this process (determining what the important characteristics of the existing environment are and what type of information is needed to describe them) is a major analytic task only an overview is included here; a more detailed discussion of this step is provided in Section 8.4.

Establish the Purpose, Scope, and Level of Detail of the Assessment

Determining what is important to know about the existing environment is critical to the entire assessment effort since it determines what information will be available for analyzing how the inputs from the proposed action will result in social impacts. In order to find out which aspects of the existing environment are important to the particular assessment you are conducting, you need to understand (1) the purpose of the assessment, (2) the scope of the assessment, determined in large part by the nature of the inputs from the proposed action that could cause social effects, and (3) the level of detail necessary for the type of assessment you are conducting. In addition, you need to understand how -- by what mechanisms -- the effects of the proposed action will occur.

As discussed in Chapter 6, the type and purpose of the assessment effort should have been clarified through consideration of the overall assessment process and discussions with your supervisor. The level of detail will probably be greater if the study is focusing on social change rather than on delineating social impacts. The scoping process described in Chapter 6 recommends a procedure for estimating the potential changes caused directly by the proposed action and obtaining some preliminary information about the existing and baseline characteristics of the study area communities. Through this process, the communities or areas requiring most attention can be identified and the major sources of social impact clarified. This information should be reviewed, and the estimates of potential action-related changes (or inputs) updated if more information has become available.

Because the guide has been designed for use in a variety of assessment situations, including those requiring detailed assessment of a specific project, it is important that the users of the guide continually evaluate what level of detail is appropriate for the work being undertaken. In some cases, the assessment will appropriately be conducted at a high level of generalization, where project inputs are estimated largely in terms of total population and general occupational change and only order-of-magnitude impacts are estimated. In others, much more detail will be required. As has been stressed throughout the guide, you need to think through the time, budget, purpose, and scope of the assessment and adjust your work accordingly.

Determine Which Charactieristics of the Existing Environment Are Important and What Information Is Needed to Describe Them

This step is the crux of the assessment process. In order to determine which aspects of the existing environment are important and what information is needed, you must take what information you have at hand (or can readily obtain) about the proposed action and the study communities, apply what you know about social change, and mentally walk through the analysis of potential social effects of the proposed action. Obviously, this is not a simple task, and, in fact, it encompasses most of what is involved in conducting a social assessment. Nevertheless, this is the task that needs to be accomplished.

The important characteristics of the existing social environment are those that will either (1) affect the characteristics of the proposed action or the responses made by the community to the proposed action or (2) be affected in an important way by the proposed action or by the responses made to it. As indicated previously, the social organization model (see Figure 8-1) can be used to provide a conceptual framework determining what these important charcteristics are and to provide guidelines for conducting this analysis.

Because the use of the social organization model for this purpose requires fairly extensive discussion, Section 8.4 is devoted entirely to this topic. At this point, it is sufficient to make clear that a major step in the process of developing a description of the existing environment is to determine what you need to know about the study area, the study area communities, and the people living in them.

Decide How to Obtain the Necessary Information and Implement the Research

Introduction

Once the information you need about the communities in the study area has been identified, you should once again review your schedule and the purpose of the assessment before taking the next step -- developing a plan for obtaining the necessary information. The steps that can be followed during this phase of the process include the following:

1) Critically review the level of detail/aggregation that should be utilized in the assessment. If the level of aggregation is high, don't waste time collecting or analyzing unnecessarily detailed information. Rather, focus on the major factors and relationships.

2) Summarize the information requirements and identify the possible sources, noting whether the information is available from a secondary source, from another team member, or from field work.

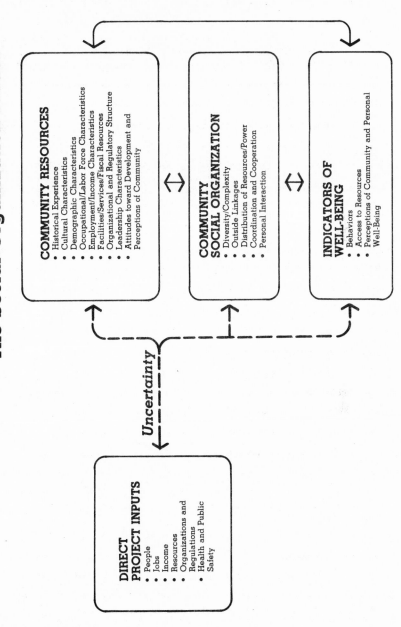

Figure 8-1

The Social Organization Model

COMMUNITY RESOURCES

- Historical Experience
- Cultural Characteristics
- Demographic Characteristics
- Occupational/Labor Force Characteristics
- Employment/Income Characteristics
- Facilities/Services/Fiscal Resources
- Organizational and Regulatory Structure
- Leadership Characteristics
- Attitudes toward Development and Perceptions of Community

COMMUNITY SOCIAL ORGANIZATION

- Diversity/Complexity
- Outside Linkages
- Distribution of Resources/Power
- Coordination and Cooperation
- Personal Interaction

INDICATORS OF WELL-BEING

- Behaviors
- Access to Resources
- Perceptions of Community and Personal Well-Being

Uncertainty

DIRECT PROJECT INPUTS

- People
- Jobs
- Income
- Resources
- Organizations and Regulations
- Health and Public Safety

3) Review the available sources and techniques for obtaining information, and determine how any primary data will be gathered.
4) Identify the field instruments that need to be prepared.
5) Develop a detailed research plan and schedule.
6) Implement the research.

Summarize the Information Requirements

In order to plan your research, you need to review the process you followed in determining the important characteristics of the existing environment (discussed in detail in Section 8.4) and prepare a summary of the assessment's information requirements. If you are examining multiple communities, this summary could take the form of a table similar to that shown in Figure 8-2. This summary will give you a good indication of the scope of information that you will need to obtain either from (1) primary field work or (2) secondary sources that might have addressed these characteristics.

Using the summary, it will be useful to review your available secondary sources, particularly any preliminary work done for the same proposed action, to identify how much of the necessary information is already available. Based on the summary of information and the suggestions for sources of data (provided in Section 8.4), you will be ready for the next step, a review of the available sources and techniques for obtaining information.

Review Available Sources

The basic techniques used to gather the information necessary for an assessment are discussed briefly in this section. The techniques include the following:

1) Analysis of secondary sources
2) Interviews
3) Questionnaires/surveys
4) Workshops/meetings
5) Field trips and observation

A more detailed discussion of these techniques is provided in chapters 12-14.

Secondary Sources

There are numerous secondary sources that can provide information about communities and social change. These secondary sources are particularly helpful in defining the economic/demographic characteristics of the community, identifying the existing institutional structure and level of facilities and services (including additional requirements), and gaining some knowledge of the community's history. Normally, secondary sources cannot give you the "soft" data about community attitudes, values, and organization, although in

Figure 8-2

Summary of
Information Requirements

CHARACTERISTIC	TYPE OF INFORMATION	POTENTIAL SOURCES
Community Resources		
Social Organization		
Indicators of Well-being		

some cases special reports can be extremely useful for this type of information as well. Consequently, while secondary sources provide an essential part of the information needed for social assessment, they must always be used in combination with one or more of the other techniques in order to obtain a more complete understanding of the community and its organization. Unless you are experienced with the type of community and type of proposed action being assessed, you will need to seek secondary sources -- often published articles or other research reports -- that can give you the informational base needed to anticipate project and worker characteristics and the interaction patterns that are likely to occur. Specific references have generally not been included in the guide because the pertinent literature varies according to the geographic region and project type, though some suggestions are included in Section 8.5. It is again emphasized, however, that your forecasts and assessment can only be as valid as the information and analytic rigor upon which they are based, so you are strongly urged to identify and utilize the pertinent literature.

Some secondary sources can profitably be reviewed before visiting the study area. These include the more theoretical sociological material, published research reports, and analyses of social change processes in similar settings or circumstances. There are others, usually available only in the community, that are useful to review before any interviews are conducted. Reviewing these materials in advance enables you to be more knowledgeable when talking with people in the community. Advance preparation not only helps build credibility, it also enables you to collect better information by identifying important issues or questions that should be covered in the field work. As the work proceeds in the community, new sources of information will be found. It should be kept in mind that reviewing secondary sources is a continuing activity, not simply advance work.

A useful skill to develop in this work is an ability to scan documents and abstract the pertinent information without getting bogged down in extraneous material. Particularly in areas where extensive resource development has occurred, a great number of lengthy reports have often been prepared. An incredible amount of time can be spent if those reports are read in detail instead of scanned for information relevant to social concerns. You should be sure to budget your time to allow adequate time in the field and in the analysis and report preparation. There is frequently a temptation to extend review of secondary sources into time that is needed for careful thought and writing.

The range of possible secondary sources is wide and varies from site to site. Among the most useful types of secondary sources are the following:

1) **Records of public meetings, scoping sessions, public comments, and surface owner consultations, as well as other bureau or agency plans or data sets on the community or project.**

2) **County comprehensive plans.** Many counties have prepared comprehensive plans that provide valuable background information about the area, the institutional structure, and the

expectations and preparations that have been made for the future. These plans are generally available in the local library or from the area planning board.

3) **Census data.** Data from the most recent U.S. censuses can provide a good indication of the type of change that has occurred in the area over the last several decades. It is useful to obtain data from any special censuses that have been conducted for communities or counties in the study area. These data are generally available in local libraries or planning offices or at libraries serving as federal depositories. In some areas, it will be necessary to interpolate community or study area characteristics from county level data.

4) **Published literature and research reports.** As in any scientific research, your work must utilize and build upon previous research and analyses. Review of pertinent literature concerning social organization, social change, well-being, and economic development can be extremely valuable. In many cases there will be extensive literature on the social and economic consequences of similar projects whose theory and research findings can be applied to the particular analysis you are conducting. It is essential that you avail yourself of this existing information and use it judiciously in your analysis. Even if the literature fails to provide the specific data you need, it will help you identify the **type** of information you need and suggest methods for its collection. Your particular needs will vary according to your training, the type of project being assessed, the type of community being affected, and your field and research experience. General literature review skills can be used to identify pertinent materials. It should be kept in mind, however, that much of the applied research that will provide the most specific and current information is not published in academic journals but remains as working papers, research reports, and technical supplements to decision-making or policy summaries (such as environmental impact statements). Identification and utilization of this body of secondary sources is discussed further in chapters 13 and 14 in Section III.

5) **Environmental impact statements/socioeconomic studies.** Many times, state or federal agencies or private companies have prepared environmental impact statements or other socioeconomic studies as part of other proposed activities in the same geographic area. These often provide detailed background information about the area. Local chambers of commerce or economic development authorities may have commissioned other economic studies as well.

6) **Local histories.** Local authors frequently have written and published histories of the area. These documents can be helpful, but it is important to remember that they have often been written by people with a particular point to make (such as demonstrating the importance of their own family in local history), or by people who are unwilling to create conflict with their neighbors. Some of the more

controversial community events or issues may consequently be
distorted or downplayed in these documents. Local histories
can be helpful, but they should be viewed with caution, and
important facts or perspectives should be verified from
other sources.

7) **Maps.** Accurate maps of the towns and counties included in
the potential study area should be reviewed. These can often be obtained from state highway departments.

8) **Lists of public officials.** Developing a list of local
elected and appointed officials, major agency directors, and
their principal functions can prevent unnecessary social
errors and enhance understanding of the institutional structure of the area. Usually such lists can be compiled from
materials available from state agencies, the local chamber
of commerce, or city or county administrative offices. Back
issues of these documents can also be useful.

9) **Local newspapers.** Scanning local newspapers is one good
way to identify major stakeholder groups, major controversies, and how the community deals with issues. For example,
long-standing or unusual levels of conflict between groups
or jurisdictions will usually show up in some form in the
local newspaper. Normally it is useful to review at least
two or three weeks' worth of recent newspapers and the most
recent annual edition of the newspaper before beginning
field work. More extensive analysis of the newspaper can be
conducted later, as appropriate. Local newspapers are usually available at local libraries or at the newspaper
office. Newspapers, especially the editorials, can often
provide additional information and a different perspective
on the important issues and events identified in local histories. Centennial issues can provide extremely useful summaries of the history and influential figures of a community.

10) **Local telephone directories.** Current and past issues of
the local telephone directory can provide much information
about the community. It is recommended that you obtain current and previous directories for the study area communities
as a source of information about the economic and organizational structure and recent changes that have occurred.

Given the wide array of potential secondary sources and the
possibility that previous work has been done on the study area by
someone else in your office, an important first step in this task is
to compile the available materials, review them, prepare a bibliography, and note additional studies or reports that should be obtained for review. An important second step is to review this
material and utilize its information.

Interviews

Interviewing is a technique frequently used in social assessment. There are many different kinds of interviews, ranging from
the very unstructured to the very structured, utilizing formal questionnaires. The approach generally recommended by this guide falls

somewhere in between and can be called "semistructured", meaning
that the social assessor prepares an interview guide and initiates
the interview with a clear idea of what he or she wants to learn
from it. The advantage of this approach is that the interviewer can
adapt the wording and sequence of the questions to the kind of information being received and can pursue information or topics that
are raised during the interview even if they were not among those
originally specified. However, it is important to make sure that
the original topics are covered.

Even though the interviewing style proposed here is relatively
informal and adapted to the person being interviewed, with no
pretense that the results constitute a statistically valid representation of the population, it is essential that standards of pro-
fessionalism be observed in conducting the interview and selecting
the people to be interviewed. These topics are discussed more completely in Chapter 13. The assessor must avoid biasing the responses by asking questions in a way that clearly implies a "right"
answer or by expressing personal views that shape the direction of
the conversation. The assessor should also select the people to be
interviewed with methods that meet reasonable sampling requirements.

Questionnaires/Surveys

Formal survey techniques can be used to obtain statistically
valid estimates of the characteristics of a population. This is
generally the only way to quantify the distribution of characteristics among the population -- particularly characteristics such as
attitudes, perceptions, and social affiliation, for which other
sources are usually unavailable. In order to claim validity, rigorous procedures must be followed to eliminate bias and sampling
errors. Unless stringent procedures are followed, formal surveys
have no greater validity as an indication of population characteristics than a series of informally conducted interviews. Since surveys
are generally less flexible than other interviewing techniques, it
is particularly important to clarify objectives and review methods
before initiating a survey effort.

Practically speaking, formal surveys which utilize questionnaires or standard questions are tools that are currently not available for regular use by federal employees. The Office of Management
and Budget (OMB) must approve all formal questionnaires or surveys
whenever ten or more members of the public will be interviewed;
quotas are established for each federal department in terms of the
number of public contacts allowed. Unless the project is of considerable significance and there is sufficient time to plan and implement a survey in a professional manner, including obtaining OMB
approval, a large-scale survey may not be appropriate. This does
not mean that questionnaires or surveys are not useful or that they
are not sometimes vital to an assessment, but only that they are not
always necessary and that they require planning and attention to
technical detail.

Useful survey data may be available from other sources, for example, from local universities, from studies sponsored by a chamber
of commerce or economic development corporation, or from studies

conducted by other state or federal agencies. While the information is not always available in exactly the form desired, it is often very helpful. One must be cautious, however, in using survey results without careful examination of the procedure which was followed in conducting the survey and compiling the results. If the survey or questionnaire was not properly designed, the results may be badly misleading. Additional guidance about surveys and questionnaires is presented in Chapter 13.

Workshops/Public Meetings

Workshops and public meetings can also be a rich source of information about both community values and the expectations residents have about the impacts of a proposed action. Care must be taken, however, to recognize that information gained in this manner cannot be assumed to be representative of the entire community. Participants of workshops and public meetings may represent only particular stakeholder groups. Public involvement techniques are not addressed in this guide. Those interested might refer to one of the handbooks developed for public involvement. References are provided in Section 8.5.

Field Trips and Observation

The principal way to obtain much of the information necessary for the description of the existing environment and the impact assessment is through field trips to the study area where you interview local residents and officials and observe how the residents in the community behave toward one another. Much of the important information about how a community is organized and how it functions is most readily available through observation -- how the neighborhoods are laid out and maintained, how local residents greet one another, the condition of public buildings and recreational facilities, and how public meetings are conducted. Consequently, it is important to prepare for your field trips and to make careful records of the observations made while in the community. Particularly if the assessment involves work in a number of communities within a short time period, it is important to develop a method for organizing your observations and perceptions so they don't become confused. Specific guidance for organizing and conducting a field trip is provided in Chapter 12. Based on this review and examination of the information requirements, the best approach for obtaining the necessary primary data -- structured, formal survey; semistructured survey; or semistructured interviews -- can be determined. The discussion in Chapter 13 can assist you in making those decisions.

Develop a Detailed Research Plan and Schedule

The purpose of developing a detailed work plan is to lay out the tasks required to obtain the necessary information so that they can be organized in a logical and efficient manner.

As a general rule, it is preferable to review and analyze information from available secondary sources before developing the specific instruments to be used in the field. This avoids both revision of the instruments and wasted interview time. If you are participating in an environmental impact assessment, it is likely that the economic/demographic and facilities/services analysts are gathering secondary data and planning field trips on about the same schedule. It is important to make sure that the efforts are coordinated.

Although other approaches could be used, it is recommended that the social organization model and the summary of information requirements developed previously be used to organize the data collection and field work. The information on the proposed action's potential to cause change in the study area communities (see Chapter 6) should be reviewed with the economist to ensure that it represents the most current thinking.

Following review of available secondary sources and discussions with the other members of the assessment team to coordinate the contacts made with community residents, the field instruments can be designed to ensure collection of all pertinent material, and the field trips can be scheduled. It is recommended that the field trips be kept brief, with adequate office time scheduled to write up and review the information gathered in the field. For large study areas, it is preferable to schedule several shorter field trips rather than one long trip, if possible.

When preparing the work plan and schedule, allow a generous estimate for the time it will take to analyze the information and write up the report. Extensive information will be gathered; much of it will be wasted if adequate time is not allocated to the analysis. To ensure careful and uninhibited analysis, it is recommended that a draft working paper be prepared prior to any of the final reports that will be formally submitted.

Implement the Research

Once a satisfactory work plan has been developed which allows adequate pacing of the effort, the research plan can be implemented. Throughout the research process, it is important to continually ensure that a focus on information pertinent to the assessment is maintained while at the same time remaining alert for any information that would indicate that revisions in the information specifications are warranted. Obviously, information that would significantly influence the forecasts of the direct inputs from the proposed action or for the baseline should be noted, but it is vital not to be enticed into collecting extensive data on topics that are either extraneous to the assessment or that are excessively detailed.

Decide How to Document Your Work and Prepare the Description of the Existing Environment

Introduction

Because the description of the existing environment provides the key information necessary for assessing and evaluating the effects of the proposed action, it is important to approach the information you have gathered in an analytic fashion. For this reason, it is recommended that you prepare an inventory of all the information about the existing environment that has been gathered. An inventory organizes the data that have been collected compactly and concisely so that it can be used. The inventory can be in the form of brief summaries (a sentence or two) organized into relevant categories. One possible schema would be to inventory data about the existing environment according to the major topics in the social organization model -- community resources, social organization, well-being indicators -- and to develop summaries describing the inputs for each of the alternatives being considered. For the with-action alternatives, it is useful to describe the inputs due to the baseline and the proposed action separately as well as in total (baseline plus proposed action) to clarify the attribution of effects to the proposed action. A few examples of what is intended for each of these areas are shown below.

1) **Community Resources**

    History. The community has not changed demographically or economically to any degree for the past two decades. It has had no experience with development.

    Attitudes. Most of the residents of the community favor the project (program) because they see it as a means for the economic revival of the town. Those opposed to the project are well organized but come from a limited population, while those who favor the project are unorganized and from a diverse population.

2) **Social Organization**

    Distribution of Resources/Power. Most of the youth leave the community after graduating from high school in order to further their education or get jobs. Those who stay mostly go into ranching. Ranchers are the elite in the community. Land is the principal basis of wealth and the principal criterion for status. There are no obvious deprived minorities.

    Coordination and Cooperation. The town and county have not demonstrated the ability to coordinate their efforts to resolve common problems. There is continuing dispute over police/sheriff jurisdictions and inability to collaborate on a decision about the jail. Animal control remains nagging unresolved issue.

The few newcomers to town remain generally isolated; no effort has been made to coordinate their entrance into community affairs.

In general, leadership has not been able or willing to take a decisive role in coordinating community positions or efforts.

Personal Interaction. Almost everything gets done on an informal basis. Most residents say they like it that way; they don't like any type of "red tape" or formality in conducting the business of everyday life. Most things get done on a slow or "as convenient" time schedule.

3) **Indicators of Well-being**

Behaviors. None of the behavioral indicators were noted as unusual, although alcohol abuse is a recognized problem.

Resources. Per capita income levels are low for the state, and community resources are limited. Most family incomes are clustered at the low end, with the usual small-town concentrations of wealth -- doctor, lawyer, banker, and a few wealthy ranchers.

Attitudes. Generally people report feeling that the community is economically depressed but has good personal relationships and lifestyle.

After the inventory has been completed, the information can be analyzed and synthesized into a draft working paper. Based on the analysis performed in the development of the working paper, you will be in a position to target your formal reports specifically to the needs of the particular assessment, summarizing the information if only a brief description is necessary. For this discussion, it is assumed that the assessment requires the development of both a detailed technical report and a shorter summary that will be included in an environmental report or environmental impact statement. As was stressed earlier, it is important to understand and keep firmly in mind the purpose and requirements of the assessment and to prepare your reports accordingly.

Analyze the Data and Prepare a Draft Working Paper

If the information about the existing environment has been obtained utilizing the social organization model, it is recommended that this model be used to organize the analysis and the draft working paper. The purpose of the draft working paper is (1) to provide a mechanism for working through the information you have obtained and (2) to enable you to develop a better understanding of your information. Preparing a working paper will also allow you to explore your information more thoroughly and to candidly develop your analysis about community leadership, distribution of resources, and community coordination.

Analyzing this complex and abstract data will be hard work. It is inevitable that there will be contradictions and gaps in the in-

formation and that it will take several passes through the material
before your conclusions become clear. The draft working paper is
intended to encourage you to struggle with the data, to check information from different sources, and to try out different analyses.
As mentioned before, guidance on the use of secondary data sources
and analysis of interview data is provided in chapters 13 and 14.
Once you have worked through the draft working paper and are satisfied that you have a good understanding of the major characteristics
of the communities and/or the area residents, including the prevailing attitudes about the proposed action and changes of the type that
may result if the proposed action is taken, you will be in a good
position to assess the consequences of the proposed action and to
prepare a formal report describing the existing characteristics of
study area communities.

Prepare the Existing Environment Chapter of the Technical Report

The purpose of a technical report is either to provide back-up
material for the environmental report or the environmental impact
statement or to serve as a stand-alone document presenting the social assessment information. Before you start to prepare material
for the technical report, it is worthwhile to make sure that you
clearly understand the purpose of the document, the intended audience, the current outline of the document, and any format specifications you will have to follow.

Once you have established the procedures and format for the social section of the existing environment chapter, you should check
with the economist and facilities/services analyst to review what
they will be including in their section of the report if your reports are to be combined into a single document. It is very likely
that some of the material that you have described in detail, especially the description of community resources and indicators of
well-being, will overlap substantially with their reports. It is
necessary to reach an agreement about who will discuss what so that
the technical report is neither redundant nor missing pertinent information.

Once this has been done, you should be in a position to prepare
the technical report quite quickly, since it will be based on the
analysis you developed in the draft working paper. It is important
to remember that the description of the existing environment presented in both the technical report and the final environmental
statement are to be analytic, not exhaustively descriptive. Report
the information that matters in your assessment of the proposed action, but don't include a lot of background or explanatory material.

Prepare the Existing Environment Section of the Environmental Im-
pact Statement

The purpose of the environmental impact statement is to summarize and highlight the information that is pertinent to the decision
about the proposed action. You will probably be given stringent
specifications about length and format. In many cases this will

require you to synthesize the most important aspects of the description of the existing environment into a very brief and succinct statement. The focus in this summary should be to provide a basis for the conclusions you reach in the forecast and evaluation of impacts (discussed in Chapter 10).

8.4 Determining the Important Characteristics of the Existing Environment: Use of the Social Organization Model

General Approach

This section presents a detailed discussion of the use of the social organization model to determine what characteristics of the existing environment need to be described and what information about the existing environment needs to be collected for your particular assessment. To facilitate this process, we suggest that you utilize a matrix similar to that shown in Figure 8-3. This matrix provides a good mechanism for systematizing and documenting your analysis. It is useful both here, in determining where to focus your efforts in describing the existing environment, and later, in forecasting the likely consequences of the proposed action (see Chapter 10).

The matrix identifies all possible combinations of project (or baseline) inputs and community characteristics. As you work through the elements of the social organization model in the remainder of the chapter, this matrix can be used to summarize your conclusions regarding the potential for each direct project (or baseline) input to affect community resources, social organization, and well-being. (It can also highlight where community characteristics are likely to affect project inputs, an aspect of the analysis addressed more thoroughly in Chapter 9). In addition, the completed matrix can be used to indicate which aspects of the social environment need to be examined in detail because they are likely to be directly affected by baseline or direct project inputs.

Since community resources, social organization, and well-being are interrelated (see Figure 8-1), one community characteristic may affect another. The matrix of major relationships can also provide a format for considering (1) whether the effects of the direct project input on a particular community characteristic could be prevented or altered by some other characteristics of the community, and (2) whether the effect of the direct project input on particular community characteristics could cause changes in other community characteristics. It is this analysis which identifies what needs to be included in the description of the existing environment, informs the forecasts of baseline and direct project inputs, and provides the basis for forecasting the social impacts of the proposed action.

The Social Organization Model: Community Resources

The purpose of analyzing community resources is twofold. The first is to assess the community's ability and willingness to respond to the demands created by the direct project inputs. The second is to determine how the community's resource base will change as

Figure 8-3

Matrix to Identify Major Relationships

COMMUNITY _____
ALTERNATIVE _____
PHASE _____

	DIRECT PROJECT INPUTS					
	People	Jobs	Income	Resources	Organizations/ Regulations	Health & Safety
COMMUNITY RESOURCES						
• Historical Experience						
• Culture						
• Demography						
• Occupations (Livelihood) Labor Force						
• Employment and Income						
• Facilities/Services/Fiscal						
• Organizations and Regulations						
• Leadership						
• Attitudes and Perceptions						
SOCIAL ORGANIZATION PROCESSES						
• Diversity/Complexity						
• Outside Linkages						
• Distribution of Resources/Power						
• Coordination and Cooperation						
• Personal Interaction						
WELL-BEING INDICATORS						
• Behaviors						
• Access to Resources						
• Perceptions						

a result of the proposed action. In some cases, project inputs will have little or no effect on community resources. In these cases, the lack of effect needs to be documented, but only limited attention needs to be given to description of existing community resources.

The adaptive capacity of a community depends not only on the availability of material resources (e.g., housing, classrooms, health care facilities, money, etc.), but also on a composite of relatively intangible things such as previous experience with development, political leadership, attitudes toward development and growth, and attitudes toward the particular project.

The major community resources that can be considered include the following:

1) Previous experience with development
2) Cultural characteristics, particularly the presence of unique populations such as American Indians, land grant Hispanics, or communities with a strong religious base, such as Mennonites or Mormons
3) Population size and demographic structure
4) Occupational and labor force characteristics, paying particular attention to the dominance of particular livelihoods and/or technologies
5) Employment and income characteristics of the community
6) Existing (or planned) facilities and services and fiscal resources
7) Institutions and organizations and the regulatory structure of the community
8) Leadership characteristics of the community
9) Residents' attitudes toward and response to development

Historical Experience

Variables

An understanding of the community's history is needed to understand the context in which community residents will experience a proposed action. It also provides information about the community's response to any similar projects or forces for change that have occurred previously. The historical review should focus on determining social attitudes, understanding the social structure of the community, and predicting how the community may respond to project inputs. Of particular importance is past experience with (1) similar projects, (2) other, related types of development, or (3) community emergencies and disasters. A community that has experienced previous projects or other situations that required coordinated response may be far more effective in responding and adapting to change than one without such experience. On the other hand, if the previous experience was bad, it may signal strong resistance and fear of change. In addition, community residents, having experienced growth, may have developed strong attitudes regarding these issues.

To save time, the review of the community's history should also be used to gather a variety of information that will be used in other areas. Particular attention should therefore be paid to information about:

1) Community origin
2) Previous experience with development
3) Current or recent political controversy regarding development
4) Major actors in previous development issues
5) Names and characteristics of influential persons, groups, or families
6) Important events (conflicts or achievements) in the community
7) Distinctive characteristics of the community that are strongly valued locally
8) Prominent stakeholder groups with a history in the area
9) Recurrent and unresolved problems that continue to plague the community

Data Sources

Local histories are often available. Although these histories must be viewed with caution and care should be taken to corroborate the important facts, they help to identify local issues. The library -- and in particular, local librarians -- are major sources of information about local history. Other sources include local newspapers, local historical societies, longtime residents, and archives at state libraries or universities.

Cultural Characteristics and Social Groups

Variables

A detailed analysis of cultural characteristics and lifestyle is not likely to be warranted for most impact assessments unless the study area population includes residents with unique racial, ethnic, religious, or occupational characteristics whose lifestyle would be affected by the proposed action. In many cases, even when such groups are present, time and budgetary constraints limit the depth of analysis that can be conducted. If the proposed action has the potential to affect the livelihood or lifestyle of a unique cultural group, the assessment design must be adjusted to allow time and resources to address the analytically difficult and often politically sensitive issue of cultural impact. If such time and resources are not available, decision makers should be alerted to the potential for problems later on. The preliminary steps in identifying and describing unique cultural groups are similar to those recommended for developing an overall social/cultural profile of the community.

One of the first problems facing the assessor is to determine what types of social groups are present in the study area communities and to ascertain whether or not any are sufficiently unique to

require special cultural attention. For large, clearly distinctive
groups such as Native Americans or Spanish Land Grant residents,
identification of the group is not such a problem. Other, less con-
spicuous groups may be more difficult to identify. In general, it
is recommended that community histories be examined to identify the
major social groupings of community residents and to delineate the
attributes which have set the groups apart. Understanding the
criteria used to distinguish the important social groups, the patterns of interaction among them, and the evolution of social groups
over the history of the community goes a long way toward establishing a framework for describing the contemporary social organization
of the community. Among the characteristics that can serve as the
basis for the formation (or perception) of social groups are the
following:

1) Ethnicity/race
2) Language
3) Religion
4) Livelihood/occupation
5) Income/wealth
6) Property ownership
7) Residential location
8) Length of residence
9) Age/sex
10) Special interests/political positions

Developing a profile of the distinguishable social groups according
to these types of characteristics and summarizing the nature of
their relationship to one another and the community is an excellent
way to organize the collection of information about community resources and community social organization.

When determining the attention to be focused on each of the
identified social/cultural groups, the following kinds of questions
need to be considered:

1) Will the unique characteristics of the group or community
cause them to be affected by or react to social change differently than a more typical group or community would?
2) What are the unique attitudes of the group or community toward development?
3) Will the proposed action alter the unique cultural characteristics of the community?
4) Will the proposed action change the relationships among the
groups or their relative position/role in the community?

Data Sources

If they are unique, most cultures found in the United States
have generally received substantial research attention though much
of it may be quite dated. There are numerous documents in university, state, and local libraries that discuss the culture of most of
the unique groups likely to be encountered. Interviews with community residents and members of the unique cultural group can provide

another primary source of information. If the assessment involves a unique cultural group, it may be useful to either consult an anthropologist with experience in the area or include an anthropologist on the study team. Local histories, newspapers, political records/minutes, and interviews with area residents provide the sources for delineating and profiling the major social groups of the community.

Population Size and Demographic Characteristics

Variables

The basic demographic characteristics of the study area communities will usually be described by the economic/demographic analyst, with the social assessor responsible for interpreting their meaning. Many actions do not cause large enough changes in population to result in a large change in a local community's demographic characteristics, aside from an increase in total numbers. Although it is useful to review as much information as available on the social characteristics of the affected area, the assessor's work should focus on those demographic factors that will change as a result of the proposed action. The level of effort must be tailored to the task. There is no value in an exhaustive demographic analysis if it is already clear that the project will have little population impact and if the demographic factors do not discriminate between alternatives.[1] Usually the scoping process described in Chapter 6 will provide sufficient information about the proposed action to indicate whether or not any demographic characteristics are likely to be significant. Examples of demographic characteristics that could be important are:

1) The total population size of the community
2) Recent trends in population size
3) Age/sex distribution of residents
4) Degree of ethnic or racial homogeneity
5) Educational characteristics of residents

The kinds of questions that will determine which of these characteristics are important include the following:

1) Could the proposed action cause a substantial change in the total population of any community?
2) Could the proposed action reverse recent population trends? For example, would communities with little experience with population change be faced with major changes?
3) Could the population change due to the proposed action result in changes in the overall age/sex, ethnic, or occupational distribution of any community, thereby affecting social relationships or service demands?

---

[1]Unless, of course the purpose of the study is to examine, in detail, population/demographic effects.

Data Sources

Typically, data to document preproject population size and demographic characteristics are provided by the economic/demographic
analyst or are available from secondary sources such as the U.S.
Census, although it may be difficult to obtain intercensal data at
the community level. Special surveys or studies may have been
conducted in the area. Interviews with local service agency personnel may be helpful in identifying these additional materials and in
assessing the importance of any anticipated demographic changes in
terms of facilities and services. Additional reference sources are
identified in Appendix A.

Occupational and Labor Force Characteristics

Variables

The labor force and occupational characteristics of the local
communities will also usually be described by the economic/
demographic analyst. Although the economic/demographic analysis
focuses more on industrial sector employment characteristics (see
below) than on occupational characteristics, sufficient information
is generally provided to identify the important occupational and
labor force characteristics and trends. As with population size and
demographic characteristics, many actions do not cause substantial
change in occupational, labor force, or livelihood characteristics.
If the occupational or labor force changes which would be caused by
the proposed action are small, this characteristic is likely to be
unimportant in the assessment. However, perceived threats to established livelihoods can occur even when the forecast changes are
relatively slight, so particular attention to this issue may be necessary. Examples of occupational and labor force characteristics
that could be important include the following:

1) The presence of high or low unemployment rates, which indicate a need for additional jobs or the lack of available
   labor.
2) The occupational distribution of residents. Especially notable are heavy concentrations in particular occupational or
   livelihood categories, such as forestry or farming, or a
   high degree of diversity.
3) The labor force participation and employment characteristics
   for particular population groups, such as women, youth, or
   ethnic groups. These data demonstrate existing distributional processes and can identify groups that may require
   special attention in the analysis.

Questions that would indicate which of these characteristics are
important include the following:

1) Could the proposed action provide needed jobs to an economically depressed area, or could it aggravate competition for
   scarce labor?

2) How many local residents would be qualified and able to obtain employment from the proposed action? Who would those residents be?

3) Would the proposed action affect an important livelihood in a way that would threaten (or be perceived as threatening) its viability?

4) Could the proposed action cause sufficient change in the area's occupational/livelihood characteristics to affect local lifestyles or social groupings?

5) Could the proposed action increase the labor force participation rate of particular groups, such as women, to an extent that would affect demand for services, such as child care, and interpersonal relationships?

6) Is the proposed action likely to result in a substantial change in the organization of labor? For example, would it affect the importance of labor unions or the relationships between occupational groups?

Data Sources

Data to document preproject labor force and unemployment characteristics are usually provided by the economic/demographic analyst. Data on occupational characteristics are available in the U.S. Census and can be abstracted, to some extent, from the employment characteristics published annually by the U.S. Department of Commerce, Bureau of Economic Analysis. The economist will usually have these documents. Other sources of data about dominant occupational groups and socially important livelihoods can be obtained through interviews with area residents, from the local employment security division office, or from secondary sources describing the area. If particular livelihoods or occupations dominate in the study area or would become important as a result of the proposed action, you should plan to review any literature that describes the work environment and lifestyle characteristics of people engaged in those types of occupations. This literature can provide data and insights that will be useful in making your forecasts and evaluations of change as well as in describing the existing environment.

Employment and Income Characteristics

Variables

From a social perspective, changes in employment characteristics (as they are usually presented) are of less interest than an area's occupational characteristics and the characteristics of the businesses located in it. However, changes in employment characteristics can be used as an indication of changes in the economic base of the community and the area's economic diversity. These data have the advantage of being available on an annual basis at the county level. In addition, they frequently are the variables that the economist uses in the baseline and with-action forecasts. Consequently, employment characteristics will often be compiled, forecast, and analyzed by the economic/demographic analyst and therefore be readily available to you. Changes in income are directly applicable to the social assessment, since changes in income level and income distribution are important indicators of change in the material well-being of the community. Examples of employment and income characteristics that could be important are the following:

1) Distribution of employment by industrial sector
2) The numerical and size (number of employees) distribution of businesses by industrial sector
3) Wage rates for workers in the various industrial sectors
4) Per capita income for the area, especially if it is substantially lower or higher than the state or regional average
5) Estimates of income distribution, especially the annual income of families
6) The extent of unionization in the various industrial sectors

Examples of questions which would determine whether these characteristics are important include:

1) Do the income or wage distribution data indicate unusually wide disparities in income compared to state or national averages?
2) Do the sectoral wage rates indicate wide disparities in income and/or that some sectors will have difficulty competing for workers?
3) Do the employment data indicate large numbers of workers in sectors that would be affected by the proposed action, or do they indicate that the proposed action could substantially alter the area's employment and industrial characteristics by introducing a new type of employment or industry or an employer of much greater size than those currently present?
4) Do local residents oppose the presence of particular types of jobs (and/or workers or worker organizations) because of their perceived social characteristics?

Data Sources

Typically, data on these variables are provided by the economic/demographic analyst. Annual per capita and per worker wage income and employment by industrial sector data are available from the U.S. Department of Commerce, Bureau of Economic Analysis. State employment security divisions usually compile this type of data also. Attitude information must be obtained from local or regional sources. For most analyses, the economist will have the statistical documents and will be preparing a description of employment and income characteristics for the study area.

Facilities/Services and Fiscal Resources

Variables

Changes in population will affect the demand for facilities and services. Changes in resources, economic activity, or income can affect the supply of services and facilities. The cost, quality, and availability of public and private services has an important influence on the distribution of effects and on perceptions of well-being and the community. In particular, changes which result in increased cost and/or decreased availability and quality of facilities and services are important not only because they affect material well-being, but because they can affect interpersonal relationships, political organization, and attitudes. Therefore, although the analysis of facilities/services and fiscal effects is usually done by the economic/demographic, facilities/services, or community affairs analysts, this information is very important to the social assessment. It is often the responsibility of the social assessor to identify organizational, leadership, or attitudinal factors that would affect the community's ability or willingness to respond in a timely, cost effective manner.

If demand exceeds supply, the price of a service may be driven up and/or a deterioration in service quality or availability may occur. If demand falls below supply, per capita costs can increase or service providers can go out of business. For public services, increased supply of facilities or services requires increased revenues. If demand increases faster than the tax base, then either the supply of facilities/services will be inadequate or the tax rate will increase. If the tax base increases faster than demand, additional services can either be provided or tax rates reduced.

In some cases, the time required to provide an additional service is so long that the service cannot be available when it is needed, resulting in periods of shortages. In other cases, the short duration of the demand or the uncertainty of the demand makes it uneconomical or politically risky to expand to meet it. This also results in periods of shortages. In some instances, local suppliers do not have the capacity or the financing to meet the demand, resulting in the introduction of outsiders. (Further discussion of facilities/services analysis is provided in Appendix B.)

Examples of facilities, services, and tax base characteristics that could be important include the following:

1) Current service levels and organizational and budgetary characteristics of public services such as
   -- general government administration
   -- schools
   -- health care
   -- roads, water, sewer, and solid waste
   -- social services (welfare, mental health)
   -- law enforcement
   -- health
   -- recreation

2) Current service levels and response capabilities of private
   sector services, such as
   -- housing
   -- medical care
   -- mental health
   -- household services (plumbers, electricians, telephone
      installation/repair, day care)

Questions which would determine whether these characteristics
are important include the following:

1) Are there current problems with service availability that
   indicate resource constraints, the community's inability to
   cooperate or obtain funds, or institutional problems?
2) Are there current problems with service availability that
   indicate inadequate demand to support the service?
3) Would the increased demands created by the proposed action
   result in inadequate service or increased costs?
4) Would increased demands and/or revenues from the proposed
   action result in increased availability of facilities or
   services?
5) Would the increased demands created by the proposed action
   require major changes in the organization of service provision or the operation of general government? Would response
   entail introduction of outside businesses or agencies?
   Would attempts to control development substantially alter
   governmental structure (the establishment of planning departments, full time paid administrative positions, etc.)
   and regulations (zoning, permits, animal control)? Are the
   government officials and service providers prepared to implement these changes? Is financing available?
6) Would the changes in facility and service availability and
   cost result in special hardships or benefits for any particular groups? For example, people on fixed incomes might
   suffer greatly if property taxes were increased by the proposed action. People owning real estate would benefit from
   rising real estate prices, while newcomers and young people
   establishing new households would suffer accordingly.
7) Would the action-related changes in the population's occupational and age/sex composition cause changes in service
   demand that would affect the supply of services or the ability of service providers to respond? For example, an influx
   of young married couples to a community that had previously
   experienced out-migration of this cohort could require the
   community's medical focus to change from care for chronic
   ailments and geriatrics to industrial accidents and
   obstetrics/pediatrics.
8) Are there potential combinations of attitudes or cultural
   orientation, service availability or costs, and changes in
   income levels that will aggravate the distributional effects
   and result in special hardships for a particular group? Be
   alert for differential use of facilities and services.
   Longtime residents are often less affected by inflation in

the cost of housing and durable goods because they generally have little demand for these facilities -- they already own them -- but they are strongly affected by increased property tax rates. Groups at particular risk from the economic effects of rapid growth (as well as general inflation) are (1) poorly-paid newcomers, (2) poorly-paid, young, longtime resident families, and (3) fixed income residents. Property tax increases often have greatest effect on fixed income residents and other longtime residents.

Data Sources

The usual sources of information about facilities, services, and the tax base are the service providers themselves. Keep in mind their political and economic stake in the information they provide and their perspective on the community. Agencies can provide not only specific estimates of impact, but also guidance on how service demands are estimated. Because multiple levels of government are frequently involved, it is often possible to get some measure of the appropriateness of your estimates and methodology by discussing the problem with several agencies that provide similar services. In general, this information will be gathered and analyzed by the facilities/services analyst and/or the economic/demographic analyst. Attitudes and expectations about current service levels and governmental organization can be obtained from community residents themselves. Interviews with political leaders can provide an indication of their assessment of local attitudes and expectations as well as an insight into the decision-making processes that have created the current service/facility conditions. The project sponsor is usually responsible for providing estimates of the tax payments that would result directly from the project. These data are helpful in assessing what governmental units will be affected and whether fiscal effects will be large.

Institutions, Organizations, and the Regulatory Structure

Variables

The institutions, organizations, and regulatory structure of a community are an expression of important social processes within it. If an organization has been formed, it can be assumed that it represents a force or activity in the community. Consequently, examining these institutions and organizations can provide information about the important social processes operating in the community. Institutions, organizations, and regulations are also important in the implementation of projects and in the community's response to the project's social effects.

As indicated in earlier chapters, one of the significant factors in a community's ability to cope with development is whether the institutions and regulations necessary to control and monitor change are in existence and persons with the necessary expertise are present. Institutions and regulations may be formal, such as a planning department with zoning controls and building permits, or they may be informal, such as a banker who will not fund projects that are unacceptable to the local business establishment. The institutions which do exist may be limited legally and unable to fully cope with change. For example, taxing authorities may be limited in the kind and amount of taxation they can impose; water management may be limited to surface water and not include groundwater; and tax monies may go to the county while the service demand occurs within the city. Therefore, the analysis of the existing environment and the characteristics of the proposed action should include an examination of the institutional, organizational, and regulatory context to identify whether there are impediments to the alternatives themselves or to the community's ability to manage the social change introduced by each alternative.

Among the institutions, organizations, and regulations that could be important are those involved in the following:

1) **Planning policy.** Institutions having jurisdiction or an interest in patterns of development or resource use that would result from implementing these alternatives; regulations concerning planning and development.

2) **Financing authority.** Institutions having the legal authority or economic capability to raise taxes, sell bonds, or otherwise finance facilities or services connected with an alternative; regulations specifying financing authority and restrictions.

3) **Land or resource acquisition.** Institutions that are concerned with the procedures necessary to acquire land, water rights, etc., necessary for implementation.

4) **Monitoring and surveillance.** Institutions involved in enforcement, inspection, maintenance of standards, and permitting.

5) **Coordination.** Institutions responsible for coordinating or managing other institutions involved in any of the functions above; regulations enabling or restricting the ability of governmental units to establish cooperative agreements.

Questions that will help determine which of these characteristics are important include the following:

1) Is there evidence of conflict between the institutions or organizations which would be required to respond to the changes introduced by the proposed action? Would this conflict limit their effectiveness? Is it indicative of a larger conflict in the community as a whole that will affect response to the proposed action?

2) Do the necessary institutions, organizations, and regulations exist to respond to the changes that could be introduced by the proposed action? For example, management of water rights, resolution of conflicts regarding land use, and joint powers agreements to share revenues and provide services. Are they adequately funded and staffed, or are there gaps where the absence of such institutions or regulations would cause problems, but where their provision

would represent a substantial change from existing conditions?

3) Are the existing institutions and regulatory mechanisms appropriate for the increased population and other changes that would result from the proposed action, or would substantial change be required or introduced by the proposed action? For example, the informal controls which exist in many small towns are workable only as long as a large proportion of the population know one another.

4) Would the proposed action directly change an existing regulatory policy, or would it impose an entirely new regulation on the community that would affect or be perceived to affect local control or access to resources?

Data Sources

The primary sources of information about institutions and organizations are governmental documents describing the structure and authorities of the various governmental entities and interviews with agencies and officers of the organizations themselves. It should be noted that the publications describing the activities and authorities of the various institutions are frequently difficult to obtain and may not clearly address the issues of concern in the assessment. Similar studies for other communities in the same state may provide useful information. Much of this information will be collected by the facilities/services analyst.

Leadership

Variables

If the community is going to be called upon to respond to the changes introduced by the proposed action, the leadership characteristics of the affected community can be an extremely important determinant of the nature and effectiveness of that response. Just as economists estimate whether taxing districts have sufficient revenues to purchase needed goods and services, a social assessor determines whether the affected communities have the political power to take the actions that will enhance the benefits and minimize the problems that could result.

"Political power" is used here to mean both the political authority and the political mandate or will of local officials and leaders. The question of authority is simply whether or not local officials have the legal authority they need, via taxing, siting, or land use laws, to impose requirements on project sponsors, control growth, and obtain revenues. The question of mandate or will is more complex. The first question is whether sufficient consensus exists or can be created in the community to provide local officials with a political mandate to establish mechanisms for controlling the kinds of changes introduced by the proposed action. In some communities this may require a change in philosophy and a substantial increase in the role of local government. In rural areas, for example, government control of private land use has often been considered a grave threat to personal liberty. In communities facing these changes in governmental authority, there may be conflicts which prevent the leadership from acting in a unified manner, especially on such issues as land use control and zoning. Such issues can be used as a platform from which one element in the community challenges another. This may result in division within the community that seriously limits the community's power to take action or to communicate clear preferences to the project developer or outside regulators. The failure of local officials to exercise the authority they have is a clear indication that the problem is not one of authority, but of mandate or will to exercise these powers.

The characteristics of the existing leadership are particularly important in determining whether or not the changes caused by the proposed action are likely to result in a change in leadership or the use of political power within the community. One of the fears frequently expressed by longtime residents is that a large influx of newcomers will cause longtime residents to lose political control to newcomers who have a different philosophy about government or who may not share their commitment to the community. According to the literature review and community studies conducted for the Bureau of Land Management's Social Effects Project, there is some evidence to suggest that whether or not this happens depends to a great extent on how the existing leadership responds. If the existing leadership does not respond or responds ineffectively, a change is likely to occur, with either different longtime residents or newcomers acquiring power. If the existing leadership responds effectively and is perceived as using its authority responsibly, it is likely to maintain its position, but its membership will be expanded to share power with newcomers. One frequent pattern is for longtime residents to retain informal power and elected policy positions, but to incorporate newcomers as administrators, investing them with considerable formal power (Thompson and Branch 1980, Thompson, et al. 1982).

Leadership response affects not only the material resources and organization of the community, it also affects residents' attitudes about the community and the effects of the proposed action. For example, Branch (1982), Albrecht (1982), Hooper and Jobes (1982), and Wilkinson (1982) found that longtime residents who were part of a political leadership group that responded effectively and shared its power with newcomers generally did not report feeling a loss of personal position or familiarity in the community. However, longtime residents who were not part of the political leadership frequently, and sometimes bitterly, reported that they had lost their access to the political structure of the community and had a reduced sense of familiarity with others in the community.

Newcomers who do not belong to the decision-making structure are very much affected by community residents' attitudes toward them and by the decision makers' ability and willingness to create a positive environment for them. This is particularly important because recent or incoming residents rarely have any political power, and decisions affecting them are usually made by others. The well-being of the community appears to be best served if accommodation, acceptance, and fairness are used in dealing with newcomers. Depending upon the magnitude of the project-related change in population and resources, this usually requires that the leadership establish mechanisms to ensure that the newcomers pay their own way so that longtime residents do not feel overburdened and resentful.

Changes in leadership seem to be somewhat more likely to occur when the newcomers to the community have skills, interest, and experience in voluntary associations, management, and community organizations, and when they expect to be in the community for some time. However, evidence from previously impacted communities in the rural West shows that newcomers (especially newcomers associated with large-scale projects) tend to be sensitive to fears of a "takeover" and often participate in ways which support or supplement the existing leadership, rather than trying to "grab" public positions or political power.

A potential source of conflict between long-term residents and newcomers exists if an important determinant of political power and leadership has traditionally been membership in a distinctive ethnic or religious group, such as membership in a tribe or in a particular church. One of the key factors determining whether or not this conflict will occur is the degree of similarity between the demographic and cultural characteristics of the newcomers and those of the existing population. If their characteristics are greatly different, the chance of conflict increases.

Another political leadership issue that is raised by the introduction of new sources of income, power, and resources is the potential conflict of interest between community leaders' official roles and their personal economic self-interest. Since holding a position of political leadership in a small community is often associated with status and wealth, rapid development may present unique opportunities which create conflicts of interest that previously did not exist. It can be difficult for the community and the leadership to establish a method for dealing with this conflict and to simultaneously develop a coherent program for handling growth and for instituting new and complex administrative programs.

Examples of leadership characteristics that could be important to describe include the following:

1) The extent to which local leaders are knowledgeable about the range of their responsibilities and authority and whether they have in the recent past demonstrated an ability to implement this authority.

2) The stability of leadership in the community/county over the last several years, and, in areas with substantial populations of newcomers, whether newcomers are included among community leadership.

3) Evidence that there has been cooperation, conflict, or little interaction between various officials and community leaders and between the informal and formal leaders in recent years.

4) The experience of current leaders with the types of changes likely to be caused by the proposed action and the way they responded previously.

5) If newcomers have entered the community, it is important to know if they were well-received and if the leadership made

an effort to make them feel welcome and to integrate them
into the community.

6) The association of leadership with ethnicity or religion.
   For example, is there a balance of power between two or more
   groups or does one group dominate the leadership positions?

7) The history of community leadership style. Does the commun-
   ity/county have a history of active, aggressive leadership
   that has taken the initiative to resolve local issues or a
   history of passive, indecisive, or quarrelsome leadership?
   Are there areas or groups that are neglected by the leaders
   or is there a serious attempt to attend to the needs of the
   entire community equitably?

8) The extent to which current leaders have the support and
   confidence of the community.

9) The extent to which local leaders control opportunities for
   accommodating change (i.e., Do they have a monopoly on
   scarce resources, or do they control zoning regulations that
   have this effect?).

Questions to ask to determine the applicability of these characteristics include the following:

1) What types of changes would be caused by the proposed action
   that would require leadership response? How clear-cut will
   the leadership's decisions be? How much uncertainty is
   there about the proposed action and its consequences?

2) Has the current leadership had experience with the types of
   problems likely to be caused by the proposed action? Were
   the problems handled adequately and easily? Did they result
   in long-lasting community issues or conflict?

3) Have the current leaders thought through the consequences of
   the proposed action? Have they formulated a clear set of
   community goals and an approach to the problems?

4) Are there other activities occurring at the same time as the
   proposed action that would affect the leaders' abilities to
   deal with action-related changes?

5) Would the proposed action introduce people with characteristics that would affect the current leadership structure and
   balance of power?

6) Do current leaders have sufficient authority to deal with
   the changes introduced by the proposed action?

7) Do current leaders perceive that the proposed action represents a threat to their leadership or to their ability to
   perform adequately? Do factions exist that could use
   project-related issues for political purposes?

8) Have the sponsors of the proposed action indicated a willingness to cooperate with community leaders and interest
   groups or is their role still unclear or antagonistic?

Data Sources

The legal authority and responsibilities of local officials can
be determined by reviewing documents summarizing local laws and

powers and by interviewing local officials. The facilities/services analyst will frequently have much of this information, although for a somewhat different purpose. Local officials often can specify the areas where additional powers are needed, but in some cases they may be unaware of the authority they have if they have not had occasion to use it. Local newspapers and interviews with community residents and leaders can provide information about the type of issues that have occurred in the past, how the leadership responded, and whether the administrative structure to deal with such issues has been established.

Assessment of the existing political mandate or will can be based on secondary sources (newspapers and reports), observation, and interviews. Discussion of recent political campaigns or controversies in which growth or development issues played a role may be particularly helpful in understanding the political forces at work in the community. Local officials can describe the mandate they personally perceive, although their willingness to discuss their views will vary from official to official and their perceptions are likely to be somewhat idealized.

One of the difficulties in analyzing the process of political organization is that it is sometimes easier to obtain the information than it is to report it in a way that is not viewed as meddling or provocative. As a rule, the social assessor should never comment on the personal ability of local officials or appear in any way to be telling the local community how it should be organized politically. On the other hand, since the response of local leadership has been shown to be one of the most important factors determining social effects, the social assessor has an obligation to indicate when it appears that the response will not be adequate, either because of (1) a lack of legal authority or a lack of mandate or will due to philosophy about government's role and/or a stand-off between conflicting interests, or (2) a fragmented community with no mechanism to reach concensus or allocate authority. Because there can be local reactions to such a statement, the social assessor must be confident of the findings, present the findings in an objective and professional manner, and be satisfied that the consequences of the political leadership problems are important enough to justify the criticism that may result from having an outsider identify these problems. It may be appropriate to present this information in a form other than the official assessment document, such as a policy paper, memorandum, or briefing. (Further discussion of the presentation of the description of the existing environment was presented in Section 9.3.)

Attitudes Toward Development and the Proposed Actions: Perceptions of Community and Personal Well-being

Variables

The attitudes community residents have toward development and the specific actions being proposed as well as their perceptions of community and personal well-being are important determinants of the social effects of a proposed action. Attitudes not only influence actions, they also influence perceptions and the interpretation of actual events. Much of the information about attitudes and perceptions will be available only from secondary sources or from interviews or surveys with community residents about current attitudes and perceptions. This information is generally used as a basis for forecasting the response longtime residents and newcomers will make to the proposed action and their evaluation of the changes caused by it. Information about attitudes and perceptions should not be gathered only from community leaders, though their attitudes are certainly important, but from the general population and each of the distinguishable social groups as well. Special attention may need to be given to the attitudes and positions of influential stakeholder groups; those with a particular interest or stake in the decisions regarding the proposed action, since they are likely to serve as the representatives of the community (or outside interests) in any public debate and can dramatically affect community opinion.

The type of information that is needed about the residents' attitudes toward development and the proposed action includes the following:

1) Position regarding development or the proposed action (favor, oppose) and the strength of that position
2) Reasons for this position
3) Anticipated effects from development or the proposed action and evaluation of those effects

Obtaining this information and comparing the patterns of response given by members of the key stakeholder groups to those of each social group (presuming that they are different) and to the general population will clarify how well the stakeholder groups' responses reflect community-wide attitudes. It will also give you an indication of how diverse the attitudes of the stakeholder groups are, what kind of constituency each stakeholder group has, and how much support there is for the various sides of each issue.

Care should be taken not to equate residents' anticipations and expectations with impacts. Attitudes indicate how residents feel about the proposed action and what they think will happen. In addition, attitudes can influence what will happen, but they often do not accurately reflect what actually will happen. Forecasting what is likely to happen is the purpose of the assessment. Information about attitudes is part of the description of the characteristics of the community that can be used to forecast the manner in which the community and the various stakeholder groups will interact with and respond to the direct project inputs. It is also used to help determine the probable meaning of the resulting changes. Many of the issues that emerge in response to a proposed action are expressions of concern that an undesirable outcome may result. An important function of the assessment process and the public involvement component is to identify and respond to these concerns.

Perceptions of the community and well-being (or community satisfaction) are quite a bit different from attitudes toward development. The interest here is (1) to discover how residents perceive their community, (2) to discover how they think it will change with the proposed project, and (3) to obtain community perceptions about

some objective indicators (discussed later in this section). All of
this information is essential to understand how residents relate to
their community, how they like it, and how they think it will
change. This information is needed to evaluate the meaning of the
community changes that are forecast to occur.

Different people have different perceptions of their community.
While some may feel it is the best place in the world to live,
others may not care for the size, the diversity, the appearance, or
the general character of the place in which they live. There are
some who would like to know and be known by everyone in town while
others would feel uncomfortable with this level of familiarity.
Knowledge of how people perceive and define their community will
allow you to make more valid judgments about how the effects of the
proposed project will be interpreted by different groups of residents and what meaning these effects will have to them.

The following information about attitudes and perceptions may
need consideration:

1) Stakeholder groups will usually have definite opinions and
   public positions about development and its effects on the
   community. These groups may or may not be formally organized, but their attitudes are likely to be important in
   forecasting response. The size, membership characteristics,
   and attitudes of the stakeholder groups toward development
   and the proposed action could therefore be important.

2) The attitudes of the various stakeholder groups may be generally similar, or they may be seriously at odds. Information about the attitudes of each group and how it compares
   with those of the leaders, the general population, and the
   various social groups, may be important for forecasting community response and distribution of effects and for determining how different groups will evaluate the effects.

3) Residents, leaders, and stakeholder groups may have misperceptions about the proposed action and the likely effects
   that influence their attitudes (and potentially their response). Information about the residents' understanding of
   the proposed action, the likely project inputs, and their
   effects can therefore be useful in forecasting and evaluation.

Questions that would help indicate what information is necessary
and in what detail it should be gathered include the following:

1) How large and important are the effects of the project likely to be? If they are anticipated to be large, more attention to attitudes is warranted, and information may be
   needed in more detail to properly assess and evaluate the
   effects on different groups.

2) Does the proposed action involve a significant policy decision? This often creates a situation where public opinion
   is particularly important to the decision maker and it is
   likely to warrant collecting more detailed information about
   the attitudes of the general population as well as stakeholder groups.

3) Has there been controversy over the proposed action? Controversy generally indicates not only intense feeling but disagreement among groups. In situations where there has been controversy, it is often unclear how the general public feels about the proposed action. In some cases this may indicate a need for detailed information and perhaps a sample survey.

In addition to community satisfaction, information about how residents think their community will change with the proposed project can be useful. This requires more focused questions than those addressing community satisfaction, and the answers may need to address an entirely different dimension. For example, a person may state that what they like about the community is its "small-town atmosphere," but say that the biggest change with the proposed project will be "an increase in business." This illustration points out that the question on satisfaction deals with the present situation while the question on changes deals with expected futures. It is not the assessor's job to "correct" people if they anticipate a community change that is not likely to occur, although it may be desirable to provide respondents with descriptions of the types of objective changes that the assessment team does anticipate and solicit their comments and evaluations of them. A content analysis of public meeting records, letters to the editor and local newspaper articles may help identify the dimensions of public concern and project-related issues (see Chapter 13 for a more detailed description of content analysis).

As will be discussed later, the assessor will need to collect and analyze data on some indicators of community well-being. The interviews conducted to collect the community satisfaction and anticipated change information can also be used to obtain residents' interpretations of current community well-being measures, and their expectations for the future. Large discrepancies between residents' perceptions of the statistical social indicators, and/or the preliminary forecasts need to be accounted for and explained. The assessor may want to ask residents why they feel as they do about these aspects of community life, and to compare residents' expectations and their projections against the experience of other similar communities. Based on this closer examination and review of the literature, assumptions, and projection techniques can be refined.

In gathering and analyzing all this information, the assessor should be looking for patterns in the responses according to the characteristics that correspond with social groupings and stakeholder group membership -- age, sex, occupation, length of residence, etc. To the extent possible, the assessor should be able to explain the differences that appear. All of this information will enable the assessor to discuss what the changes due to the proposed project will mean to the community residents: how it will affect their daily lives and their sense of and attachment to the community. This information will allow you to address the human meaning of social change.

Some issues that need to be taken into consideration are the following:

1) Community satisfaction is typically very important to people in rural communities. The community tends to be very important to residents of rural communities.
2) Why people like their communities and what they like about them are different in rural and urban areas and in different regions of the country.
3) Service availability is usually fairly low in rural areas, and residents don't generally expect a high level of service.
4) Residents may have preconceived ideas about changes in rates of behavior such as crime, divorce, drug abuse, etc., that will occur because of the project. Although these perceptions may be accurate, they may also be based on little knowledge; overestimates or underestimates are likely to be made.

Questions which would help indicate what information is necessary and in what detail it should be gathered include the following:

1) What do community residents like about their community? What do they like about the general area? Why? What don't they like about the community? What don't they like about the general area? Why?
2) Are residents satisfied with community services? What services would they like to see in addition to what is available? Do they use the community services? Which ones?
3) What do residents think will happen to the community if the development occurs? What do they feel will be the most important changes? Why?
4) What kinds of changes in behavior (crime, divorce, etc.) do community residents anticipate? Why? How do they feel about these anticipated changes?
5) What is the pattern of response to all these questions? Do answers differ by age, sex, occupation, length of residence? How can the pattern be explained?
6) What local issues have emerged as a result of the proposed project? What have been the dimensions of disagreement? Which groups have taken what positions? Are the positions consistent with previous patterns in the community or are new alliances and divisions being formed?

Data Sources

The appraisal of local attitudes toward development and perceptions of the community and well-being can be made as part of the interviews being conducted to investigate other attitudes, community resources, and social processes. In addition, any records of public response -- consultations, public meetings, correspondence files, hearings, and public comments -- as well as newspaper accounts can be reviewed and analyzed for attitudes and issues about the proposed or similar actions. However, it is important to be cautious in utilizing this type of information. Any claim that data represents the attitudes of the community requires that the interviewing techniques and data sources meet the standards of probability sampling described in Chapter 13. Multiple sources of data, methods of data collection, and methods of analysis should be used as often as possible. The primary data collected from field interviews should be compared to and used in conjunction with any other available studies of the area.

Ordinarily, a structured survey or other quantitative instrument is not necessary to obtain sufficient information about community attitudes and perceptions for an assessment if interest is limited to ascertaining the major, dominant attitudes and perceptions in the community. However, the limitations of this approach need to be recognized. There are occasions when a formal survey approach is warranted. These generally occur (1) with major projects, where the anticipated effects will be large; (2) with actions involving significant policy decisions, where public opinion is particularly important; (3) where controversy has been intense and it is not clear how the "silent" majority feels; or (4) where a representative sample of attitudes and perceptions is important to the assessment itself. Chapter 13 discusses the use of structured sample surveys. When a quantitative approach is taken, it is important that a good sampling design and questionnaire be used, that an adequate pretest be done, and that reliability and validity measures of the items be completed before the results are released.

When planning your research, it is important to remember that the same sources may be called upon to provide information about all aspects of the community -- resources, social organization, and well-being. Consequently, it is advisable to consider all your data and information requirements before starting your research. Social change research requires an integrated rather than a serial or compartmentalized approach.

Social Organization Model: Social Organization Structures and Processes

This component of the social organization model contains much of what is "social" about a community. Change in any social system or community can only be understood by considering all of the major elements that compose the system; that is, the "inputs" into the community (project inputs), the resources available to the community (community resources), and the "outputs" of the system (social organization and the well-being of its members). The way in which these elements are combined and related is largely determined by the social structure and processes which have evolved over time and are particular to each system or community. The social organization of a community interacts with other elements in the social system, simultaneously influencing and being influenced by the characteristics of these other elements.

Social organization is difficult to study because it is an abstraction. Since social structures and processes are not directly measurable, they must be inferred from objective actions and outcomes and from statements about motives and feelings. Thus, we cannot directly measure the process of coordination and cooperation in the community; the process must be inferred from the outcomes and patterns of behavior, from the statements of participants, and from

the observation of analysts. Social processes such as coordination
and cooperation have very real effects, as do their absence. If,
for example, a new jail is needed, but the coordination does not
exist to get city and county officials to cooperate by sharing revenues and agreeing on a design, then it may be impossible to build
the new jail no matter how much it is needed. It is this abstract,
emergent quality of social organization that makes the study of
sociology and social change difficult for many people. But the
social organization of a community is very real and has real and
measurable effects.

People in potentially impacted communities know that their communities are made up of more than objects and individuals and they
know that it is the way people behave toward one another that determines the reality of a social group or community and establishes the
meanings that actions have for the residents. People generally know
this, but because of the abstract nature of social processes, many
cannot articulate clearly what changes they foresee as a result of a
proposed project or why they feel so strongly about having this aspect of their life change. When people in impacted communities talk
about how development has changed their lives, how their sense of
community has been affected, or how their communities are losing
their small-town qualities, they are talking about their interpretation of changes in the social structures and processes that have
evolved over time to organize their social or community life. The
study of social organization is complex, constantly evolving, and
never complete. That which can be learned by examining the existing
environment can be very useful in forecasting how a proposed action
will affect a community.

To understand a community before development (the existing environment), the major social structures and processes must be at
least reasonably well understood. To forecast how development will
change a community, an understanding of how existing social structures and processes have evolved is necessary. In this guide, five
major social organizational processes are identified which can be
used to study the social organization of a community:

1) Diversity/complexity
2) Outside linkages
3) Distribution of resources/power
4) Coordination and cooperation
5) Personal interaction

This set of social organizational processes was derived from an extensive review of the literature on social organization, rural development, and social impact and change (Wilkinson 1980, Thompson
and Branch 1980). It was tested by the authors and others in small
communities throughout the intermountain West where it was found to
provide a useful framework for understanding the social organization
of the communities and for forecasting the social impacts of large-
scale resource development or comprehensive planning decisions
(Thompson, et al. 1982). The particular set of processes utilized
in the guide could be collapsed or expanded to suit the specific research interests of the user or the distinctive characteristics of a
proposed action or study community. Indeed, the user of the guide

is encouraged to build upon this framework, adapting it to apply more precisely to the task and communities being addressed.

The five social organization processes are described below, along with methods for observing and measuring them. A discussion is also provided to clarify how to determine whether these processes may be impacted by a proposed action and how they interact to produce social change.

Diversity/Complexity

Increases in population, employment, and income usually increase the diversity and complexity of a community as both the number and types of activities and groups in the community expand. As a town grows, for example, the population may become large enough to support an additional clothing store, thus increasing the number of businesses in the community. There is also likely to be an increase in complexity as well. There may now be enough business to justify a sporting goods store (separate from the hardware store) or a liquor store (separate from the grocery store) and a diverse enough population to result in the establishment of new voluntary associations such as churches or clubs and to change residents' interaction patterns and their basic perceptions and definitions of the grouping of people within the community.

An increase in diversity and complexity can be both positive and negative; it can be viewed as creating opportunities or increasing competition, as a source of interest or a threat to simplicity. On one hand, a great deal of diversity in services, groups, and activities can mean that a community is able to satisfy the needs of a larger and more diverse population. But, on the other hand, an increase in diversity is also likely to mean that the community has become less simple and more complex. Greater complexity can mean that a community becomes less personal in some areas. For some people, this may create a sense of impersonality. In a town that is structurally simple, people tend to feel they know everyone and everything in their town. They know how to get things done. As the town becomes more complex or diverse, they may feel that they no longer know their community and that they are no longer known by others.

Increases in diversity/complexity can be examined for the (1) economic, (2) political, and (3) social/cultural (including religious) sectors of the community, as discussed below.

Economic Diversity/Complexity

Variables

The creation of new and different jobs in a community is likely to increase the purchasing power of the community, which in turn increases the number and kind of services provided locally. Existing stores, restaurants, and service establishments can expand, since they have increased their clientele and/or business volume.

Uncertainty about whether the increased purchasing power is temporary, as it would be during the construction phase of a large project, can limit this expansion. When the increase in purchasing power is expected to be temporary, business and financial people are less willing to invest in expansions or new businesses because the increased activity may be too short-lived to return an adequate profit.

If small communities are far from additional markets, any expansion or specialization of business is likely to take place almost exclusively in fields that serve the people or activities associated with the proposed action. Under these circumstances, although the local economy may grow in size and the number and type of businesses may increase, the community frequently does not diversify its economic base very broadly. The local economy thus remains fragile in the sense that changes in the one or two major sectors affect the entire economy. This cycle has been repeated many times in communities relying heavily on a single type of business.

As a result, the increase in economic diversity in small isolated towns has historically been limited, even when major industrial projects have been located nearby. This is particularly true if an aggressive regional center is located within commuting distance. However, the degree of diversity and the ability of local business to compete with regional centers can be influenced by the presence of key resources (such as financing) and the actions of community leaders and business people to provide an attractive business climate and develop a specific diversification policy. Also, changes in the number and type of financial institutions can have an important effect on the ability of local businesspeople to obtain funds for expansion and on the economic control that can be exerted by area bankers.

Unless a community has previously experienced a project similar to the proposed action, implementation of the project is likely to increase the economic diversity of the community to at least some degree. At the same time, it will almost inevitably increase the number of businesses or agencies with strong outside linkages. In very small, isolated communities or with very big projects, these changes can be substantial even though the total number of businesses remains small.

An increase in complexity and an associated major increase in outside linkages results when a community passes the threshold from serving only its local residents to being a "regional trade center," capturing business from a much larger geographic area. Conversely, a substantial business decline and reduction in diversity/complexity can result if a nearby town reaches this threshold and becomes a regional trade center, particularly if it takes over this role from the study community. Characteristics which could be useful in understanding the economic diversity/complexity of a community include the following:

1) The number of businesses located in the community and recent trends in these data.
2) The number, type, and size of businesses producing goods and services that are sold outside the local region (basic industry) and recent trends in these data.

3) The market area of the community -- do community businesses serve primarily community residents, or do they serve residents of other communities as well?
4) The shopping patterns of local residents -- where do they go to do their shopping, in town or elsewhere?
5) The number of banks, supermarkets, and movie theaters in each town.

Questions to ask to determine which of these characteristics would be useful to the assessment include the following:

1) Does the proposed action have the potential to substantially affect the number of businesses in a town?
2) Would the proposed action introduce a significant number of new types of businesses, result in the loss of existing types of business, or prevent opportunities for business expansion in the future?
3) Would the proposed action substantially affect the market area of the town? Would it cause it to increase or decrease its trade area?
4) Would the shopping patterns of local residents be affected? Would there be major increases or decreases in local business or business in nearby towns?
5) Would the proposed action affect the number of financial institutions in the community? What about supermarkets and movie theaters?
6) Would the proposed action significantly alter the diversity of "basic" (export) industry in the town? Would it substantially broaden its employment and income base or would it make employment and income more dependent upon, and vulnerable to, fluctuations in business cycles.

Data sources

The data on the number and types of businesses can be obtained either from the project economist, from the U.S. Bureau of the Census County Business Patterns, from the yellow pages of phone books, or from the local chamber of commerce. Information about the market area and shopping patterns can be obtained from the economist or from local business people in the community. The boundaries do not need to be exact. The point is to understand generally the type of business activities present in the community, where residents shop, and what area local businesses serve. The analysis of potential effects of the proposed action (and changes in the baseline) should be obtainable from discussions with the economist.

Political Diversity/Complexity

Variables

Changes in employment and income, along with an influx of people, often create a need for an increased role of local government and for a more elaborate and more professional governmental structure. These changes often require local government to deal with issues of regulating growth and development such as zoning problems, compliance with state or federal regulations, and regulation of subdivision developments. In small communities, many administrative tasks are performed by officials who serve without pay; consequently, the increased complexity and related increase in governmental responsibilities create time demands which often mean that the community must pay its officials and hire professional staff for the first time.

Both town and county officials are also often required to deal with many new actors, including corporate representatives and state and federal agencies, many of whom have extensive outside ties or are actually located outside the community. In order to comply with the needs and regulations of these other agencies, as well as to enforce new local regulations, the decision process is likely to become more formalized and legalistic in nature. This occurs because decisions can no longer be based on personal knowledge of all the participants and because the sheer number and scope of the decisions that have to be made become overwhelming if each is dealt with as a unique case. Increased formalization tends to increase the number and diversity of linkages between the community and outside political/governmental organizations. Major indicators that these transitions have taken place are when a town or county hires a professional town administrator, when a planning department is established, when elected political positions become paid and/or full time, or where there begin to be formally recognized stresses and strains between town and county governments.

An increase in political complexity and diversity is often one of the changes felt most intensely by longtime residents in towns that are moving away from a relatively informal organization. Increased political complexity and diversity very often means increased governmental control and the imposition of formal procedures for conducting business with the local government where previously the government was little involved and informality and personal acquaintances prevailed. Since this increase is generally driven by an increase in population and is therefore accompanied by other substantial changes in local government activities -- such as the imposition of land use regulations, the expansion of facilities and services, or changes in the tax regulations -- and in interpersonal relationships, it is frequently perceived by longtime residents as confusing and as an indication that their role and importance in the community has diminished. On the positive side, the establishment of more formal procedures, if thoughtfully formulated and justly implemented, can serve to prevent favoritism and unfair treatment and can be an essential tool for controlling growth. The existence of rules and procedural requirements can be particularly useful for local leaders when their official responsibilities require them to deny friends' requests.

In most cases, the transition from informal to formal, from simple to complex in local government is not accomplished smoothly or without regret. There is generally a strong desire to retain the personal and comfortable qualities of simplicity and informality. However, the pressures and demands of responding to and dealing with the multiple changes that occur during a period of rapid community change appear to require this transition. The research conducted for this guide concluded that the most effective leaders in impacted communities have generally been those who recognized when such a transition was necessary and who made it occur with efficiency and decisiveness (Thompson, et al. 1982).

The characteristics of political diversity/complexity that might be important for an assessment are primarily those that delineate the current role of local government and indicate the degree of formalism and regulation in the local government activities. They include the following:

1) Which government officials (both city and county) are in full-time, paid positions and how long this situation has existed.

2) Whether the community or county has a full-time administrator and/or planner who is professionally trained and how long that position has existed.

3) Whether there are formal local procedures (forms to fill out, meetings to attend) for the issuance of building permits and subdivision developments, and whether there is a planning department.

4) Whether the participants at town council or county commission meetings make formal presentations, or whether the meetings are informal discussions.

5) Whether regular town/city council and county commission meetings are held, and whether decisions are actually made or presented at the meetings or are made informally elsewhere.

6) The extent to which local officials are accustomed to dealing with outside agencies.

7) The extent to which relationships between the various local governmental jurisdictions are formalized by explicit cooperative agreement, joint boards or commissions, and regularly scheduled meetings.

Questions that can be asked to determine which characteristics of the existing environment need to be described include the following:

1) Would the proposed action cause regulatory demands on the local government that would introduce new organizations, agencies, or regulations?

2) Would the proposed action cause an increase in population that would necessitate major expansions of facilities and services or raise the issue of zoning and land use control?

3) Would the proposed action substantially affect the local government's budget to the extent that an administrator or comptroller would be required?

4) Would the changes introduced by the proposed action be precipitous (large and fast) and/or would there be major fluctuations in action-related inputs by year? Both would increase the administrative burden on local political officials and increase the pressure for greater complexity.

Data sources

The principal sources of data are local government officials, rosters of government employees, local newspapers, and interviews with local residents. Answers to many of the questions can be developed in collaboration with the person responsible for the facilities/services analysis.

Social Diversity/Complexity

Variables

Typically, as population increases, so does the social diversity and complexity of the community. Often there is a greater variation in ethnicity, religious preference, age, or race for larger populations than for smaller ones. A large influx of people inevitably results in increased diversity in personal background and frequently in the norms or values which govern people's behavior. In fact, a frequent fear expressed by longtime residents is that the influx of new people will cause the community to lose its current, shared rural orientation and goal structure. Parents in communities undergoing large population and economic change often express concerns that their young people will get jobs or be in classrooms which bring them together with people holding different values.

One thing that large-scale development often does that affects the complexity of small towns at least temporarily is to introduce "transients." The introduction of people who are not residentially stable into a small, residentially stable town causes change and frequently some conflict. If the number of in-migrants is large, the change can be great. Longtime residents in small towns often can't imagine residential mobility and see newcomers who do not make a long-term commitment to the community as "strange" and threatening to the community orientation they value. This can result in antagonistic behavior and stereotyping. Because transiency tends to be linked to particular occupational groups (especially construction workers), it is often difficult to separate the issues of transiency from those of actual occupational and lifestyle differences. It does appear that projects which will have a high worker turnover and which will introduce large numbers of temporary residents into a community will create a greater sense of social disorganization and (at least temporarily) complexity than those with smaller and/or more stable work forces. The number of new faces that community residents have to deal with is important. A high turnover among newcomers has been found to contribute strongly to the loss of the sense of "knowing and being known" in a community that is so important to many longtime residents of small towns and to the social processes of these communities.

It must be remembered that social diversity means different things to different people, since one of the tasks of the social assessor is to determine how changes will be viewed by different social groups within the community. The homogeneity which is valued by one person may be seen as confining and restrictive to another. An increase in the diversity of the population may "liberate"

existing minority groups in the community by moderating the social
pressure to conform to the patterns of the dominant group or by
reducing their visibility as the "other" group. The regional and
ethnic characteristics of any in-migrating population associated
with the proposed action are therefore very important to the determination of potential changes in social diversity. Consequently, it
is recommended that these matters be discussed with the economist
when the alternatives being assessed involve the in-migration of any
substantial number of people.

Characteristics to consider include the following:

1) The ethnic and religious diversity of the existing population, with particular attention to situations where there is
   one dominant and one subordinate group and where recent
   large changes have occurred.

2) The residential stability of the current population (an estimate of the proportion of life-long residents in the population would be ideal).

3) An indication of the number of different voluntary organizations in the community, membership patterns, and the extent
   of change during the last five to ten years.

4) An indication of the extent to which community residents
   view the community as composed of factions or separate
   groups (for example, do residents divide their community
   into townspeople, ranchers, Mexicans, newcomers, transients,
   etc?). These often correspond to the important social
   groups and may identify key stakeholder groups. Such description can also provide useful information about residents' perceptions of the community.

5) The patterns of attitudes toward the proposed action. Do
   they follow established patterns or do they represent new
   coalitions or divisions?

6) The extent to which the community is experienced in dealing
   with transients (for example, through the presence of resource development projects, military bases, tourism, or
   universities) and the overall perceptions about transients
   (previous negative experience could predispose the community
   to antagonism).

7) To what extent is the community accustomed to dealing with
   labor unions?

Questions to ask that would determine the relevance of these
characteristics include:

1) Do residents in the community take opposing positions regarding the proposed action in a way that could result in
   the enhancement or establishment of a "we-they" distinction
   between people?

2) Will the proposed action introduce (or remove) a sufficient
   number of people to substantially alter the residential
   stability of the population?

3) Will the proposed action introduce large numbers of transients (5 percent of the existing population or more would

be large)? Is the community accustomed or unaccustomed to
transients? Are they prepared to deal with them pleasantly?

4) Will the population in-migrating (or out-migrating) due to
the proposed action have demographic characteristics relatively similar to the rest of the population or will it have
substantially different characteristics in terms of age,
sex, ethnicity, religion, and regional origin? Is this
change in population (or related changes in income or occupation) going to affect the number or characteristics of the
social groups in the community? Will it affect the relationships between groups?

5) Will the new jobs and/or the in-migrants substantially
change existing labor relations practices? Will unions
become more or less important as a result of the proposed
action?

Data sources

Data on demographic and residential stability variables are
available from the U.S. Census at a community level, but only for
census years. If the assessment is being conducted some years after
the census, these data can be used as a basis for discussing recent
changes with community residents. School and law enforcement personnel often provide helpful information about demographic characteristics and recent changes. They can also often provide a good
indication about transient populations and particular community social groups, especially if they correspond to geographic neighborhoods, occupations, or income levels.

Telephone directories and local newspapers can provide a quick
indication of the numbers and types of major permanent voluntary
organizations such as churches, fraternal organizations, and
unions. Local chambers of commerce frequently compile lists of such
organizations and can also provide information about organizations
serving transient populations. Interviews with local residents and
the review of local newspapers and other public documents will be
the principal sources of information about attitudes toward the
project and perceptions about the social groupings in the community. If the community or region has been the subject of previous
studies, the study reports and articles can provide useful, sometimes very detailed data and analyses. If attitude data are
reported, it is important to examine the research methods and questions carefully so that you do not misinterpret or misrepresent
them. Additional guidance on the use of secondary data and surveys
is provided in chapters 13 and 14.

Estimates of the characteristics of the project-related population will generally be developed in collaboration with the economist
and the facilities/services analyst, since the estimates depend upon
the type of employment, wage scales, job duration and location, competition with other projects for workers, availability of housing
and other amenities, and employment policies. Knowledge about the
community and its likely response to newcomers can provide useful
information for these estimates.

Outside Linkages

Variables

One of the important aspects of a community's social processes is whether decisions about investment, distribution of resources, new projects, and regulatory controls are made by people in the community or by people outside the community. Large scale industrial or resource development often increases both the number of outsiders making decisions that affect a community and the relative importance of those decisions to the community's ability to function and respond. For example, when a federal agency or a major industrial developer initiates a project, important decisions about the number of employees, development plans, schedules, and hiring policies are often made at the regional or national headquarters of the company, far from the local community. In addition, large-scale projects frequently require that a variety of state, regional, and national government agencies be consulted or involved in evaluating, monitoring, providing assistance, and regulating conditions in study area communities. Union hiring agreements can dictate the location of hiring halls and significantly affect the accessibility of project-related jobs to local residents as well as the specific working conditions and agreements. These outside linkages influence the degree of local participation in decision making and affect the community's adaptive capability.

Outside linkages can have both positive and negative effects locally. On the positive side, linkages to outside groups -- state, regional, national, international -- can enhance the community's ability to acquire assistance such as federal grants, loans, information, or political support. Outside agencies may be in a position to alleviate specific local problems. For example, it is not unusual for towns in the West to feel boxed in by federally managed lands. Land for expansion can be very scarce, creating difficulties for the community. On occasion, land exchanges or sales have been arranged to help solve such problems. By providing technical know-how and political support, private companies may help local communities obtain assistance, grants, or loans.

Many communities experiencing rapid growth need additional financial assistance to provide the expansion of capital facilities that the increased population requires. A notable difference between the small, western communities that were able to provide these facilities during the rapid growth period of the 1970s and those that were not was the ability of local leaders to establish effective linkages outside the community and draw additional resources from the outside into the community. In a number of cases, locally initiated outside linkages provided access to badly needed resources that would otherwise have been unavailable. In other cases, the initiative of state government was crucial in establishing these outside linkages and assisting local governments to obtain resources.

On the negative side, outside linkages can mean a loss of local autonomy and the withdrawal of resources from the community or area. An increase in federal presence can usurp local people's

control or ability to govern themselves. Large industries and
agencies are likely to have greater political power and economic
resources than local political leaders, and they may use this power
to overrule or bypass local decisions or to drain resources from the
community.

Similarly, large nationwide chain stores, which may be attracted
to the area by the increased population and buying power generated
by some projects, frequently have better access to financing and a
broader sales base than their locally-owned counterparts. Their
superior access to materials and larger size can make it difficult
for local businesses to compete. At the same time, the presence of
such large, high-sales businesses has advantages for the community,
such as a wider selection of goods, lower prices, and the ability to
expand rapidly to meet increased demand.

The influx of large numbers of new residents can also change the
outside linkage characteristics of a community. These new residents
frequently have ties outside the community that can serve as links
to additional information, to emergency assistance, and to emotional
support. They can also reduce the density and intensity of personal
contact among community residents and diminish newcomers' affiliation with the local community.

A principal purpose of analyzing outside linkages is to determine how the community's existing and potential outside linkages
would affect its ability to obtain and control resources and to respond to change. An additional purpose is to identify the potential
for significant change in outside linkages that would affect the
other social organization processes or indicators of community well-
being and community perception.

Characteristics of a community that might be important for the
analysis include the following:

1) The existence of local ties to state government, for example, local residents holding state positions; personal
   relationships between local leaders and state government
   officials.

2) Demonstration that the community has effectively obtained
   state or federal grants or programs during the last five to
   ten years. This could take the form of being selected as
   the site for state institutions or programs (schools, fairs,
   rodeos, conventions) or of obtaining state or federal
   assistance for economic or community development.

3) The number and type of national or international businesses
   or agenies located in the community, such as national energy
   companies, chain retail stores, national financial institutions, state or federal agencies, or national voluntary organizations.

4) The proportion of local workers who are union members.

5) The proportion of local residents who are relative newcomers
   to the community (five years or less).

Questions that would indicate which of these characteristics
would be important for analysis of the proposed actions include the
following:

1) Would the proposed action increase the local presence of federal or state agencies, especially in roles which would affect local control of resources?

2) Would the proposed action alter the economic conditions in the community in a way that would increase or decrease the number or role of nonlocal businesses? Would this change result in competition between locally and nonlocally owned businesses? Would it introduce union activities into a previously nonunionized area?

3) Would the proposed action create sufficient strain on local resources that the community's ability to respond would depend on its ability to obtain outside funds or technical assistance?

4) Would the characteristics of the proposed action introduce large numbers of workers with strong outside ties whose duration of stay in the community would be short enough to discourage them from affiliating with the community?

5) Would the sponsor of the proposed action use its outside linkages to increase the resource base and economic diversity of the community, or would it use them solely or primarily to extract additional resources from the community?

Data Sources

Analysis and interpretation of data on outside linkages is difficult. One reason is the potential for linkages to function in both positive and negative ways -- for providing resources or for extracting resources, for supplementing local political power or for diminishing it. Another reason is that some of the most important linkages are informal and hence are extremely difficult to identify and assess. National trends toward increased outside linkages were very strong during the last decade. This has made it difficult to determine what proportion of the change observed in communities undergoing large-scale development were attributable to growth. In addition, this is an area where it has been found difficult to avoid making unwarranted value judgments; there is often a tendency to favor local control and to overestimate the adverse effects of outside linkages.

Information about the number and types of businesses, agencies, or organizations that represent formal outside linkages can be obtained quite readily from the yellow pages of the local telephone directory. It is generally not necessary to be exact; the question is one of major changes. Much of the available information about externally linked businesses and their role in the community can be obtained by interviewing an official of the local chamber of commerce or a local developer. If the community is large and the listing would be a substantial task, it is probably not necessary to make more than a rough estimate.

Information about the community's ties to state and federal government will probably be most readily available from interviews with community leaders, although local newspapers may also be helpful. Information about the community's ability to obtain state and federal programs and monies may be available in summaries of

resource distribution published by the states or agencies, or it may
have been compiled by a local government official. Otherwise, this
information can be obtained through interviews with local officials. As with the externally linked businesses and organizations,
the list does not have to be complete. The point is to determine
whether or not the community has a demonstrated ability (or inability) to obtain outside assistance.

Information about the characteristics of project-related workers
will probably be available from the economist, as will estimates of
the expected changes in externally linked businesses. Estimates of
the with-project changes in the presence and role of state and federal agencies or large-scale industry can be derived from an evaluation of the institutional and regulatory characteristics of the
proposed action, in consultation with the legal council of the proposed action's sponsor. Examination of legal requirements and
records documenting what has happened with similar projects in the
same state will also provide useful information.

The availability of information about the characteristics of the
sponsor of the proposed action and its use of outside linkages will
depend very much on the type of assessment being done. Unless a
project sponsor has been specified, this factor remains highly uncertain, although a summary profile of companies undertaking similar
projects in the recent past could be informative.

Distribution of Resources and Power

Variables

Throughout the guide, the term "stakeholder" has been used to
indicate those groups or classes of people who have a vested interest or "stake" in the decisions or activities being assessed. Although the term has typically been used in the public involvement
process to indicate groups that have taken a public position advocating the decisions they believe best represent the interests of
their group, it applies in the broader sense to all members of communities whose environment, economy, or social organization could be
affected by the proposed action. Social assessment has the respons-
ibilty to identify and, in many cases, to provide public visibility
to the full range of potential effects so those who will be affected
can understand what their stake in the decision really is. For this
reason, the broader definition of stakeholders is appropriate for
social assessment. At the time of the assessment there is likely to
be a great deal of uncertainty about the characteristics of the proposed action and its likely consequences. Many stakeholder groups
may therefore not yet be prepared to represent their interests; some
may not even be aware that they have a stake in the decision.

The issue of stakeholder representation and the difficulty of
balancing conflicting interests is nowhere more clearly manifest
than in the analysis and presentation of the social processes by
which status, power, and access to resources are distributed among
community residents and outsiders. There are also few instances
where the social assessment is so likely to feel the political nature of the assessment process. To clarify and make public without

advocating, to describe diplomatically without equivocating, to analyze without criticizing are particular challenges when dealing with
these issues.

One important function of social assessment is to identify
changes that are likely to occur in the patterns of access to
resources and to assess the probable reaction of different groups to
these changes. If a proposed action introduces relatively small
changes, the likelihood of a significant effect on the distributional processes is slight. A concern in these cases would be to ensure
that the unique problems faced by distinct groups would not be exacerbated by the changes that are introduced. If the proposed action
will cause major changes in population, jobs, and income, the processes by which resources are distributed may be a very significant
factor determining the social outcome for various stakeholder
groups. In addition, the distributional process itself may be substantially affected by the changes. Four aspects of the distribution processes can be particularly important for forecasting and
assessing social consequences: (1) equity, (2) criteria for status
or power, (3) basis of obtaining wealth, and (4) distribution of
services.

Equity

One of the crucial issues a social assessment must address is
that of equity. Usually equity means that the resources of a community are distributed justly and fairly among all its members.
Since "just" and "fair" are culturally defined terms, with one person's definition varying substantially from another's, the analysis
of equity is complex and difficult. In social assessment, attention
tends to be focused on three aspects of equity. First, the assessor
attempts to determine what criteria govern the distribution of costs
and benefits of the type that would occur with the proposed action.
As part of this analysis, an effort is made to assess whether the
various social groups in the community feel that these criteria are
fair and just. The second task is to determine whether the prevailing distributional processes will result in a relatively commensurate distribution of costs and benefits. That is, those who reap the
benefits are also those who pay the costs -- as opposed to a situation where the costs fall upon those with little chance to obtain
benefits. Of particular interest is an analysis of the balance of
benefits and costs for each of the community social and stakeholder
groups in order to (1) identify any groups for whom the costs would
constitute a hardship, (2) to anticipate the emergence of new, organized stakeholder groups, and (3) to anticipate the likely nature
of public response to the project. The third aspect of the analysis
is to determine whether the changes introduced by the proposed action will be sufficient to alter the distributional criteria and
processes themselves.

Each stakeholder group will normally resist erosion of its absolute or relative status, power, and wealth. If an increase in the
wealth, status, or power of one group will occur at the expense of
another, some degree of conflict is inevitable. Even the fact that
the distribution would increase equity is unlikely to diminish the

conflict in the community, although it might alter the way it is expressed. The one condition under which it may be possible to increase equity while not significantly reducing the standing of an existing stakeholder group is when an economy is expanding, as it might when a major new development such as an energy project occurs. In reality, it appears unlikely that the benefits of a project will be distributed equally to all residents because of the powerful distributive processes that have been established; some people are likely to be in a position to ensure that they will gain a disproportionate share of the new resources. Consequently, unless there are substantial forces for change, existing inequities may be reinforced rather than eliminated.

In some areas, unique cultural groups are being exposed to development in a particularly intense way. Large-scale projects are being introduced on or near the lands they hold by special, generally nontransferable legal rights and cultural beliefs. This can present genuinely new, unfamiliar, and possibly culturally incongruous means for acquiring wealth, status, and power that the group cannot completely avoid. This has been particularly true for some Native Americans and Hispanic land grant holders. In some cases, the creation of new paths to wealth, status, and power is viewed as an opportunity to alter the existing pattern of resource distribution. In others, it is viewed as an unwanted imposition by outside actors which constrains the decision-making capability and autonomy of the group.

Criteria for status or power

There are several potential criteria for status or power in a community. These include: wealth, property ownership, a family name or family role of historical prominence, and role played in the community (e.g., major accomplishment, etc.). Different communities may put a slightly different emphasis on each of these factors, but if the population in a community remains stable or if the majority of the in-migrants are from within the region and share the same general criteria, the status criteria of the community are likely to change only slowly.

In communities where status is largely determined by family name, blood relationship with other community members, or other factors which generally favor longtime residents, introduction of even a large project may create no significant change if the majority of the newcomers ascribe to the same type of status criteria as the longtime residents. This is because the newcomers cannot challenge longtime residents for status within the existing framework. However, in communities where status is largely determined by employment or wealth (an unusual situation in most small towns), the introduction of a number of highly-paid managerial and technical people may cause disruption in the relative standing of longtime residents. The effects of a proposed action on the relative status of longtime residents (and on the prevailing status criteria) will depend upon several factors: (1) the number of newcomers, (2) the status of the newcomers relative to the longtime residents according to the status criteria of the longtime residents, and (3) the status of the newcomers relative to the longtime residents according to the status criteria held by the newcomers.

Research in ten rural western communities which had experienced moderate or large-scale resource development found that no marked change had occurred in the basic status structure although some broadening in the criteria for obtaining status or power had appeared and the stratification systems had frequently become more complex (Thompson, et al. 1982). The changes that had occurred had been relatively gradual, indicating that such development may initiate a long-term change, rather than an abrupt short-term modification. Those groups or individuals who might be losing relative status or position had generally anticipated these changes, resisted them, and expressed concern about additional changes that might result from further development. (In an assessment, such concerns could be addressed in the section on attitudes toward change and perceptions of community well-being.)

Basis of obtaining wealth

In many rural communities, land and property ownership has been the primary basis for obtaining wealth, with some opportunity in professional or service careers such as medicine, law, real estate, or banking. People successful in these occupations often hold property as well. This means that the basis for wealth and its associated status and power is tied to the geographic area and natural resources in a very physical way.

A new basic economic activity in an area can change the basis for acquiring wealth and provide new opportunities for particular groups of local residents. In general, the shift that occurs with large-scale development is from agriculture to industrial activities. If development activities have been under way in an area for a long time and have progressed gradually, there is a reasonable possibility that those who have wealth in the community will be participating in the development as investors.

However, most of the truly large-scale development now occurring in rural areas is controlled by large, multinational corporations which relocate managers and workers into the area to implement their project. The newcomers, even the managers, are generally neither the owners of the resources being developed nor the ultimate decision makers regarding their use. But managers and senior technical people do control access to the decision makers whose decisions may have considerable impact on the community and its residents. Managers, senior technical people, and skilled workers generally receive large salaries compared to the norms of rural towns. To the extent that wealth is a significant determinant of status or power, these management, technical, and skilled crafts jobs present an alternative path to acquiring wealth and an alternative means to status and power not controlled by the existing community. The cumulative effect of these alternatives may be to modify the existing stratification system over the long term.

It should be noted, however, that although industrial/corporate employment may not have been prevalent in the community prior to the resource development, many small rural communities have a long history of having young adults leave the community for employment in these types of jobs. Access to industrial employment may therefore not be new; what may be different is its visibility and immediacy in the community.

Distribution of services

Public services are not used equally by all stakeholder groups and are not equally important to each group. Typically, those groups with relatively low incomes are more dependent upon public sector services and resources than are the more wealthy, although the wealthy may utilize some of the public services more heavily than the poor (schools, roads, etc.). If necessary, people with wealth are generally able to obtain the services they need in the private sector. A proposed action that results in poorer quality or diminished availability of services can place a greater burden on those groups that are highly dependent on these services than on those groups who have access to services in other ways. For this reason, in assessments where service availability problems are expected to occur, it is not enough just to know the cumulative effect on facilities and services, it is also necessary to know which groups in the community utilize those services, what alternative means they have for obtaining them, and what the loss or degradation of these services would mean to each group.

Characteristics of the existing environment that could be important in assessing the distribution of resources and power include the following:

1) Definition of the prevailing criteria for attaining status, wealth, and power, with attention to the possibility of distinctive sets of criteria for any unique cultural groups and to the various groups' assessment of the fairness of these criteria.

2) Indication of the relative positions of the major social groups in terms of wealth, status, and power. The presence of economically, politically, or socially disadvantaged groups indicate a need for careful analysis of distributive effects. Potential effects on absolute or relative wealth, status, or power indicate a need to identify and characterize stakeholder groups.

3) Description of public services utilization patterns by the major social and stakeholder groups.

4) Identification of the types of changes (and potential conflicts) in wealth, status, and power anticipated by each of the major social groups. These anticipations can influence the development of organized stakeholder groups, the responses of community residents, and their attitudes toward the proposed action and the newcomers.

Questions that would help determine the relevance of these characteristics for the particular assessment being conducted include the following:

1) Would the proposed action change the employment or income characteristics (either by creating new jobs with different earning potential or by affecting the earning potential of existing jobs or resources -- for example, real estate or commercial activities)?

2) Would the proposed action introduce people who would challenge the existing status criteria or compete with longtime residents for status?

3) Would the proposed action introduce a sufficient number of people to affect service provision characteristics?

4) Would the proposed action be perceived as a threat by powerful stakeholder groups? Would it be a threat to vulnerable social groups?

5) Would the presence and policies of the action's sponsor affect the distributional processes established in the community?

Data Sources

One place to start compiling data on community distributional processes is from the federal census, where income, occupation, and housing characteristics can be obtained for the population as a whole and for major ethnic groups -- blacks, the Spanish-surnamed, and Native Americans. If social groups (or stakeholder groups) reside in geographically distinct areas, tract data from the federal census can be used to identify differences in these characteristics by group. A drive through the area to observe the neighborhoods can also be helpful, although one must be cautious about assumptions derived from housing type, neighborhoods, and income. The agricultural census may provide useful information about characteristics of the rural residents that is often more difficult to obtain from field interviews.

Interviews with service providers can be used to identify and provide a qualitative description of groups with particular resource utilization characteristics and to provide estimates of current usage patterns and latent needs by social or stakeholder group. Although these estimates will not be exact, they are generally sufficient.

Definition of the prevailing criteria for status, wealth, and power and information about the relative positions of the social groups can be obtained by a combination of observation and interviews with local residents. Organized stakeholder groups can also be identified and interviews conducted with their members and official representatives. These interviews, public documents, and local newspapers can be used to identify anticipated changes and conflict.

The effects of the proposed action on income, housing, service availability, and the characteristics of the in-migrating population can be estimated in collaboration with the facilities/services analyst and the economist by examining information about the proposed action and reports describing similar actions. It should be stressed that these will be estimates. The purpose is to get an idea of what types and magnitude of change might be introduced.

Coordination and Cooperation

Variables

The ability of a community to adapt to and control change is determined to an important degree by its ability to coordinate its efforts and resources and to establish cooperation among the various elements of the community. Of all the characteristics of the existing environment, few are more important for assessing the consequences of a proposed action than the extent to which the community can and will coordinate its efforts to influence its future.

The coordinative characteristics of a community are closely interrelated with the characteristics of the other social organization processes. Coordination involves the processes of establishing a commonality of perspective and managing and controlling conflict in the community. Coordination is made more difficult by high levels of conflict and by increased complexity and diversity. The need for more complex coordinative mechanisms generally corresponds with an increase in the complexity of the community.

The ability of a community to coordinate its efforts and resources depends upon the interaction of five major factors: the characteristics of the community leaders, the characteristics of the community's organization in terms of diversity/complexity and cooperation, the extent to which local resources are controlled by outsiders, and the characteristics of the issues to be addressed. Although all five are important and interrelated, the personal characteristics of community leaders were identified in the community research as the single most important factor in the ability of energy-impacted communities to organize, cooperate, and address community problems (Thompson, et al. 1982). Unfortunately it is also the factor that is the most difficult and politically sensitive to predict.

Since the ability of a community to coordinate its efforts and obtain cooperation can have a major influence on its ability to successfully respond to problems, it is important to determine how this process is currently operating in the study area communities and then to estimate (1) how this characteristic of the existing social organization will affect the development process and (2) how it will be affected by the project.

In most assessments, the objective will be to determine the extent and effectiveness of the coordinative process in the existing community prior to the project and to understand how the community is likely to respond to the changes introduced by the proposed action. This involves understanding avenues that are available to the community for affecting the outcome of the proposed action. Characteristics of the existing environment that could be useful for this aspect of the assessment include the following:

1) Identification of community projects that have been initiated in recent years (such as schools, libraries, courthouses, recreational facilities, water or sewer plants, roads, economic development, community events), and description of how the effort and resources were coordinated to

make the project succeed or how the coordination effort failed and why the project was abandoned.

2) Identification of specific coordinative or control mechanisms that have been established in the community to solve problems (for example, joint-powers boards, task forces, councils, zoning, animal control), and description of the process by which they were established.

3) Identification of major and persistent conflicts or issues in the community, and description of how the conflict is being controlled or exacerbated. Here it is especially useful to examine the mechanisms that have been developed to control or contain conflict between major stakeholder groups, particularly those which share political power, and to incorporate newcomers into the community.

4) Identification of the mechanism available to the community to affect the changes introduced by the proposed action (for example, limiting in-migration by prohibiting new water connections, mobile homes, or subdivisions, or requiring that local residents be hired rather than outsiders) and the effectiveness of the community's response.

Questions which can be asked to help determine which of these characteristics will be important include the following:

1) To what extent could the outcomes of the proposed action be different if the community responded in the most effective instead of the least effective way possible?

2) To what extent could the outcomes of the proposed action be affected if the community responded in the most antagonistic and coordinated way possible, in the most supportive and coordinated way, and in the least coordinated way possible?

3) To what extent could the changes introduced by the proposed action reduce or enhance the coordinative processes in the community?

Data Sources

Some information about the coordinative mechanisms and the cooperative processes in the community can be obtained through review of documents describing community political structure over the last several years and examination of local newspapers, but the primary source of information will be interviews with community residents (particularly those involved in community affairs and decision making) and observations about how the community approaches problems and how successfully local projects have been completed. It should be remembered that local politics are notoriously erratic and idiosyncratic. Consequently, the objective in the examination of previous community response is to abstract patterns; it is important not to be distracted by all the details of the local political process. In addition, it is important to remember to listen analytically to the interviews with local residents and to get the perspective of a variety of different people. Guidance on selecting respondents and conducting informal interviews is provided in Chapter 13.

Reporting about how coordination and cooperation are affecting a community can be politically explosive and has the danger of being perceived as meddling in local affairs. This is a sensitive area which requires the continual exercise of judgment. The purpose of an assessment is not to dictate to local governments and private groups how they should provide for the health and welfare of their constituents. The responsibility of agencies under NEPA and other legislation is to ensure that potential harmful effects are identified and taken into consideration in the decision process. Obviously, determining what and how to present information about the effect of existing coordination and cooperation processes on social outcomes is a judgment area. Questions about the appropriate way to deal with this topic should be discussed with colleagues, the project manager, and the assessment team leader.

Personal Interaction

Variables

Personal interaction has been included as a separate category, although in many ways it summarizes aspects of the other four social organization processes. Personal interaction is used here to mean the way in which people in a community identify and respond to one another. It has been kept separate because changes in the process of personal interaction have often been identified as an important consequence of introducing large-scale projects in rural areas. Longtime residents of impacted communities consistently identify changes in personal relationships as one of the most personally meaningful consequences of the project's effects.

The nature of personal interaction is affected both directly and indirectly by the types of changes introduced by large-scale development projects or technological change. Changes in the size of the community, demographic characteristics of the residents, the complexity and diversity, the mechanisms by which resources are distributed and shared, and the extent to which community residents have to deal with outsiders can all affect the patterns of personal interaction. Consequently, a proposed action that affects those characteristics of the community is likely to affect its personal interaction characteristics as well.

There are several particular effects on personal interaction that can occur in impacted communities. With an influx of a large number of people, particularly if there is high turnover among them, community residents will not know everyone in town. Interaction based on personal knowledge will no longer be possible in many areas of community life. In communities where people can no longer interact informally on the basis of who they are, the dominance of personal interaction in the patterns of everyday life will decline. Although it is unlikely that primary relationships will be lost, the proportion of strangers encountered will increase; in public exchanges, people will begin to be treated similarly, according to established formal rules.

Associated with the loss of personal recognition and informal interaction is a change in the basis for identifying and categorizing people. Residents become identified and categorized not on the basis of personal knowledge (knowledge of their character, attributes, and status), but on the basis of their organizational affiliations and memberships. This happens because an increased proportion of the daily activity of community life is conducted in and through organizations. Changes in the procedures for check-cashing or paying by check are an excellent example of how and why this change takes place. In many small, rural communities, most residents can cash personal checks with no questions asked and without need to present personal identification. However, these privileges are not necessarily accorded to all residents equally. Some residents may not be allowed to cash checks or buy on credit. The basis for these distinctions is knowledge about the person. This informal system works only as long as the participants feel they have sufficient knowledge about each other to make accurate judgments about whom to trust. Such knowledge generally takes a long time to acquire.

When new people enter the community, several things happen that cause this informal system to change. The first and most obvious change occurs when newcomers arrive in the community. Many of these newcomers want to use personal checks to purchase goods and services. Since no personal relationship has been established that would allow the merchant to judge the newcomer's trustworthiness, the newcomer may be asked to provide identification and may be required to have a local address and phone number, even to use checks drawn on local banks. At first, longtime residents can usually continue to use checks as before, although the use of counter checks may be eliminated.

The next changes occur when newcomers begin to work in local stores and banks. The newcomers are usually unfamiliar with community residents and are not able to distinguish longtime residents from newcomers. Consequently, they are likely to ask everyone wishing to use a check to show identification. If growth or turnover remains high, this may become an established procedure, both to minimize confusion and to avoid the appearance of discrimination.

The final step in the process occurs when new businesses enter the community, especially those headquartered elsewhere. The policy of these businesses may be to cash no checks, to cash checks only for persons showing two pieces of identification, or to cash checks only for persons with a check guarantee card. At this point, there are few differences in the way longtime residents and newcomers conduct everyday business in the community, and the basis of recognition has essentially shifted from knowledge of the individual to trust in an organization.

When this happens, both newcomers and longtime residents must find organizations that can be used to help identify and characterize themselves. For some newcomers, especially management personnel who can be sponsored by the company or agency implementing the action, this may create no problems and represent no change from accustomed practice. For others, such as blue collar workers who lack such company affiliation, this can be more difficult, although it is probably not unfamiliar. For most longtime residents, obtaining organizational affiliation may not be difficult, but the necessity is likely to be distasteful, since it represents a loss in their sense of community and personal prestige. For many, the necessity to submit to such regulations constitutes a significant irritation.

The high degree of shared background, experiences, and values along with the personal familiarity usually found in small stable communities create another characteristic of personal interaction that can be affected by the in-migration of newcomers. Residents of such communities generally have little need to spell-out their expectations or perspectives to one another in matters of every day life. They are usually correct in assuming that both parties will know and abide by the implicit standards of local behavior. Newcomers, of course, do not share this "common knowledge" and may therefore require different, more explicit communications and may unknowingly violate some of the unstated norms of interaction or behavior. Longtime residents tend to be sensitive to nonconformance in areas that are highly valued or that have become symbolic of the community's way-of-life. The protocol of (and overall approach to) outdoor recreation, especially hunting and fishing, is such an area for many longtime residents of the intermountain West. The manner in which residents greet one another and exchange pleasantries when meeting on the street or in stores is another. The protocol followed when driving and parking in town is yet another. If the number of newcomers is small, their effect on this aspect of personal interaction patterns is likely to be noted and viewed as a nuisance or irritation. If the number of newcomers is large, the entire context of public interaction may change as the assumption of implicit communication and common understanding can no longer be made.

Characteristics of the existing environment which could be useful in addressing this aspect of social organization include the following:

1) The extent to which local residents share a common background, especially in terms of residential location
2) The extent to which community interaction is informal, idiosyncratic, and implicit, as opposed to formal, explicit, and based on rules or procedures
3) The extent to which informal interaction and informal ways of getting things done are valued as a way of life

Questions which will be helpful include the following:

1) Will the proposed action result in sufficient change to cause the informal way of doing things to be replaced with more formal procedures?
2) Will the proposed action result in changes that change the extent to which residents know one another and the implicit rules governing social conduct?
3) Is the potential for decreased familiarity, informality, and trust a concern?

Data Sources

Informal interviews and observation will provide the major sources of data on personal interactions unless a survey covering this topic has recently been conducted in the area. Some data on the changes in personal interactions that are caused by growth are available in secondary sources, but evidence is frequently limited. Schools, banks, and law enforcement agencies are good places to look for indications of the prevailing nature of interpersonal relationships.

The Social Organization Model: Indicators of Social Well-being

In the final analysis, the whole purpose of analyzing direct project inputs, community resources, and community social organization is to determine whether and in what manner a proposed action will alter the social well-being of the community. In a very real sense, the purpose of the social well-being component of the model is to integrate and summarize the consequences of the changes that have been analyzed in the previous three components -- project inputs, community resources, and social organization. In the well-being component, the focus is on integrating this information to determine how the changes that have been identified will affect the well-being of individuals and groups in the study area or community.

The concept of well-being has both objective and subjective components, each of which can be represented by indicators. Objective indicators of well-being are aggregate measures of the incidence or occurence of social behavior, socioeconomic characteristics, or physical conditions. Objective indicators include such things as crime occurrence and crime rates, divorces and divorce rates, personal income distribution, housing characteristics, and so on. They are defined as objective indicators because they are measures or statistics of factual or "objective" conditions or events. Subjective indicators, on the other hand, are aggregate measures of the attitudes, perceptions, and values of the people in the community. Subjective indicators include satisfaction with community services, support or opposition for population growth, the importance of participation in community decisions, and so on.

Gathering data to compile objective and subjective indicators can be difficult, but the real difficulty comes in interpreting the meaning of the data, which is not as easy as it might seem. The concept of "well-being" is complex and ambiguous. It is used to indicate the net effect of a combination of subjective and objective factors whose composition, let alone relative importance, remains unclear. Does well-being exist merely because people perceive themselves to be well off, or are there some objective measures that must be applied? Does the fact that people perceive changes in well-being mean that they have occurred? Inevitably there is a kind of tension between the subjective and objective determinations of well-being that makes the analysis difficult. Objective and subjective indicators are not independent. Objective indicators are interpreted by community residents, influencing their attitudes, values, expectations, and fears. Attitudes, values, and expectations influence behavior, thus affecting objective conditions and indicators. At the same time, well-being is a relative term. Comparisons of past to future, this community to another, and reality to expectations all play a role in determining perceptions of

well-being and complicate the interpretation of both subjective
statements and objective indicators.

Analyzing the objective and subjective indicators within the
framework of the social organization model can help you interpret
their implications and meaning. As indicated in the model, well-
being indicators both affect and are affected by direct project (and
baseline) impacts and by changes in community resources and social
organization. For example, an influx of young, male adults might
cause a rise in crime rates in a community which had previously had
little incidence of crime. The rise in crime rates could lessen
community integration, introducing a degree of mistrust between newcomers and longtime residents, and increasing local demand for increased law enforcement. Or, the combination of rapid population
growth, the demographic and social characteristics of the newcomers,
and the inability of local officials to coordinate an effective response may cause residents to lose confidence in their leaders, experience declining service quality and facility availability, and
suffer anxiety and frustration. The social organization model has
been designed to help you identify these possible relationships and
to interpret the implications of your analysis.

A critical difficulty is determining what the complex consequences of those linkages will be. There is also a difficulty in
that people experience well-being as individuals, while the responsibility of the assessment is to determine effects on well-being in
the study area or community as a whole. In social assessment, it is
generally not possible to study or take into explicit account individual personality characteristics. Yet obviously individual personality characteristics play a role in determining what changes in
well-being an individual will experience as a result of a particular
project. Practical constraints thus introduce substantial uncertainty into efforts to describe well-being or to forecast effects on
well-being for social groups much less entire communities.

Nevertheless, the assessment must attempt to take into account
both the objective and subjective components of well-being. The
objective indicators can be divided into two components: rates of
behavior and access to resources. The subjective indicators include
attitudes and perceptions. The discussion of well-being can be organized as follows:

1) **Rates of behavior**, such as suicide, divorce, crime, and
   family violence
2) **Access to resources**, such as per capita or family income,
   public services, recreation
3) **Perceptions of community and personal well-being** held by
   area or community members, focusing on their interpretation
   and evaluation of the changes caused by the proposed action

Where possible, it is desirable to compile time series data for
all the communities and counties in the project region as well as
for the state(s) and the United States. This allows the study area
to be compared with other jurisdictions over time, and provides a
more understandable basis for description of study area characteristics.

The following section discusses each of these three categories of well-being indicators, with guidance on how to determine which characteristics of the existing environment will be analytically important to the assessment of social effects.

Rates of Behavior

Variables

When considering behaviors, it is necessary to consider both the incidence (the total number of times a behavior occurs) and the rate (the ratio of the number of times a behavior occurs to the population size).

The analysis of behaviors serves two purposes, which have somewhat different data requirements. The first purpose of analyzing behaviors is to develop a measure of the existing and future social environment of the community in order to evaluate the quality of the environment for community residents. For this analysis, rates of behavior are usually the most revealing and useful measures. High rates of problem behaviors are an indication of a (comparatively) poor social environment and of problems in the community. High rates of problem behaviors adversely affect residents' sense of personal security and comfort and their satisfaction with the community as a place to live. High rates of problem behaviors may reflect structural or resource problems in a community that increase the likelihood that people will behave in personally destructive or socially unacceptable ways. However, high rates of problem behaviors may also result from particular demographic characteristics of the population (for example the age-sex structure) that have little to do with community resources or organization. It is very difficult to determine the relative importance of these two factors for the rate of behavior that is observed or forecast. This is a topic of continuing debate in the literature and its lack of resolution makes forecasting or interpreting changes in rates of behavior very uncertain.

The second purpose of analyzing these behaviors is to determine or forecast the demands being placed on service providers and community resources. Problem behaviors generally require some type of service response -- law enforcement, judical, public assistance, counseling, health care. An increase in these behaviors will thus have implications for service providers and the community budget. In an assessment, one of the tasks is to determine the demand for community resources and whether adequate resources will be available. For the social assessor, this analysis is important in evaluating resource availability and in determining whether resource inadequacies will occur. Such inadequacies could adversely affect the social environment of the community and/or increase the rate of problem behaviors. For this analysis, measures or estimates of the incidence of the behaviors is most useful.

Despite the problems with the data that are discussed below, there is general agreement that the following are among the important rates of behavior to consider in assessing resource development projects:

1) Crime
2) Divorce
3) Suicide
4) Infant mortality
5) Family violence and mental health
6) Alcohol and drug abuse
7) Public assistance and welfare
8) School dropouts and student turnover
9) Unemployment

Even though there is a general consensus that analysis of these behaviors can be useful in the assessment of effects on social well-being, there are three important qualities to remember in utilizing and analyzing information about them.

1) **Lack of clear cause-and-effect relationships.** The number of social variables is large, and the interaction among them is consequently complex. It is virtually impossible to say one single thing causes another. Does a dramatic increase in population cause divorces? It may be possible to answer "Sometimes -- under some conditions -- it depends." It may be more likely that the addition of a large number of young, single males is likely to increase crime, but an honest researcher will once again have to conclude that it depends. The social assessor usually finds him- or herself dealing with indirect relationships and probabilities, not clear and direct cause/effect relationships. This increases the difficulty of making clear distinctions between the probable effects of various alternatives and of forecasting outcomes for situations in which many aspects remain uncertain.

2) **The behaviors are indicators, not a direct measurement of well-being.** It is possible to infer that if suicide, divorce, crime, and family violence all increase, social well-being declines, but since social well-being is intangible, that is simply an inference -- there is no direct measurement of social well-being. These rates of behavior indicate, but they do not measure. One of the problems is that all of these indicators look at individual or family behaviors, while the thing to be measured, at least in part, is community well-being. When a crime is committed, it is committed by an individual who interacts with a community; the reasons for committing the crime are both highly individual and yet related to conditions in the community. Because the individual and community components cannot be clearly separated (and, in fact, is the subject of considerable academic and political debate), inferences can be made, but uncertainty about the net balance remains that is difficult to resolve.

3) **The available data are often not good.** First, the indicators that are used typically reflect the availability of data; they are frequently not the measures that constitute the best indicators of well-being. For example, the emphasis tends to fall on rates of undesirable behaviors because

those are the ones measured. There aren't any available
measures of how often neighbors or families help one another
or work to improve the community. Yet obviously the incidence of positive behavior is as important to well-being as
the incidence of problem behavior.

Second, fluctuations in the data may be the result of
differences in reporting procedures rather than in actual
rates of behavior. Take crime rates, for example. Many
rural communities did not report crime rates systematically
until the mid-1970s, and the quality of reporting continues
to vary substantially from jurisdiction to jurisdiction. As
a result, apparent differences in crime rates between communities or between time periods may reflect differences in
reporting procedures, not actual differences in the incidence or rate of crime.

Finally, the population of rural communities and counties
is often so small and the incidence of the behavior so low
that many of the commonly used measures are unstable and
difficult to analyze at a community or county level. If the
number of burglaries in the community in a year increases
from four to eight, there has been a 100 percent increase in
burglaries. But does that increase affect well-being? If
it drops back down to four burglaries the next year, does
that indicate that well-being has improved?

4) **Well-being is related to expectations.** Since so much of
well-being has to do with perceptions, people usually think
well-being is changing in the direction they expect it to
change. People who expect a proposed action to improve
their well-being are likely to concentrate on those indicators which correspond to their expectations. Those who
expect well-being to decline can usually find evidence to
support that expectation. This obviously increases the
difficulty of interpreting the meaning and importance of
changes in the various objective well-being indicators.

Crime

Crime is one of the indicators that has consistently been found
to have an important effect on perceptions of well-being. Actually,
what is crucial is not the number of crimes that are committed as
much as the number of people who will feel themselves or those close
to them to be victims of crime. As indicated above, there are significant problems with the crime data that are available for use in
the description of the existing environment since they are influenced by reporting procedures and often do not reflect the actual
number of crimes committed. Additionally, rate calculations in
rapidly growing communities are often suspect because accurate population data are unavailable. This may make the data from other communities experiencing similar change less reliable for forecasting
the consequences of the project in the study community.

Several factors associated with rapid growth are thought to contribute to an increase in crime:

1) An influx of large numbers of young adult males who, as a group, tend to exhibit higher than average crime rates.
2) The presence of incoming workers who often experience a period of low income and high expenditures when they first come into the community. This appears to be associated with bad check writing and theft.
3) Situations where services are inadequate, localized inflation exists, or personal interactions are poor, making newcomers (or longtime residents) feel stressed, frustrated, angry, and out of control.
4) A high turnover among newcomers that decreases familiarity and reduces the effectiveness of informal mechanisms for controlling crime, such as watching out for strangers, and that encourages theft, bad check writing, and vandalism.
5) Poor law enforcement due to inadequate or untrained personnel.
6) The juxtaposition of persons from different groups in situations (like bars) that encourage the development of arguments and fights.

There is a widespread perception that crime increases dramatically in communities experiencing rapid growth. For communities in the West, the available data leave little question that the incidence of crime has increased, and there is considerable evidence that the rate of theft (of various sorts) and personal assaults (usually reflecting bar fights) have increased because of the growth. However, there is little indication that the rate of other violent crimes against persons have increased. Most of the increase appears to have occurred in property crimes such as burglary and misdemeanors. One problem in interpreting the widely held belief that crime is related to large-scale development is that crime rates increased dramatically throughout the nation during the 1970s, the same period that many large-scale projects were initiated. In future assessments it is important not to attribute crime rate changes to large-scale development projects that are caused by other, unrelated factors.

An increase in the number of crimes has definite implications for the number of law enforcement officers, jail space, and judicial services required. In such circumstances, law enforcement personnel often report feeling caught in the middle and expected to respond to situations that are beyond their control. This can cause morale, high turnover, and behavior problems among law enforcement personnel and it can adversely affect residents' perceptions of community well-being. In small communities, an increase in the number of crimes appears to affect perceptions of safety and personal security, whether or not the rate of crime increases.

Divorce

Divorce is one of the indicators for which data at the county level are usually readily available, though reporting problems still exist. The problem is that changes in the divorce rate are hard to interpret. When an increase does occur, it isn't always clear what

it means. One argument is that divorce is related to rapid growth
because it reflects stress on family relationships due to poor living conditions (especially housing) and lack of community or social
support. An alternative theory is that growth creates greater social diversity in a town, causing the social sanctions against divorce to be relaxed, thus permitting termination of unsatisfactory
relationships. In addition, increased job opportunities for women
may permit them to end unsatisfactory relationships. The question
is whether a particular change in the divorce data indicates a decrease or an increase in social well-being. It should be noted that
an argument can also be made that economic development should reduce
the number of divorces, since it may alleviate economic pressures, a
major source of marital stress.

Those factors potentially related to resource development that
may have an impact on divorce rates are the following:

1) An influx (and retention) of young adults in the early
stages of the family cycle, the group with the highest risk
of divorce. Since most divorce figures are not broken down
by age, this could produce a dramatic increase in divorce
rate that is more a function of the population composition
than a change in any individual's behavior.

2) Problems of housing availability or other resources and services that can create high stress and a poor living environment and can increase interpersonal conflict and lower
coping ability.

3) Extensive overtime, shift work, a sudden increase in expend-
able income, and other work-related changes that may strain
family relationships.

4) A relaxation of social sanctions against divorce either because the community norms change or because informal controls are less effective.

5) Increased employment and marriage opportunities for adult
women.

6) Less social and personal support provided by family and
friends.

An increase in the divorce rate and the number of divorced persons has definite implications for community services and facilities, and for residents' perceptions of community, including the
following:

1) Increased need for household support services and child care
as the number of female-headed households (frequently having
low incomes) increases

2) Increased demands on the judicial system and on those responsible for enforcement of child support payments

3) Increased demand for marriage and family counseling as the
number of persons involved with family dissolution or formation increases

4) Increased dissatisfaction (and disgust) on the part of those
who view such occurrences as indication that the community
is failing

Suicide

Another indicator of social well-being is the number and rate of
suicides, although suicide clearly reflects both personal and social
problems. Regrettably, the data on suicides and attempted suicides
are notoriously unreliable. Since suicide is a rare event under any
conditions, the small populations in most communities being studied
for assessments, combined with the poor data, make valid determination of trends in suicide rates or how suicide rates have been affected by previous development activities very difficult.

Historically, suicide rates have generally not been found to
rise during periods of rapid growth. If the growth is managed reasonably well, most residents of rapid growth communities (particularly those that previously were stagnant or declining) report a new
sense of vitality and activity that, while stressful, is stimulating
rather than depressing. Groups that do appear to be susceptible to
depression are the wives of newcomers, particularly construction
workers who find themselves in poor living conditions with few support systems and who presumably despair that they will get out of
this situation, and persons who are forced against their will to
change their residences (through eminent domain purchases, etc.) or
their livelihoods.

In those towns showing a strong economic downturn after rapid
growth, there have been reports of increased suicides attributed to
severe economic pressures, disrupted plans, and a sense of failure
due to job loss. This phenomenon has been documented on the national level during periods of economic depression. Suicide clearly
represents an extreme in personal and familial tragedy, and the potential for such consequences as a result of the down cycle of
resource-based growth warrants further examination. Data from the
recent recession should begin to be available soon.

Infant mortality

While acknowledged as a valid indicator of the availability of
adequate maternal nutrition and health care, community case studies
have generally not shown any indication of substantial changes in
infant mortality due to rapid growth. Infant mortality rates appear
to be most affected by economic conditions and medical care; the
level of these two factors in most areas of the United States is
apparently such that only very major changes will affect the rate.
The exceptions may be in areas with high populations of Native Americans, Hispanic land grant residents, or other particular cultural
groups whose economic or health care practices may be affected in a
major way by the proposed project. Infant mortality rates, which
are available from U.S. Vital Statistics and state divisions of
vital statistics, are therefore not recommended as a particularly
useful indicator in most assessment situations, with the exceptions
noted above. Nevertheless, it may be worthwhile to compare the infant mortality rates in the study area communities with state and
national levels for several years to check for anomalies that may
indicate special adverse or favorable conditions.

Family violence and mental health problems

Family violence includes such behaviors as spouse beating, child abuse, child neglect, and incest. While case studies reveal that law enforcement, mental health, judicial, and public welfare personnel in rapid growth communities consistently report concern about family violence and community mental health, the statistical evidence to justify these concerns is not clear. There is a continuing debate among social scientists about whether (and how much) family violence and mental health problems have actually increased over the last decade and what factors are responsible for this increase, if it has occurred. There is some feeling that increased use of services primarily reflects the fact that services have become more readily available and that people are simply more sensitive to these problems and more likely to seek assistance or report offenders. As with crime, there has been nationwide concern over the perceived increase in family violence that has occurred throughout the United States during the decade of the 1970s.

Although the link between rapid development, family violence, and mental health problems has not been clearly established, several hypotheses have been formulated:

1) Construction workers, due to cultural/social background or family characteristics, are more prone to family violence and mental health problems than most residents of western towns. An influx in construction workers will therefore cause an increase in the level of family violence and mental health problems in the community.

2) Housing conditions, lack of recreational facilities, and other resource availability problems and increased uncertainty created by rapid growth conditions lead to frustrations and stress which are expressed in mental health problems and family violence. These problems affect both newcomers and longtime residents.

3) Work characteristics such as shift work, overtime, and the development of work-related rather than family-related friendships all strain marital relationships in a way that provokes violence and neglect.

4) An increase in the number of single parents and families with stepchildren as a result of higher divorce and remarriage rates creates family situations that aggravate stress and are susceptible to violence, neglect, and incest.

5) Changes in long-established patterns and way of life along with high levels of uncertainty distress and upset longtime residents, increasing their mental health problems and, perhaps, provoking increased violence.

Increased family violence and mental health problems can cause increased demands on law enforcement and medical and judicial facilities. In addition, the establishment of counseling services for both the abuser and the victim and the provision of shelters can increase the demand on social services and mental health services.

As with many of the behavioral indicators, there is some evidence that family violence and mental health problems increase during periods of economic disruption, job loss, and residential movement such as would accompany the down cycle that often follows rapid growth.

Alcohol and drug abuse

Alcohol abuse has been a long-standing problem in many rural communities. Construction, oil, and gas workers, as well as university students, for example, are generally assumed to use alcohol as well as drugs at a somewhat higher rate than the resident population, and drugs are often thought to be introduced into the schools in greater quantities by their children, although data to document these perceptions are scarce. However, few communities in the West have reported that large-scale development during the 1970s has done much but slightly aggravate a problem that already existed and was already increasing in response to national trends and pressures. Even in rapid growth communities where drugs have been a major problem -- such as Rock Springs, Wyoming and Grants, New Mexico -- law enforcement, school, and public assistance personnel have not attributed the major source of the problem to the development activities.

From the little data that are available, drug and alcohol use patterns among the workers do not appear to change significantly in a new community. Workers with problems tend to bring those problems with them, rather than developing them because they are living in a rapid development area.

An increase in alcohol and drug abuse is generally associated with increases in other problem behaviors. Consequently, any substantial increase in alcohol and drug abuse would increase the demands on law enforcement and judicial services, medical and mental health services, and public assistance. The major concerns expressed in communities that have experienced rapid growth are the exposure of children to drugs and the increase in drunken driving. Increases in the number and violence of barroom fights are also often mentioned. In general, blue-collar newcomers have been perceived as heavy users of alcohol and drugs who contribute to an already serious community problem.

Public assistance and welfare rates

In a number of communities experiencing rapid growth due to energy resource development, public assistance and welfare personnel have reported that development tends to reduce the number of chronic recipients due to improved working conditions, but that it increases the number of persons requiring short-term or emergency assistance.

Apparently, the reasons for this increased short-term, emergency demand are the following:

1) Newcomers need assistance to cover the period between arriving and receiving the first paycheck. Many agencies report

high caseloads but also very high turnover and short-term
dependency.
2) Workers often come to an area before jobs are available and
may remain for a period after the work has been completed or
shut down. In addition, people who are genuinely
unemployable may be attracted by the prospect of jobs. In
all cases, emergency funds may be needed.

Major demands are made on public assistance services during
"bust" conditions. There is generally no indication that resource
development creates conditions which substantially increases the
number of persons permanently dependent upon welfare, although lack
of child care sometimes prolongs the welfare dependency of female
heads of household. Other proposed actions such as urban renewal,
technological change, or public policy decisions could have much
more pronounced and prolonged adverse effects on particularly vulnerable groups.

School dropouts and student turnover

Parents and schools in energy resource communities often express
concern that youths will drop out of school to take high-paying
jobs. Their fears are that future occupational and personal opportunities will be lost to the communities' children and that valuing
high pay over education will reinforce a materialistic orientation
that they find objectionable. While these concerns are understandable, the social meaning of dropping out of school is unclear if, as
has generally been the case in energy-impacted communities at least,
the dropouts are profitably employed and can enter an occupation
with high future earning potential. In the West there has been little indication that either parents or school personnel feel that
youth are dropping out of school because of growth-related effects
on the quality of schooling, though this possibility must be considered for some alternatives. Changes in technology may make particular school programs more desirable while decreasing the market
value, and hence attraction, of other programs.
Statistics regarding school dropout rates are not commonly
available. If compiled, they can be obtained from state departments
of education or from the local school systems. Unfortunately, although some school systems are now collecting the data necessary to
measure student turnover rates, this information is seldom compiled. School officials may be able to provide some indication of
historic levels, but quantified data are not likely to be available.
Student turnover creates problems for schools that are similar
to the problems residential turnover causes for communities -- a
constant need to orient students, decreased familiarity, increased
difficulty in coordinating activities and integrating students, and
a tendency for short-term residents to mistreat school property. It
also creates problems for the transient student similar to those for
the transient community resident -- disruptions of personal and social ties and a great increase in the time and energy that must be
spent getting oriented and settled.

Unemployment

Although unemployment could be considered a measure of access to resources, it is included here since questions have been raised about the extent of "voluntary" unemployment created by an influx of workers before project start-up or an influx of "ne'er-do-wells" attracted by the easy money of rapid growth communities. As with many of the indicators, the available data on unemployment are not an actual measure of unemployment but rather a measure of "covered unemployment" -- those qualifying for unemployment compensation. Others, such as discouraged workers who are not actively seeking work, are not included in these statistics.

Evidence from communities that experienced resource-related growth during the 1970s indicates that unemployment rates will normally decline during the growth period, although with population increases the actual number of people unemployed may not fall, and the influx of job seekers may prevent unemployment from declining dramatically. Although particularly rapid development may sometimes lead to labor shortages that cause difficulties for employers, this effect appears to be reduced by the extensive communication systems and high worker mobility found throughout the United States. During periods of labor shortage, competition for labor tends to increase worker turnover and make it difficult for employers to obtain needed workers. In general, personnel in local unemployment compensation and welfare departments in communities which have experienced energy-related growth report little or no increase in the number of "hard core" unemployed. (There are generally relatively few who fall into this category; they are primarily people with long-standing family responsibilities, behavioral characteristics, or physical problems that prevent them from holding a job). The general conclusion of these personnel is that the conditions generated by growth, particularly rapid growth, are such that newcomers who remain unemployed tend to leave the community after a relatively short period.

Employment services, generally provided by the state, have experienced an increase in service demand associated with large-scale projects, since the number of workers and worker turnover tend to increase during growth periods. In general, this increased demand has not been viewed as a problem. What has been a problem, though primarily at the state level, has been the high demand for unemployment compensation during periods of slowdown or following project shutdown. During periods of national recession, when workers may not find alternative employment elsewhere, they may stay in the local area for some time, substantially increasing state costs for unemployment compensation.

Information on rates and incidence of behavior that could be useful for the assessment include the following:

1) Total number and per capita crime rates (from the FBI Uniform Crime Index, Parts I and II and local or state records) and calls for service for each community and county in the study area as well as for the state and nation for the most recent five years available.

2) Total number and per capita divorce rates for each county in
   the study area and the state for the most recent five years
   available.

3) Average monthly case load and expenditure data and per capita average monthly and expenditure data for public assistance and welfare for each county in the study area and the
   state for the most recent two or three years. Data can be
   obtained for individual service categories. These data
   should be supplemented with indications from the public welfare personnel about particular groups or areas that are
   dependent upon public assistance. Information about program
   and policy changes should also be compiled to improve interpretation of changes in case load and expenditures.

4) School dropout rates for each study area county and the
   state, and indicators from school administrators about student turnover levels. Data for the last two to three years
   are sufficient and most useful.

5) Total number of unemployed persons and unemployment rates
   for each county in the study area as well as the state for
   the last two to three years. These data should be accompanied by an indication of unusually high unemployment rates
   by any social groups, based on interviews with local employment security officials (or the study's economist).

6) Annual infant mortality rates for each county and the state
   for the last five years, broken out by ethnic group, if
   possible (if the study area includes one of the high risk
   groups).

Questions that will help determine which information is useful
for the assessment include the following:

1) Will the proposed action result in any of the factors identified in the preceding discussion as potential causes of
   behavior problems?

2) Do the data or local perceptions indicate existing behavioral problems? (The reason for compiling all the data for all
   the study area communities and the state is to allow comparisons and to identify discrepancies.)

3) Is there concern in the community that the proposed action
   will result in increases in any of these behaviors?

Data Sources

It is frequently difficult to obtain data for communities because many of the statistics are compiled only at a county level.
Sources of information regarding crime rates are community, county,
and state records of crime and calls for service as well as the FBI
Uniform Crime Index, Parts I and II (contained in the FBI Uniform
Crime Annual Reports, which are available at most university and
college libraries). As a result of the rapid increase in crime during the 1970s, the criminal divisions of many state governments are
now conducting crime analyses and should be contacted before

starting any primary data collection. To protect against the data problems indicated above, it is important to discuss your data and analysis with the law enforcement and criminal justice personnel in the local area before publishing conclusions.

Data on the number of divorces filed per year in each county are available from **U.S. Vital Statistics** and from the division of vital statistics in most states. Rates are generally not published and therefore must be calculated using these data and population estimates (generally available from the economic/demographic analyst).

Suicide information is available from **U.S. Vital Statistics** and the division of vital statistics in most states. In general, these numbers are small and unreliable and therefore do not constitute a valid indicator.

Statistics related to family violence and mental health problems are generally not compiled in a standard form. Available data can be obtained from mental health agencies or private mental health facilities, law enforcement agencies, court records, welfare/social service departments, and special organizations focusing on family violence and mental health problems. The provision of mental health and family violence services by private or voluntary organizations makes accurate estimation of case loads and problem levels very difficult.

Statistics on alcohol and drug use are generally poor and may not be available. Possible sources include law enforcement agencies, school administrators, health departments, and court records. In some communities, special data collection procedures have been instituted to compile statistics on alcohol and drug problems. Finding comparable data for comparison remains difficult, however.

Public assistance and welfare statistics can be obtained from the state's department of social services and public welfare. The data are generally compiled at a county level. Community level data may be available from local service agencies.

Statistics regarding school dropout rates are only sometimes available. If compiled, they can be obtained from the state department of education or from the local school systems.

Unemployment figures can generally be obtained from state or local employment service offices. Analysis of this data should be discussed with the economic/demographic analyst. The main task of the social assessor will be to determine whether unemployment is a disproportionate problem for any particular ethnic or occupational groups.

Access to Resources

Variables

It is difficult to analyze overall social well-being effects because of the complexity of the interaction between community characteristics (including resource availability and social organization), individual behaviors, and resource distribution. The availability of resources such as income, community services, and a clean environment comprise a recognized component of social well-being. In fact, adequate resources are generally considered a principal requirement for well-being. Consequently, the major purpose of this part of the description of the existing environment is to summarize the information about community resources, community population characteristics, community social organization, and individual behaviors and to analyze it in terms of access to resources. Where appropriate and possible, similar data should be prepared for each of the social groups in the community, and for the key stakeholder groups (if they are different).

To determine which of this information will be pertinent to the assessment, you will need to (1) summarize the net consequences of the project-related changes in community resources, community population characteristics, community social organization and individual behaviors thus far identified to see if they could have a significant effect on access to resources, and (2) evaluate whether the existing characteristics or expectations of resource availability will alter the behavior or response of any of the social groups in the community. This analysis will be useful in refining the estimates of baseline and direct project inputs and will serve as the basis for forecasting the changes in access to resources likely to result from the proposed action. It is also important for analyzing attitudes toward the proposed action.

Most of the indicators regarding access to resources will have been estimated by the economist or facilities/services analyst in his/her analysis of community resources. The purpose here is to re-evaluate this information in light of the analysis of the community's social organization and behavioral indicators, to disaggregate them to the group level, where possible, and to present them in terms appropriate to the analysis of well-being. The principal factors to be addressed are the following:

1) Access to income (per capita and per family), accounting for local inflation if possible
2) Access to community services, especially mental health, public assistance/welfare, medical care, law enforcement, recreation, education, and roads
3) Access to environmental resources

Access to income

The effect of a project on access to income varies substantially according to the type of proposed action being assessed. Per capita and per family income has risenly substantially in many energy growth communities. It may be lowered for families affected by modifications of grazing regulations. For most proposed alternatives, the distribution of income will not be even; some groups will benefit or lose substantially more than others. Interviews in energy growth communities indicate that most longtime residents feel that both their families and their community have benefitted economically from the development. Ranchers express grave concern about the effects of grazing reductions on their income levels. To date, no detailed analysis of income distribution effects of energy development on resource management decisions has been made. Summers et al. (1976) and Summers and Selvik (1979) provide a useful review of the effects of industrial development in nonmetropolitan areas.

Computations of per capita income or purchasing power will usually be provided by an economic/demographic assessor. Estimates of the current distribution of the income may be made by the economist but should be confirmed in general terms through the process discussed above under distribution of resources. Data will not generally be available to make more than qualitative estimates. Normally high per capita income and increasing levels of per capita income are considered a social good, although some care should be taken to evaluate the distributive effects of increased income and purchasing power.

Access to community services

Another major indicator of social well-being is the accessibility of services in the community. Usually, the analysis of facilities/services availability is conducted by someone else, though in case you become responsible for this analysis, guidance for conducting facility/services/fiscal assessments is provided in Appendix B. The analysis of potential change in access to services usually focuses on the following:

1) The present level of services in the community
2) The current distribution of services in the community (to social groups)
3) The likely needs and access of the future population
4) The organizational or coordinative problems which are being encountered or may be encountered in future service delivery
5) The implications of future service and facility requirements and revenue sources on tax levels, net fiscal balance, and service quality

The most important facilities and services to be considered for inclusion in the social assessment are the following:

1) **Mental health -- number of personnel and types of services.** The adequacy of these services and their accessibility are frequent problems in rural areas. Often, mental health centers serve a multicounty area; distances between communities can make it difficult for many in the area to utilize the services.
2) **Public assistance and welfare -- number of personnel and type of service.** The service loads for this agency can change drastically with a large increase of new people, both due to problems of transients and increased payments for Aid to Families with Dependent Children (AFDC).
3) **Medical care -- number of physicians by type, number of hospital beds, and utilization rates.** An underlying problem in most rural areas is that the population cannot support a wide range of medical specialties or facilities. This can change only with major increases in population or substantial shifts in governmental policy. The result is

that in most small towns, many medical needs are met by re-
ferring patients to distant centers. Low utilization rates
of local hospitals may mean that many patients are being
referred to urban areas. Calculating the community's ability to provide medical services presently and in the future
requires a thorough understanding of the medical personnel
and facilities in the area and how they are used in relation
to facilities in distant urban areas.

4) **Law enforcement agencies.** The normal indicator for law
enforcement agencies is the rate of professional officers
per 1,000 population. However, in anticipating future demand, it is also necessary to consider whether present officers have the qualifications and training to deal with the
kind of problems brought by a larger population. Organizational and administrative problems which would inhibit the
provision of expanded services should be identified. Large
population growth in unincorporated areas and in widely
scattered developments can create problems for county law
enforcement agencies. Patterns of population growth may
raise issues of law enforcement consolidation and expansion
of prison facilities.

5) **Recreational facilities.** Information about existing recreational facilities will probably be compiled by the person
responsible for land use, the facilities/services analyst,
or the economist. Access to indoor and outdoor recreational
facilities has been identified as important to perceptions
of well-being. Conflict over the use of open land and outdoor recreational areas between newcomers and longtime residents has occurred in communities that have experienced
rapid growth. The anticipation and potential for this type
of conflict should be examined. It is also important to
determine what plans are being made to provide additional
recreational facilities to meet the needs of any newcomers.

6) **School facilities.** Information about classroom space and
staff will probably be compiled by the person responsible
for facilities/services assessment. Quality education has
been identified as important to perceptions of well-being.
It is useful to determine what special effort is being
planned to welcome newcomers and to provide any special
counseling support that might be necessary.

7) **Roads.** Increased traffic and heavier utilization of county roads is frequently an issue in rapid growth communities. Traffic congestion and the presence of newcomers on
rural roads that previously received little use can become
symbolic of the intrusion of development and the presence of
strangers. It is important to determine whether the proposed action has made or could make provisions for staggered
shifts or for road maintenance programs to alleviate some of
these problems.

Of the characteristics of the existing environment concerning
access to resources, those that have been identified as being potentially important for the assessment include the following:

1) Per capita and per family income levels, with estimates of the relative position of the major social groups and comparison to state and national data.

2) Descriptions of the services offered and the number of personnel available at the nearest mental health center and its distance from the community. This should include evaluations from service personnel, local residents, and the facilities/services analyst about adequacy of service for each social or stakeholder group.

3) Descriptions of the services offered and the number of personnel available at the local public assistance and welfare agency and its distance from the community. Discussion should include evaluations from service personnel, local residents, and the facilities/services analyst about adequacy of service for each social or stakeholder group.

4) Description and the utilization rates of the nearest hospital, its distance from the community, as well as the number and type of primary care physicians and the ratio of physicians per 1,000 population. Discussion should include evaluations from physicians, local residents, and the facilities/services analyst about adequacy of services for each major social or stakeholder group.

5) The total number and number per 1,000 population of uniformed law enforcement officers along with a description of the organization of the department and an evaluation of service adequacy and the capacity to administer an expanded department. The adequacy of current facilities should also be considered.

6) Evaluations by community leaders and residents of the adequacy of existing recreational facilities and programs (for major stakeholders, with special attention to age groups), and a description of the mechanisms available for planning and providing recreational services.

7) The adequacy of school facilities for the increased population, with special attention to the problems of space and personnel if a large temporary peak in school enrollment is expected.

8) The current condition and traffic levels on municipal and county roads.

Questions which can help determine whether these characteristics will be important to the assessment include the following:

1) Do any of the indicators point to inadequate service provision? Could this be aggravated or alleviated by the proposed action?

2) (If the schedule for the proposed action indicates) have the service providers formulated a plan for responding to the demands generated by the proposed action? Are those plans realistic? Have they solved the problem of peak temporary requirements?

3) Do the characteristics of the existing services indicate that the demands created by the proposed action would be difficult to meet?

4) Do residents anticipate problems in any of these areas or express particularly high value for the current service characteristics?

5) Do the characteristics signal current or potential problems for any community or stakeholder group, given the characteristics of the proposed action?

Access to environmental resources

If the proposed action is expected to substantially alter the supply or accessibility of an environmental resource, such as would result from modification of grazing regulations, wilderness designation, or dam construction, those aspects of the environment that would be altered should be included as part of the description of the existing environment. Data on resident's attitudes about and use of the affected component would have to be gathered as a basis for forecasting the consequences of the alteration. You will probably want to consult with specialists in the environmental sciences, if this aspect of the assessment appears to be important.

Data Sources

Economic and income data should be available from the economist, based on census or U.S. Bureau of Economic Analysis data. The information about income distribution should be available from the interviews and from data collected for analysis of the distribution of resources.

The information needed to assess access to resources should already have been obtained as part of the interviews with agency personnel described in the earlier portions of this chapter which discussed community resources and coordination. As part of the analytic process, it is helpful to develop some preliminary conclusions which can be discussed with agency personnel to be sure (1) that the data are appropriate and correctly analyzed and (2) that you have a proper understanding of the organizational issues and problems that could occur and how they would be addressed if the proposed action were implemented.

Perceptions of the Community and Personal Well-being

One of the important aspects of social assessment is estimating how residents will feel about the changes that will occur if the proposed action is implemented. Since this requires the application of information about current attitudes, perceptions, and anticipations of future conditions, it is somewhat problematic and must be addressed cautiously, with recognition that attitudes and perceptions are subject to change.

The information to be used in this component comes from the interviews that were conducted to obtain community or area residents' attitudes toward change and the proposed action and their perceptions of the community and their personal well-being. Data from other secondary sources may also be available and useful. The purpose is to use this information to identify which aspects of the community and current conditions are of particular salience to the various community and stakeholder groups and to prepare to analyze the types of changes that are forecast if the proposed action is implemented. The information obtained during the examination of the existing environment should enable you to (1) identify which perceptions and definitions of community or the area will be most affected by the proposed action, how they will be affected, and why; (2) identify which groups are likely to experience decreased, enhanced, or unchanged satisfaction with their community or their personal situation and why; and (3) provide a summary discussion about the human meaning of the social changes that are forecast to occur.

Summary

Once you have worked through this process for one of the communities in your study area, a similar analysis can be carried out for the remaining communities much more quickly. As you work through the social organization model, many questions will be raised concerning the likely consequences of the various interactions. These are precisely the questions that must be answered in order to complete the assessment. By identifying them early in the process, you have an opportunity to do further research or reading on these specific topics. Given the current state-of-the-art in forecasting social change -- or even in understanding change that has already occurred -- a substantial number of questions are likely to remain unanswered. It is the responsibility of the assessor to draw those conclusions that can be made, to present them clearly and forcefully, but to refrain from misrepresenting the level of certainty associated with them.

8.5   References

The particular references that will be useful to you will be determined by the nature of the communities you are studying and the type of proposed action or policy whose effects you are trying to assess. The references provided in this section represent only an example of the type of material that you might find helpful. Numerous special bibliographies have been developed covering various aspects of impact assessment, large-scale resource or industrial development, and social change. You are encouraged to utilize your research and literature review skills to identify the sources most pertinent to you. Because they illustrate the development of the analytic framework presented in the guide, the reports prepared for the Bureau of Land Management Social Effects Project have been included among these references.

Applebaum, Richard P.
  1970   _Theories of Social Change_. Chicago: Rand McNally.

Albrecht, Stan
   1982a   BLM Social Effects Project Community Research Working
           Paper: Price, Utah. Prepared by Mountain West
           Research-North, Inc. and Western Research Corporation.
           Denver, Colo.: U.S. Government Printing Office.
   1982b   Paradoxes of Western Energy Development: Social-
           Cultural Factors. Presented at the annual meeting of
           the American Association for the Advancement of
           Science. Washington, D.C.

Anderson, B.F.
   1981   Cascaded Tradeoffs: A Multiple-Objective, Multiple-
          Publics Method for Alternatives Evaluation in Water
          Resources Planning. Prepared for the Bureau of Reclama-
          tion, Engineering and Research Center. Denver, Colo.

Bell, Colin and Howard Newby
   1972   Community Studies: An Introduction to the Sociology of
          the Local Community. New York: Praeger.

Bender, T.
   1978   Community and Social Change in America. New Brunswick,
          N.J.: Rutgers University Press.

Berger, Peter L., and Thomas Luckman
   1966   The Social Construction of Reality. Garden City, N.Y.:
          Doubleday.

Berry, B.J.L.
   1967   Geography of Market Centers and Retail Distribution.
          Englewood Cliffs, N.J.: Prentice-Hall.

Blalock, H.M.
   1979   Measurement and Conceptualization Problems. American
          Sociological Review 44: 881-894.

Blau, Peter M.
   1975   Approaches to the Study of Social Structure. New York:
          The Free Press.

Blau, Peter M. and Robert K. Merton, eds.
   1981   Continuities in Structural Inquiry. Beverly Hills:
          Sage.

Blumer, Herbert
   1969   Symbolic Interactionism: Perspective and Method.
          Englewood Cliffs, N.J.: Prentice Hall.

Bowles, Roy T.
   1981   Social Impact Assessment in Small Communities. Toronto:
          Butterworth.

166

Branch, Kristi and Pamela Bergmann
    1982   BLM Social Effects Project Community Research Working
            Paper: Grants, New Mexico. Prepared by Mountain West
            Research-North, Inc. and Western Research Corporation.
            Denver, Colo.: U.S. Government Printing Office.

Branch, Kristi
    1982   BLM Social Effects Project Community Research Working
            Paper: Douglas, Wyoming. Prepared by Mountain West
            Research-North, Inc. and Western Research Corporation.
            Denver, Colo.: U.S. Government Printing Office.

Briscoe, Maphis, Murray, and Lamont, Inc. and Mountain West
Research-North, Inc.
    1983   Generic Mitigation Program. Helena, Mont.: Montana
            Department of State Lands.

Burdge, R.J. and Paul Opryszek, eds.
    1981   Coping with Change: An Interdisciplinary Assessment of
            the Lake Shelbyville Reservoir. Urbana: University of
            Illinois Institute for Environmental Studies.

Campbell, A., and P. Converse
    1972   The Human Meaning of Social Change. New York: Russell
            Sage Foundation.

Campbell, A., P. Converse, and W. Rodgers
    1976   The Quality of American Life: Perceptions, Evaluations,
            and Satisfactions. New York: Sage.

Catton, W.R., and R.E. Dunlap
    1978   Environmental Sociology: A New Paradigm. The American
            Sociologist 13: 41-49.

Chalmers, James, David Pijawka, Kristi Branch, Pamela Bergmann,
James Flynn, and Cynthia Flynn
    1982   Socioeconomic Impacts of Nuclear Generating Stations:
            Summary Report on the NRC Post-Licensing Studies. Wash-
            ington, D.C.: U.S. Government Printing Office (U.S.
            Nuclear Regulatory Commission).

Cortese, Charles F.
    1978   The Social Effects of Energy Boomtowns in the West: A
            Partially Annotated Bibliography. Monticello, Ill.:
            Council of Planning Librarians (Exchange Bibliography
            No. 1557).

Coser, Lewis A.
    1967   Continuities in the Study of Social Conflict. New
            York: The Free Press.

Crenson, Matthew
    1971   The Un-Politics of Air Pollution. Baltimore: The Johns
            Hopkins Press.

Creighton, James
    1980   The Public Involvement Manual. Denver, Colo.: U.S.
            Bureau of Reclamation.

Dahrendorf, Rolf
    1959   Class and Class Conflict in Industrial Society. Stan-
            ford, Calif.: Stanford University Press.

Dillman, Don and Darryll Hobbs, eds.
    1981   Rural Society: Research Issues for the 1980s. Boulder,
            Colo.: Westview Press.

Dohrenwend, B.S., and B.P. Dohrenwend
    1974   Stressful Life Events. New York: Wiley.

Dixon, Mim
    1978   What Happened to Fairbanks? The Effects of the Trans-
            Alaska Oil Pipeline on the Community of Fairbanks,
            Alaska. Boulder, Colo.: Westview Press.

Duncan, O.D.
    1964   Social Organization and the Ecosystem in Handbook of
            Modern Sociology, Robert Faris, ed. Chicago: Rand
            McNally, pp. 36-82.

Durkheim, Emile
    1951   Suicide. New York: The Free Press. (Originally pub-
            lished in 1897.)

Ford, Thomas, ed.
    1978   Rural U.S.A.: Persistence and Change. Ames, Iowa:
            Iowa State University Press.

Finsterbusch, K., and C.P. Wolf, eds.
    1977   Methodology of Social Impact Assessment. Stroudsburg,
            Pa.: Dowden, Hutchinson, and Ross, Inc.

Fischer, Claude, R. Jackson, C.A. Stueve, K. Gerson, L. Jones, and
M. Baldasare.
    1979   Networks and Places: Social Relations in the Urban Set-
            ting. New York: The Free Press.

Frankena, Fredrick
    1980   Community Impacts of Rapid Growth in Nonmetropolitan
            Areas: A Literature Survey. East Lansing, Mich.:
            Agricultural Experiment Station, Michigan State
            University.

Freudenburg, William R., Linda M. Bacegalupi and Cheryl Landall-Young
    1982   Mental Health Consequences of Rapid Community Growth: A
            Report from the Longitudinal Study of Boomtown Mental
            Health Impacts. Journal of Health and Human Resources
            Administration 4: 334-352.

168

Gartrell, John W., Harvey Krahn, and F. David Sunahara
  1980   A Study of Human Adjustment in Fort McMurray. Prepared
          for the Alberta Oil Sands Environmental Research Pro-
          gram. Edmonton: Thames Group Research, Inc. and the
          Population Research Laboratory, the University of Al-
          berta.

Goffman, Erving
  1961   Asylums: Essays on the Social Situation of Mental Pa-
          tients and Other Inmates. New York: Doubleday and Com-
          pany.

Gordus, Jeanne Prial, Paul Jarley, and Louis Ferman
  1981   Plant Closings and Economic Dislocation. Kalamazoo,
          Mich.: W.E. Upjohn Institute.

Hawley, Amos H.
  1950   Human Ecology: A Theory of Community Structure. New
          York: Ronald Press.

Hawley, W.D. and F.H. Wirt, eds.
  1974   The Search for Community Power. 2nd ed. Englewood
          Cliffs, N.J.: Prentice-Hall.

Hazza, Jacqueline and Virginia Mayer
  1982   Shutdown: A Guide for Communities Facing Plant Clos-
          ings. Washington, D.C.: Northwest-Midwest Institute.

Heider, Fritz
  1958   The Psychology of Interpersonal Relations. New York:
          Wiley.

Heise, David R.
  1975   Causal Analysis. New York: Wiley.

Hillery, George A.
  1982   A Research Odyssey: Developing and Testing a Community
          Theory. New Brunswick, N.J.: Transaction Books.
  1968   Communal Organizations: A Study of Local Societies.
          Chicago: University of Chicago Press.

Hooper, Douglas A. and Kristi Branch
  1982   BLM Social Effects Project Community Research Working
          Paper: Forsyth, Montana. Prepared by Mountain West
          Research-North, Inc. and Western Research Corporation.
          Denver, Colo.: U.S. Government Printing Office.

Hooper, Douglas A. and Pat Jobes
  1982   BLM Social Effects Project Community Research Working
          Paper: Ashland, Montana. Prepared by Mountain West
          Research-North, Inc. and Western Research Corporation.
          Denver, Colo.: U.S. Government Printing Office.

Hunter, Albert
  1975   The Loss of Community: An Empirical Test Through Repli-
          cation. American Sociological Review 40: 537-552.

Isard, W., C. Choguill, J. Kissin, R. Seyfarth, and R. Tatlock
  1972   Ecologic-Economic Analysis for Regional Development.
          New York: The Free Press.

Kenney, R.L. and H. Raiffa
  1976   Decisions with Multiple Objectives: Preferences and
          Value Trade-offs. New York: Wiley.

Kuhn, Thomas A.
  1970   The Structure of Scientific Revolutions. 2nd ed.
          Chicago: University of Chicago Press.

Larson, L.E.
  1979   The Impact of Resource Development on Individual and
          Family Well-Being. Prepared fu. Alberta Oil Sands En-
          vironmental Research Program. Edmonton: Family Re-
          search and Consulting Limited.

Leistritz, F. Larry and Steve H. Murdock
  1981   The Socioeconomic Impact of Resource Development: Meth-
          ods for Assessment. Boulder, Colo.: Westview Press.

Lenski, Gerhard E.
  1966   Power and Privilege: A Theory of Social Stratifica-
          tion. New York: McGraw-Hill.

Light, Richard and David Pillemer
  1982   Numbers and Narrative: Combining their Strengths in
          Research Reviews. Harvard Educational Review 52: 1-26.

Light, Richard and P. Smith
  1971   Accumulating Evidence: Procedures for Resolving Contra-
          dictions among Different Studies. Harvard Educational
          Review 41: 429-471.

Malhotra, Suresh and Diane Manninen
  1979   Socioeconomic Impact Assessments: Profile Analysis of
          Worker Surveys Conducted at Nuclear Power Plant Con-
          struction Sites. Seattle, Wash.: Battelle Memorial In-
          stitute.

Massey, Garth
  1978   Building a Power Plant: Newcomers and Social Impacts.
          Prepared for the Metro Center, National Institute of
          Mental Health. Rockville, Md.

Merton, Robert K.
  1968   Social Theory and Social Structure. New York: The Free
          Press.

Metz, William C.
    1982   American Energy and Mineral Industry Involvement in
             Housing. Paper prepared for the U.S. Department of
             Energy. Upton, N.Y.: Brookhaven National Laboratory.

Micklin, Michael
    1973   Population, Environment, and Social Organization. Hins-
             dale, Ill.: Dryden Press.

Mohr, Lawrence B.
    1982   Explaining Organizational Behavior. San Francisco:
             Jossey-Bass.

Mountain West Research, Inc.
    1982   Back-up data prepared for the Colorado Cumulative Impact
             Task Force (CITF). Denver, Colorado.
    1981   Forecasts prepared for the Bureau of Land Management
             Fort Union Regional Coal Team. Billings, Montana.
    1979   A Guide to Methods for Impact Assessment of Western
             Coal/Energy Development. Reston, Va.: U.S. Geological
             Survey (Missouri River Basin Commission).
    1975   Construction Worker Profile. Washington, D.C.: Old
             West Regional Commission.

Murdock, Steve H. and F. Larry Leistritz
    1979   Energy Development in the Western United States. New
             York: Praeger Publishers.

Murdock, Steve, John Thomas, and Don Albrecht
    1982   Handbook for Assessing the Social and Special Effects of
             Nuclear Repository Siting. Prepared for the Office of
             Nuclear Waste Isolation, U.S. Department of Energy.
             Washington, D.C.: U.S. Government Printing Office.

Nisbet, Robert
    1962   Community and Power. New York: Oxford University Press.

Olsen, Marvin E.
    1968   The Process of Social Organization. 1st ed. New York:
             Holt, Rinehart, and Winston.

Pijawka, David and Kristi Branch
    1982   BLM Social Effects Project Community Research Working
             Paper: Salina, Utah. Prepared by Mountain West
             Research-North, Inc. and Western Research Corporation.
             Denver, Colo.: U.S. Government Printing Office.

Pillemer, David B. and Richard J. Light
    1980   Synthesizing Outcomes: How to Use Research Evidence
             from Many Studies. Harvard Educational Review 50:
             176-195.

Popenoe, David
1980   Sociology. 4th ed. Englewood Cliffs, N.J.: Prentice-
        Hall.

Purdy, B.J., E. Peele, B.H. Bronfman, and D.J. Bjornstad
1977   A Post Licensing Study of Community Effects of Two Oper-
        ating Nuclear Power Plants. Oak Ridge, Tenn.: Oak
        Ridge National Laboratory.

Sanders, Irwin T.
1975   The Community. 3rd ed. New York: Wiley.

Seiler, Lauren H. and Gene F. Summers
1979   Corporate Involvement in Community Affairs. Sociologi-
        cal Quarterly 20: 375-386.

Shields, Mark
1977   Grounded Theory Construction in Social Impact Assess-
        ment. In Methodology of Social Impact Assessment, Kurt
        Finsterbusch and C.P. Wolf, eds. Stroudsburg, Pa.:
        Dowden, Hutchinson, and Ross, Inc.

Stein, Maurice
1960   The Eclipse of Community. Princeton, N.J.: Princeton
        University Press.

Stern, Robert N. and Howard Aldrich
1980   The Effect of Absentee Firm Control on Local Community
        Welfare: A Survey. Itaca, N.Y.: Cornell University,
        New York State School of Industries and Labor Relations.

Stufflebeam, Daniel L. and William Webster
1981   An Analysis of Alternative Approaches to Evaluation. In
        Evaluation Studies Annual Review, Vol. 6. H.E. Freeman
        and M.A. Soloman, eds., pp 70-85. Beverly Hills,
        Calif.: Sage.

Sudman, Seymour
1976   Applied Sampling. New York: Academic Press.

Sudman, Seymour, and Norman M. Bradburn
1982   Asking Questions: A Practical Guide to Questionnaire
        Design. San Francisco: Jossey-Bass.

Summers, Gene and Arne Selvik
1979   Nonmetropolitan Industrial Growth and Community Change.
        Lexington, Mass.: Lexington Books.

Summers, Gene, S.D. Evans, F. Clemente, E.M. Beck, and J. Minkoff
1976   Industrial Invasion of Nonmetropolitan America. New
        York: Praeger.

Suttles, Gerald D.
1972   The Social Construction of Communities. Chicago: Uni-
        versity of Chicago Press.

Thompson, James G., A.L. Blevins, and G.L. Watts
1978   Socioeconomic Longitudinal Monitoring Report. Washing-
        ton, D.C.: Old West Regional Commission.

Thompson, James and Kristi Branch, eds.
1980   The Bureau of Land Management Social Effects Project:
        Literature Review. Prepared by Mountain West Research-
        North, Inc. and Western Research Corporation. Denver,
        Colo.: U.S. Government Printing Office.

Thompson, James G., Kristi M. Branch, and Gary Williams
1982   The Bureau of Land Management Social Effects Project:
        Summary Research Report. Prepared by Mountain West Re-
        search, Inc. and Western Research Corporation. Denver,
        Colo.: U.S. Government Printing Office.

Thompson, James G., Gary Williams, and Robert L. Kimble
1982   BLM Social Effects Project Community Report: Rangely,
        Colorado. Prepared by Mountain West Research-North,
        Inc. and Western Research Corporation. Denver, Colo.:
        U.S. Government Printing Office.

U.S. Forest Service
1978   Inform and Involve Handbook. Washington, D.C.: U.S.
        Department of Agriculture.

Vidich, A.J. and J. Benoman
1958   Small Town in Mass Society. Princeton, N.J.: Princeton
        University Press.

Warner, W. Keith
1974   Rural Society in a Post-Industrial Age. Rural Sociology
        39: 306-317.

Warren, Roland L.
1978   The Community in America. 3rd ed. Chicago: Rand
        McNally.

Weiss, Carol
1975   Evaluation Research in the Political Context. In Hand-
        book of Evaluation Research, Vol. 1. E.L. Strvening and
        M. Guttentag, eds., pp 13-26. Beverly Hills, Calif.:
        Sage.

Whiting, Larry R., ed.
1974   Communities Left Behind: Alternatives for Development.
        Ames, Iowa: The Iowa State University Press.

Wilkinson, Kenneth
    1982   <u>BLM Social Effects Project Community Report: Craig,</u>
              <u>Colorado</u>. Prepared by Mountain West Research-North,
              Inc. and Western Research Corporation. Denver, Colo.:
              U.S. Government Printing Office.
    1980   Social Organization. In <u>The Bureau of Land Management</u>
              <u>Social Effects Project Literature Review</u>, James Thompson
              and Kristi Branch, eds. Prepared by Mountain West
              Research-North, Inc. and Western Research Corporation.
              Denver, Colo.: U.S. Government Printing Office.

Williams, Gary
    1982   <u>BLM Social Effects Project Community Report: Wheatland,</u>
              <u>Wyoming</u>. Prepared by Mountain West Research-North, Inc.
              and Western Research Corporation. Denver, Colo.: U.S.
              Government Printing Office.

Woolcott, Michael and Gary Williams
    1982   <u>BLM Social Effects Project Community Report: Washburn,</u>
              <u>North Dakota</u>. Prepared by Mountain West Research-North,
              Inc. and Western Research Corporation. Denver, Colo.:
              U.S. Government Printing Office.

9. Refining the Forecasts of Baseline, Direct Project, and Total Inputs

9.1 Introduction

As discussed in Chapter 3, the effects of a proposed action are determined by comparing conditions as they would be at a future time with the proposed action to conditions as they would be at this future time without the proposed action. According to the analytic framework developed earlier in the guide, two basic sets of information are needed to forecast the social effects of a proposed action: (1) a description of the existing environment and (2) forecasts of the baseline, direct project, and total (baseline plus direct project) inputs. The description of the existing environment has been addressed in the previous chapter (Chapter 8). The forecasting of baseline, direct project, and total inputs is the subject of this chapter.

The principal direct project inputs for large-scale projects and resource-based decisions tend to be economic and demographic since it is primarily through people, jobs, income, and resource changes that the proposed action interacts with the existing environment to produce social change. Although primary responsibility for forecasting the changes in people, jobs, income, resources, organizations and regulations, and public safety that would occur under baseline and with-project conditions is often assigned to other disciplinary specialists (economists, facilities/services analysts), the social assessor has both an interest and a role in this forecasting process. The primary function of social assessment is to analyze how these inputs will interact with the community to cause social change or affect the well-being of residents. In preparing for this task, the social assessor often obtains information about characteristics of the study area communities that can improve the team's ability to make accurate forecasts of baseline and direct project inputs.

This chapter discusses how the forecasting and refinement of baseline, direct project, and total (baseline plus direct project) inputs fits into the overall social assessment process. It then discusses the major factors influencing the forecasts of the six types of inputs. It should be emphasized that some of this information may be substantially more detailed than is necessary for the

175

particular assessment you are conducting. If portions of this chapter are not appropriate or useful, they should be disregarded.

9.2 Purpose and Role in the Assessment Process

As shown in Figure 9-1, refining and finalizing the forecasts of baseline and direct project inputs occurs between the description of the existing environment and the forecast and evaluation of the social effects. It occurs at this point in the assessment process for two major reasons.

First, this position allows the focusing and screening approach utilized in chapters 6 and 8 to be applied to the forecasting of baseline and direct project inputs. Placing this step after the description of the existing environment allows information about the study area communities to be used to focus attention on those direct project inputs that may cause important social effects, to inform decisions about the precision needed in the forecasts, and to inform the forecasts themselves. Information about the existing environment provides a basis for determining whether or not the communities and residents in the study area would be sensitive to small inputs. If they would be, precise estimates might be called for. If they would not, general, more approximate estimates will probably suffice. The same distinction may hold with regard to the assessment effort as a whole. If precise estimates of baseline and direct project inputs are not available or necessary for the level of detail called for by the assessment, the detail and precision of the forecasts of project effects and impacts will of necessity also be limited.

Second, this analytic sequence allows the forecasting of baseline, direct project, and total inputs to serve as preparation for the forecasting and evaluation of social effects. Information about the existing environment can identify particular constraints (lack of housing, zoning restrictions) or resources (a particularly large pool of available workers) that can alter the anticipated inputs, possibly by modification of the proposed action. Working through the forecasts of baseline and direct project inputs in the context of the specific study area can clarify the characteristics of the inputs as well as the patterns of interaction between these inputs and community social characteristics.

As noted previously, most responsibility for preparing the forecasts of baseline, direct project, and total changes in people, jobs, income, resources, and public safety lies, in a interdisciplinary setting, with other members of the assessment team. However, description of these changes is so critical to the assessment of social impacts that it is wise for the social assessor to make sure that these responsibilities are understood, that a common set of expectations about the timing and format of the forecasts has been established, and that the knowledge of all team members is utilized in making these forecasts. Coordinating schedules in a way that provides the social assessment with forecasts of inputs when they are needed can be a fairly serious problem, since the social assessment uses as input what the other components generate as

Figure 9-1

The Social Assessment Process

Mitigation • Enhancement and Monitoring

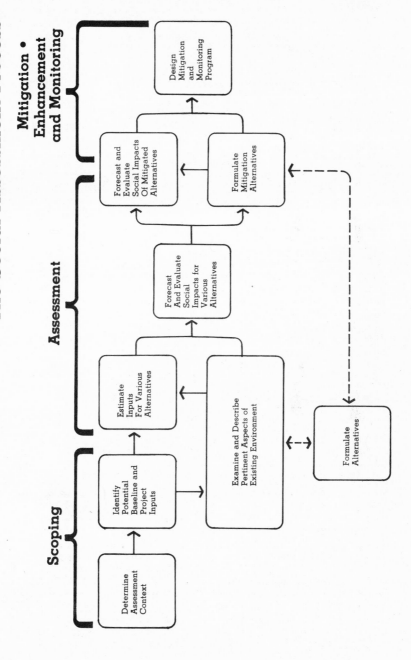

output. This is one reason that it is important to determine how precise the estimates need to be. Order of magnitude estimates can generally be obtained early in the process, either on your own or through discussions with the responsible parties. Precise estimates are often more difficult to obtain at this stage.

9.3 Refining the Forecasts of Baseline, Direct Project, and Total Inputs

This section discusses the six types of inputs and why they are important to social assessment. Some of the factors known to influence the inputs and to clarify their likely effects on the community are identified. The purpose of the discussion provided in this chapter is to alert the reader to the types of relationships or factors that affect how projects interact with communities and to promote a broader understanding of these mechanisms. This chapter does not discuss the technical methods for forecasting these inputs. (Demographic forecasting techniques are discussed in Appendix A and methods for forecasting facilities/services/fiscal changes are discussed in Appendix B). Rather, the focus in this chapter is on the interactions between the proposed action and the community that could influence the magnitude and nature of the inputs to that community. With an understanding of these interactions you are in a better position to discuss the forecasts with the other team members, to participate in refining the forecasts of baseline and direct project inputs, to anticipate the types of consequences that different projects will have, and to formulate and assess mitigative strategies.

People

Changes in the number and characteristics of the people in a community can affect every aspect of the community's social organization. Existing community characteristics influence the population effects of a project. To understand what is likely to occur, some estimate must be made of how many new people with what characteristics will come into the community, how long they will stay, and what they will do while residing there. In many cases, the characteristics of the project-related population are determined primarily by other aspects of the project, notably the job characteristics, and by the existing socioeconomic characteristics of the study area.

Newcomers who enter a community to take project-related jobs constitute the major force for social change introduced by many large-scale development projects. Consequently, the most critical baseline and direct project inputs to be estimated are often the number and characteristics of the people who will be introduced into the community. As mentioned above, an increase or decrease in population has the potential to affect all aspects of community organization. If the population influx is large compared to the existing population, the attitudinal and behavioral characteristics of the newcomers can dominate the community. Large increases in population, particularly if they are temporary, can disrupt social organization processes, create new social groups, decrease the availability of resources, and adversely affect community well-being.

Estimates of population change for most large-scale, resource-based, or industrial actions are closely tied to the estimates of change in employment. They involve a number of complex relationships between job characteristics (such as wage rates, occupational characteristics, shift schedules and overtime, duration of the project), community characteristics (for example, location, amenities such as schools, shopping, and housing, attitudes toward newcomers), and the policies of the company or agency implementing the action (provision of worker housing, training, and equal opportunity employment). Although it is not always clear how applicable earlier experience will be in the future, considerable secondary data often exists on the demographic characteristics of the workers employed by projects similar to the proposed action. For large-scale projects, detailed community-specific population forecasts are usually prepared. These typically provide age- and sex-specific estimates for each year of the study period. On smaller projects or those which do not involve large changes in population, the estimates are likely to be less detailed.

For study area communities sensitive to the level of population likely to be introduced (or lost) because of the proposed action, discussions with the economic/demographic analyst and the facilities/services analyst and a review of some of the secondary materials describing the characteristics and consequences of these types of population change are probably warranted. Since a large portion of the forecast of social change depends upon the number and characteristics of the newcomers (or outmigrants) relative to the longtime residents, it is best to understand these relationships as well as possible and to pay close attention to the forecasts. Your knowledge of local socioeconomic conditions can be very useful in refining the forecasts of population and demographic change.

A description of an economic/demographic model used to forecast population change due to large-scale projects is included in Appendix A.3. Review of the structure of this model and the sequence of analysis may help you understand the interrelationships more clearly and allow you to participate more actively in discussions with the economist/demographer.

Jobs/Occupations

Changes in jobs and occupations are often one of the major consequences of large scale projects and technological innovation. Specification of the changes that will occur in the jobs and occupations in a community is needed to answer questions about how the occupational characteristics and distributional processes in the community will be affected and what proportion of the change will be due to the proposed action.

The Number and Type of Jobs that Will Be Created (or Lost) by Changes in the Baseline or the Proposed Action

If the proposed action will be the principal source of change in jobs/occupations over the study period, most of the necessary information about the number and type of jobs can be obtained from a description of the occupational breakdown of the work force of the proposed action. This description can generally be obtained from the company or agency implementing the action or from such descriptions for other similar projects.

If baseline conditions or the proposed action will result in a substantial change in other (induced) jobs as well, specification of the characteristics of these jobs may also be important. This is a more difficult forecast to make since it requires analysis of complex economic/demographic relationships. Forecasts of these additional jobs are generally presented in terms of industry rather than occupational distribution. Since the occupational implications of the employment changes may not be evident from these forecasts, it may be helpful to discuss these forecasts with the economist to determine what types of jobs are being created or lost.

As with most of the information used in social assessment, order of magnitude and comparative estimates regarding occupational changes are generally adequate. For large-scale projects, data are generally developed as an annual series for the baseline, project, and total conditions, with the employment distributed among the study area communities. The most important things to note about the forecast changes are (1) peak levels, (2) long-term "permanent" levels, and (3) trends (whether the changes are rapid or slow, constant or up and down), since these attributes can affect both resource availability, social organization processes, and the overall ability and willingness of the community to respond. Limitations in the community's ability or willingness to respond to anticipated levels of population or employment may indicate a need to reevaluate and adjust the original forecasts.

The Number and Type of Jobs that will be Obtained by Longtime Residents versus the Number that will be Obtained by Newcomers

The economist/demographer will generally carry out the analysis of the distribution of jobs for the baseline, project, and total conditions based on consideration of the factors listed below. Although you will probably not be responsible for this analysis, you may have obtained information about the community that could help refine these forecasts. The pertinent information includes the following:

1) The number and type of jobs that will be available
2) The skill/experience requirements for these jobs
3) The number of longtime residents with the required skills and experience
4) The number of longtime residents who will want these jobs
5) The attitude of the company or agency implementing the action toward local hiring and on-the-job training

6) The distribution of union and nonunion jobs (which determines who controls the hiring policy and where hiring decisions will be made)

7) The attractiveness of these jobs to people from outside the
community (generally determined by job and wage characteristics)

8) The availability of labor from outside

The Distribution of Jobs Among Community Residents

When new jobs are made available in a community, there is a potential for change in the distributional processes and in the
diversity/complexity of economic and social life. Since occupational characteristics have a strong influence on attitudes and
lifestyles, changes in livelihood from shifts in the types of jobs
held by longtime residents can have widespread effects on the other
social organization processes as well.

Examining who in the community would get which jobs is part of
the analysis needed to determine how many jobs will be obtained by
longtime residents and how many will be obtained by newcomers, information which is critical to forecasting the population changes
that would occur. Participation in this analysis can clarify some
important aspects of the distributional processes of the existing
environment and improve the reliability of the forecasts.

Quite obviously, jobs requiring specific skills can be obtained
only by those who either already have the skills or can acquire them
through training or experience. Information about the occupational
and educational characteristics of the different community groups is
useful for determining how many and which community members might
qualify for the new jobs.

Qualifications are only part of the equation, however. Workers
can obtain jobs only if they are willing to apply for them. Available evidence indicates that adult longtime residents who are
already employed tend not to leave existing jobs for short-term construction phase jobs, although they may take a second job or
occasional short-term work if their full-time job schedule can accommodate it. If there have been major construction projects in the
area in the past, longtime residents may have developed the skills
to effectively compete for these jobs. Local youths are likely to
be available and interested in construction jobs, if hiring policies
and training opportunities permit entry level workers. The number
of women obtaining construction jobs is typically small, although it
has been increasing. The number of community residents willing to
apply for project-related jobs can be affected by the availability
of other employment opportunities and by the community's attitude
toward the project. If the community is strongly opposed to the
project, social pressure may be applied to community members not to
work on it.

An increase in the employment base of the community often results in increased opportunities in service sector jobs. These are
often filled by women, many of whom may be working for the first
time or the first time since child-bearing. Although these jobs
tend to be low-paying in comparison to the "direct" project-related

jobs, they may offer employment opportunities that were previously unavailable to women. A large increase in the proportion or number of working women can affect the distribution of income among families and create changes in service demands and patterns of personal interaction. The availability of support services (such as child care) can have an important effect on the willingness and ability of women to compete for jobs. The factors most important to consider when estimating who will get which jobs include:

1) Types of jobs created
2) Expected duration of the jobs
3) The community's skill/experience base from previous projects
4) Older workers' willingness to leave established jobs
5) Young workers' ability to obtain entry-level jobs or training
6) Traditional distribution of jobs between males and females and among social groups
7) Community attitudes towards the project
8) Other employment opportunities available to residents
9) Support facilities for working parents

Careful examination of the forecast baseline conditions may be useful in determining how the residents are likely to respond to the project-related jobs and what the jobs will mean to community residents. Under baseline conditions in many rural areas, people may leave their communities because no jobs are available. With the proposed action (or the prospect of the proposed action), some may choose to remain or to return. Under these circumstances, new jobs can create entirely different social effects than they would in a community which already has ample jobs and where almost all new jobs would have to be filled by newcomers.

If the number of jobs being introduced into a community has the potential for large social effects, it will be important to develop detailed baseline and with-action scenarios. If the number of jobs to be produced by a project is not sufficient to be a significant source of social change, such detailed estimates are generally unnecessary.

If a baseline forecast is to be prepared, it will usually be the economist's responsibility. If no other major projects are anticipated, future employment characteristics will generally be estimated by more simple methods, such as trend analysis. It should be emphasized that the purpose of this analysis for the social assessment is to determine whether there are groups in the community which will benefit in a particular way from the proposed action and to provide a basis for understanding the mechanisms affecting the distribution of resources. Thinking through the information you have about these factors can clarify the processes by which resources, particularly access to jobs, are distributed within the community and can help you make a preliminary estimate of the effects of these jobs.

Income

Change in the level of income often constitutes one of the major project-related effects. Changes in income levels, however, can generate conflict in communities if they alter existing distributional patterns. Specification of the changes that will occur in the level of income and an understanding of the potential for distributional effects can therefore be important for the social assessment. For most types of proposed actions there are three major mechanisms by which income levels and distribution can be changed. These are through (1) the wages paid to workers in jobs created by the proposed action, (2) increased business activity and windfall profits, and (3) increased or decreased cost for use of a resource (for example, modification of leasing fees or grazing regulations).

Wages Paid to Workers in Jobs Created by the Project or by Change in Baseline Conditions

If the proposed action or change in baseline conditions introduces a large number of new jobs into a community, it is generally worthwhile to examine what this will do to wage levels and, consequently, to the distribution of income from wages. These issues are relatively easy to address in aggregate by comparing existing wage rates with the wage rates forecast for the baseline, direct project, and with-project (total) conditions. Substantial changes may occur if the number of jobs with atypical (high or low) wage rates is relatively large. The distributional question is considerably more difficult and is tied directly to the distribution of jobs (discussed previously).

Large wage differentials between existing and new jobs can have several effects that are important to the social analysis. In many cases, the skill requirements for some of these high-paying jobs are such that local residents are likely to obtain at least a portion of them. The availability of higher-paying jobs can create competition for labor. This can make employers offering lower-paying jobs either unable to obtain or keep employees or force them to increase their wage rates. It can also create tension among community groups. Either consequence can have important distributional effects. If severe, it can create serious staffing problems for local government, local commercial establishments, and possibly farmers and ranchers. However, the effective communication system in the United States and the mobility of workers reduces the likelihood that a sufficient shortage of labor will occur to cause significant inflation in the wage rates of nonproject industrial sectors.

From the workers' perspective, the effects of a high wage differential can be positive (if the wages they are paid increase) or negative (if they don't increase, and the higher wages in other sectors lower their comparative economic status). Consequently, if the assessment is dealing with large changes in jobs and income, these possibilities should probably be discussed with the economist.

Income from Increased Business Activity and Windfall Profits

Another major way that the income levels and distribution in a community are affected is through an increase in business activity or inflation in the value of goods/services due to increased demand. If the number of people introduced in the community is small and the project will not make major purchases locally, this is unlikely to be an important factor. If the population increase is large relative to the existing population, the community is particularly isolated, or the wage differentials are high, it may be important. Under these circumstances the distribution of resources and, potentially, the community's ability to coordinate response may be affected by the creation of conflicts of interest and/or changes in the status relationships among residents.

The extent to which wages are spent in a community depends largely upon what goods are available there and what alternative sources are available. Consequently, pressure from excess demand due to worker purchases is likely to be greater in a small, isolated town than in a similar-sized town located near a regional center. High levels of local spending can have both positive and negative effects, often on different groups within the community. If local supply is not adequate to meet demand, prices are likely to rise. This occurs most frequently for high demand goods and services that are not easily transportable and are more expensive (such as land, housing, durable household goods) and less frequently for goods whose supply can easily be increased (such as groceries). Local price inflation benefits the sellers of the goods and hurts the buyers. Severe local inflation can create difficulties for those in low wage jobs and on fixed incomes, although their utilization of the items with inflated prices needs to be evaluated to determine the extent of this effect.

Because it usually benefits only the few, inflation of prices is generally considered an adverse effect. It can affect local residents' perceptions of the quality and relative importance of personal interactions. Especially in smaller towns with highly informal personal interaction patterns, businesses that inflate prices beyond what seems fair tend to be seen as greedy. If this is perceived as a widespread occurrence, residents may feel there has been an undesirable change in established patterns of behavior and that too much emphasis is being placed on economic rather than personal considerations.

The ability of informal social controls to impose sanctions against price inflation may influence the extent of price increases and windfall profits. Local residents' attitudes toward the project and the newcomers may also have an effect. Prices may be raised to prevent growth and the establishment of new businesses, or they may be raised to indicate protest and resentment of the activity or newcomers. These types of response affect not only "real" income levels, but also the amount of increase in business and population and the personal interaction processes in the community. Changes in these factors may in turn affect the number and behavior of newcomers.

Increased local demand can also result in the expansion of existing businesses or the establishment of new ones. Establishment of businesses by outsiders can affect the organizational/regulatory context of the community, and overall business response can substantially increase the number of new people who move into the town. Two factors that have been identified as critical to the ability and willingness of local businesses to expand are (1) availability of financing and (2) the certainty of demand. Particularly if the proposed action involves a large, temporary peak in the number of workers (which is typical of power plant or synfuels projects) or if the timing of the proposed action is uncertain because of fluctuating demand or potential regulatory difficulties, businesses may be unwilling to expand or unable to obtain financing. This can occur either because of the uncertainty of the long-term prospects, because financing capabilities are strained by the expansion and local banks are unable to lend, or because local banks are unwilling to extend their loan capabilities. If local businesses are unable to expand, the number of outside companies entering the community may increase, changing the outside linkages and distribution processes in the community.

In many small towns, expansion of commercial facilities is evaluated positively by most residents. Therefore, estimation of the effects of increased purchasing power (from increased population and/or increased income levels) on the number of establishments can be important in evaluating residents' perceptions of change in the community.

Increased or Decreased Cost of Resource Use[1]

If the proposed action involves modification of the cost or availability of resources that contribute to the income of area residents (such as federal land for grazing, subsidized irrigation water, etc.), it can cause real or anticipated effects on the income and well-being of at least one stakeholder group. (In these cases, the principal social effects of the proposed action may occur as a direct interaction between the proposed action's income effects and the well-being of individuals/families in the study area, with the effects on study area communities of minor importance.)

It is generally the responsibility of the resource management specialist or economist to calculate the effects of the proposed action's change in resource availability or cost on family/farm/business income (and to estimate the amount and type of income and employment generated or lost as a result). It is usually the responsibility of the social assessor to determine the significance of these effects for the study area residents. This task involves determining whether or not the income changes will be sufficient to: (1) affect the livelihood pattern of the area, (2) affect the social organization of the area, and (3) affect the well-being of area residents. When dealing with these types of potential effects, it is important to be sensitive to the consequences of any uncertainties about actual effects from the perspective of the affected population. In many cases, the position of the potentially affected population relative to those proposing the modification/project is such that it is to the advantage of the potentially affected population to be highly risk averse. From their perspective, their

---

[1]Income effects of this type can also be addressed as an indirect effect of change in the cost and availability of resources, as discussed later in this chapter.

potential for loss due to the uncertainties is substantially higher than their potential for gain. When this perspective is combined with the political realities of an assessment process, accurate determination of attitudes, perceptions, and positions can be both extremely difficult and very important.

Analysis of the distributional effects of a proposed action is not routinely addressed by the economist; therefore, if they appear important, it may be your responsibility to investigate them. Since many of the questions involve economic relationships, an economic perspective may be helpful and collaboration with the economist beneficial. Similarly, unless you are experienced in the area, it may also be worthwhile to get help determining the types of businesses and organizations likely to be introduced into or driven out of the community or study area by changes that are forecast for income and employment, if that aspect appears to warrant attention. Information about community or stakeholder group opposition to the proposed action, expressions of inability to plan or respond because of project uncertainties or lack of financing, or indications that community leadership is likely to take an aggressive role in coordinating businesses' response can be useful in refining the forecasts of income effects.

Resources

A major feature of some projects is modification of the resources available to the study area communities. In other types of proposed actions, resource changes are relatively small. The types of resources included in this input category range from public lands and water to recreational facilities and taxes. The major question being asked is how the proposed action will change the resources that are available to the community and the individuals in the study area.

The focus of the analysis will vary greatly depending upon the type of proposed action being assessed. Those which involve modification of a resource that is used locally (for example, grazing permits, wilderness, water) will require a substantially different analysis than those which do not. For most large-scale development projects, the resource change with the greatest immediate potential for local social effects is the change in local tax revenues, although long-term environmental consequences may also be important. For decisions involving renewable resources (timber, grazing, wildlife, wilderness), the principal source of effect is change in the cost or availability of the resource itself.

Quantification of the change in resources will generally be the responsibility of another team member. For example, the economic/demographic or facilities/services analyst is generally responsible for determining the change in taxes and for forecasting baseline, with-action, and total revenues if they are needed. Detailed analysis of changes in tax revenues is generally most important when (1) the project is imminent, (2) both the revenue base and the demands for services will change, and (3) there is a possibility that the community's ability to respond will be affected. If you are responsible for this aspect of the assessment, additional guidance is

provided in Appendix B, but the assistance of someone knowledgable
about the tax structure of the area is advised.

Two aspects -- jurisdictional distribution and timing -- are
frequently among the largest resource issues, since they determine
whether adequate resources will be available to meet demand. For
this reason forecasts should address both the jurisdictional
(county, town, school district) and temporal distribution of resource change. In these forecasts, attention must be given to the
ability of area residents and/or local or state governments to alter
resource availability and cost. The local jurisdictions in the
study area, for example, may have considerable flexibility in the
type and magnitude of taxes that can be locally imposed, or they may
be severely constrained by the state or local regulatory structures.

With many large-scale development projects, difficulties are
frequently created because the jurisdictional distribution of tax
revenues does not correspond with the distribution of demand for
services. This is most likely to occur between towns and counties
and between school districts. Some communities have addressed this
problem by coordinating their resources and service provision
through the formation of joint power boards or other collaborative
mechanisms. Specification and interpretation of the baseline and
with-action revenue forecasts can be enhanced by application of information about the community's approach to planning and controlling
the effects of the proposed action and about the ability of local
government jurisdictions to coordinate and cooperate.

The characteristics of the company or agency implementing the
action can have a substantial effect on the change in resources and
particularly on the manner in which the change occurs. Transfer of
resources by application of the right of eminent domain or by
changes in legislation, for example, often result in conflict and
long-term resentment. Tax revenues can be tremendously affected by
the characteristics and policies of the company or agency implementing the action. Public agencies or companies may be tax exempt and
thus pay no local taxes on their properties or purchases, although
they may have the ability and willingness to make payments in lieu
of taxes.

Since the timing of revenues relative to the timing of demand is
critical to the ability of local jurisdictions and residents to respond, considerable attention is often given to development of
schedules. Some communities and companies implementing action have
negotiated prepayment of taxes, special contributions to the jurisdictions (such as firefighting equipment), the provision of company-
sponsored facilities for their workers (such as worker housing with
its own water and sewer systems), or long-term, phased implementation of new regulations. Although these agreements tend to be
viewed as mitigation strategies rather than as part of the proposed
action, it may become more common to have such resource provisions
incorporated as part of the original project design. Currently, the
extent of this type of resource provision depends largely upon the
initiative taken by the local government and area residents and upon
the attitudes and experience of the implementing company or agency.
The ability of these entities to coordinate their efforts can make a
major difference in the fiscal and social consequences of a project. Information about the potential relationship between the

community, stakeholder groups, and the company or agency implementing the action can therefore be very important to the assessment. Indeed, this factor can be so important that lack of knowledge about the likely behavior of the implementor introduces a substantial degree of uncertainty into the assessment process that should be noted.

Organizations and Regulations

In some cases, implementation of the proposed action can result in a drastic change in the number and type of organizations active in the community. In others, the proposed action itself may be a policy or regulation which affects the ability of the local governments or area residents to control their activities and resources. Changes in the number and type of organizations and in the regulations under which communities and their residents must operate can have consequences for the diversity/complexity, distribution of resources, and interpersonal interactions in a community. These consequences can be of sufficient magnitude to affect jobs and income as well as perceptions of well-being. Energy development projects, for example, are most likely to cause changes through the introduction of: (1) new federal or state agencies or modifications in the visibility of their presence, (2) new businesses (including national corporations, chain stores, and franchises), and (3) voluntary organizations such as churches, fraternal organizations, and unions.

Regulations governing communities and their residents change through a similar process. Regulations can be imposed (or changed) as a direct consequence of the proposed action. As the situation in the community changes (or is anticipated to change), regulatory changes are likely to occur. For example, many small communities undergoing rapid growth experience pressure to implement or enforce planning, zoning, and land use regulations even when there may be a strong aversion to loss of personal control over private property. The chance that this pressure will result in regulatory change appears to depend upon a number of community-specific factors such as state pressure, the magnitude of growth, the coordinative ability of local leadership, and the distributional effects of the regulations. Unless the specific purpose of the assessment is to identify the effects of policy changes, it is likely that the specification of inputs regarding regulatory changes will primarily involve identifying general regulations associated with the type of development for the particular state involved and looking at the types of regulatory changes that have occurred in other communities under similar circumstances. It is probably also worthwhile to review the policies of the state government.

Health and Public Safety

For some assessments, a major purpose or desired outcome of the proposed action is to reduce risk to health and public safety. Anticipated health and safety effects (such as those resulting from a dam) are generally forecast specifically by other specialists. The responsibility for quantifying these effects rarely falls to the social assessor. Changes in public health and safety are important inputs because they can affect both the objective measures and subjective perceptions of community well-being. Unless there are particular factors in the community that would affect estimation of these effects (such as a cultural or social aversion to the use of a facility), the specialist's estimates can generally be used without extensive evaluation.

The problem is more complex when the proposed action could adversely affect public health or pose a threat to public safety. In most such cases, the reduction is rarely clearly defined or quantified; it is generally presented in terms of increased risk of adverse health and safety effects. As has been evident from public response to nuclear power plants, nuclear waste disposal sites, and other projects involving hazardous materials (chemical warfare, etc.), the level of uncertainty usually associated with the health effects, and the severity of the consequences (should they occur) create the potential for fear and strong opposition to the proposed action. Under these circumstances, special attention needs to be given to public attitudes and the social consequences of introducing such risks into the community.

9.4   Documenting the Results

When baseline, with-action, and total specifications for each of these types of inputs (for each area or impacted community in the study area) have been made, it is often useful to summarize the results into an inventory, making a brief notation about the principal factors that influenced the estimates. This type of inventory can facilitate the revision of estimates in case changes occur in the baseline conditions or the description of the proposed action, and it can also be used when forecasting the social effects of the various alternatives. An example format for such an inventory is shown in Figure 9-2.

For most large-scale projects, the single most critical project input is the total number of people. It may be helpful to use population as a proxy for change in the baseline and project inputs and to develop graphs similar to those shown in Figure 9-3, identifying the year of peak temporary population, the year in which long-term permanent population levels are reached, and the magnitude and duration of the "temporary excess" population. These simple graphs can be very useful in forecasting the level of impacts that are likely to occur in different communities, for comparing alternatives, and for guiding your evaluation of the importance of other direct project inputs.

9.5   References

To avoid duplication and scattering of reference citations throughout the guide, the materials pertinent to this discussion have been included in the reference sections of Chapter 8 and appendixes A and B.

190

Figure 9-2

Inventory of Inputs

DATE: _____

COMMUNITY/AREA: _____

ALTERNATIVE: _____

		BASELINE	PROPOSED ACTION	TOTAL WITH-ACTION	COMMENTS
People	PEAK				
	PERMANENT				
Jobs	PEAK				
	PERMANET				
Income	PEAK				
	PERMANENT				
Resources	PEAK				
	PERMANENT				
Organization/ Regulation Changes	PEAK				
	PERMANENT				
Health and Public Safety	PEAK				
	PERMANENT				
Other					

Figure 9-3

Summary of Population Change

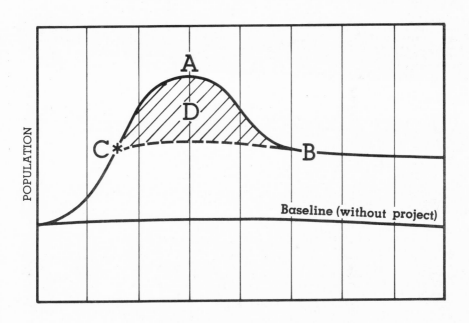

A Peak Temporary Population (with project)

B Long-term Permanent Population (with project)

C Point at which Population Reaches Long-term Permanent Size

D Temporary Excess Population

10. Forecasting and Evaluating the Social Effects

10.1 Introduction

This chapter describes some ways to forecast and evaluate the probable social effects of proposed actions. It builds upon the information contained in the previous chapters, particularly chapters 8 and 9. Forecasting and evaluating social effects is a difficult part of social assessment because it requires the assessor to make judgments for which there are no hard and fast guidelines. Two specific activities are covered in this chapter: forecasting and evaluation.

A forecast is a statement about the likely future of a particular place for a particular time. In impact assessment, forecasts are made about the likely future human and environmental conditions that would occur under the "no-action", or baseline, alternative and under one or more "with-action" alternatives. These forecasts are usually not intended to define exactly what will occur, a recognized impossibility due to our incomplete ability to foresee future events and the indeterminancy and complexity of human response. For the same reasons, forecasts also do not usually attempt to assign specific probabilities to the occurrence of a particular outcome or event, although in some cases the alternative futures may be ordinally ranked according to such criteria as maximum-high, most probable, minimum-low.

Forecasting is a risky business. It requires comprehensive understanding of the community for which forecasts are being made and correct anticipation of changes in trends and of discontinuities due to outside intervention, technological break-throughs, or natural disasters; capabilities seldom demonstrated in the past. Forecasting social conditions is especially difficult for several additional reasons. First, it deals with the consequences of the collective behavior of actors (individuals, city councils, stakeholder groups) who can alter their behaviors based on both real and perceived changes in the environment. Second, sufficient research has not been conducted to provide a firm base of information about the complex correlations and cause-and-effect relationships that determine change in social organization and well-being. Forecasters must rely on information about these complex relationships obtained from previous research and available theory. In most cases, evidence from past experience, although informative, is not sufficient to allow direct generalizations to be made with confidence, even for forecasts covering a short time frame. Third, events affecting social conditions rarely occur precisely as planned or anticipated. Communities may decide to initiate an aggressive planning program instead of "riding it out." The company or agency implementing the project may make a concession or provide information that convinces opposition groups not to actively object. The company or agency implementing the project may modify project schedules or work force characteristics. The company or the state may provide financial assistance to the local commmunities.

Since social change occurs through a linked process (the initial response influences the subsequent response which both affect the following response), forecasts of future social conditions are inherently conditional. They are therefore most appropriately addressed in the conditional, i.e., "If A happens (community leadership responds efficiently), the outcomes are likely to be X; if B happens (community leadership falters), the outcomes are likely to be Y." Unfortunately, the reporting format of an assessment may not allow such presentation.

Evaluation is the process by which meaning is attached to the social effects that are forecast to occur. Like forecasting, this is a difficult task. The purpose is to use available information and analytic skills to describe how the affected parties are likely to interpret the forecast social effects. The tension between objective change and the meaning of such change has been discussed throughout the guide. Various data sources and procedures for measuring meaning or perception (for example, interviews, questionnaires, observation, and secondary sources) have been described in other chapters. But in the end, it is your responsibility to describe the meaning that different effects will have for different community groups and stakeholders as accurately and clearly as possible.

Forecasting and evaluating the social effects that will result from a proposed action is the goal of the social assessment. Without the forecast and evaluation, the process would be only a data gathering exercise, not an impact assessment. Indeed, the forecast and evaluation are the social assessment, since they determine and describe the most likely social impacts and how they will be interpreted. They are the cumulative result of all the previous work. So, despite the problems and the difficulty, it is a task that is critical to the successful completion of an assessment. The information presented in this chapter is designed to help you plan and organize your effort and to guide you through the forecasting and evaluation process.

At this point it is important to make clear what the guide attempts to accomplish with regard to forecasting and evaluating social impacts. It does not pre-empt your analysis by attempting to delineate the outcome that would result from the interaction between particular community characteristics and specified baseline or direct project inputs. The variability in community social characteristics, baseline, and direct project inputs and the complexity of social response stymie efforts to establish universal equations for such interactions. Simplification of the system of interactions that must be considered is necessary in order to forecast social impacts: social change is so complex that forecasting would be impossible without an analytic framework that helps organize and focus the analysis. The social organization model represents the analytic framework recommended by the guide. This approach still requires complex analysis and consideration of many interrelationships, but further simplification and the use of simple decision rules were found to reduce the power and flexibility of the analysis and to encourage rote rather than analytic forecasting, thus increasing the likelihood of serious error.

The social organization model, and this chapter, in conjunction with the rest of the guide, attempt to help and guide you through the analytical process of forecasting and evaluating social effects. The goal is to enable you to identify and obtain the information that you need, to organize it in a manner that facilitates and enriches the analysis, to ask the right questions, and to apply your knowledge and information in a systematic, rigorous analysis of the likely consequences that will result from the complex interactions initated when community and project are brought together. Previous research and theory plus the data you have collected in the earlier steps of the assessment process provide the basis of information about the community, the social groups, the baseline and direct project inputs, and about the processes of social interaction and change. The complexity of community life and human response ensure that each assessment will be unique, and that the available information will often be inadequate to allow forecasts to be made with certainty. The purpose of the guide is to help you make the best, most informed judgments possible under these circumstances.

10.2 How to Forecast and Evaluate Social Impacts

Clarify the Objectives and Guard Against Biases

The forecast and evaluation is the goal of social assessment, but the goal of most social assessment is to provide decision makers or policy makers with the information they need to make an informed decision. The decision maker will feel confident in using the forecast if the methods and analysis that have been employed are sound and well documented and the assessment is directed toward the decisions being evaluated. In addition to assuring that you understand the objectives of the assessment, as you prepare to make the forecasts you should take time to reflect upon your objectivity. The forecast and evaluation should be derived from the data and the analysis -- from what the data demonstrate, not what you expected or wish the data to show. Throughout the assessment process -- from design through report preparation -- you must seek to identify your biases and guard against them while conducting the assessment and presenting your results.

Clarify the Approach

Before initiating the forecasting process, two aspects of the approach need to be clarified. First, the purpose and detail necessary for the assessment need to be reviewed. In some cases, the principal purpose of the impact forecast is to determine the general magnitude and type of social changes that will occur in order to compare a variety of alternatives. In this case, the desired level of detail in the forecasts and discussion of impacts will generally be low. In other cases, the principal purpose of the assessment is to delineate the social consequences of a particular action in sufficient detail to facilitate enhancement or mitigation. Here, considerably more attention to detail will be required. Obviously, it is important to determine which approach is appropriate for the assessment being conducted.

The second aspect of the forecasting approach that needs to be clearly established is how the comparisons between the with-project and the baseline conditions are to be made. Three approaches can be used. Since they can yield somewhat different results and involve somewhat different presentation, it is important to understand which is more appropriate to the assessment being conducted. The first comparison follows the sequence:

1) Forecast future conditions for the study period without the proposed action (baseline).
2) Forecast future conditions for the study period with the proposed action (with-project).
3) Determine the difference between the two and attribute that to the proposed action.

The second involves a somewhat different analytic process:

1) Describe existing conditions.
2) Forecast future conditions with the proposed action and determine the key factor(s) causing the change (for example, population influx).
3) Compare the future conditions to the existing conditions and derive the total change forecast to occur.
4) Determine what fraction of the key factors causing the change are due to the proposed action. Attribute that fraction of the impacts to the proposed action.

The difference between these two approaches is generally only important if there are large changes occurring under baseline conditions (e.g., other large-scale development projects) that could cause substantial change in community resources, social organization, or well-being. In this case, whether the baseline changes are assumed to have already occurred when those caused by the proposed action are considered (i.e., the project effects occur "on top of" other changes, as in the first approach), or whether they are assumed to occur simultaneously (i.e., the project effects constitute a portion of the total change, as in the second approach) can make a substantial difference in attribution.

In the third approach, forecasts are made of the change expected to occur in each component of the social environment (resources, social organization, well-being) over particular periods (current to year X; current to year Y) for each of the scenarios or alternatives being evaluated, including the no-action or baseline. The relative degree of change between the baseline and with-project alternative for each time period (the project effects) can then be determined. The analytic process is as follows:

1) Describe existing conditions.
2) Forecast degree of change in each component of the social environment that would occur for each time period without the proposed action (baseline).
3) Forecast degree of change in each component of the social environment for each time period with the proposed action (with-project).
4) Determine the difference between the changes forecast for the with-project and baseline situations for each time period and attribute them to the proposed action.

Since many aspects of the social environment are described in relative rather than absolute or scalar terms (e.g., "increased complexity", "group Y is likely to have attained enhanced status and political power", "the relative economic position of group A will probably decline") this approach is often appropriate and efficient. When combined with a brief description of with-project conditions in areas of significant change or anticipated problems, it frequently offers the most succinct and effective approach to the forecasting of social impact.

Since social forecasting rarely involves extensive or detailed calculations, it is recommended that the impacts be considered from each of these three perspectives. This use of multiple techniques can sometimes highlight aspects of the social processes that will inform your forecast and improve the interpretation of results.

Inventory and Review the Data

To facilitate the forecasting effort, it is useful to review and update the inventories prepared for the description of the existing environment (Chapter 8) and the forecast of baseline and direct project inputs (Chapter 9). In addition to summarizing the available information, the inventories serve several other important functions. First, they simplify the process of validating the data. With the summaries, it is possible to see whether the results from the interviews and observations agree with the results from secondary data analysis. If they do, the analysis can continue. If they do not, it is essential to reexamine the data to determine how large the differences are, which data sources are in conflict, and, if possible, what the reasons for discrepancy are. This procedure of comparing data of different types and from different sources is called triangulation and is an important technique in social assessment. As many data sources and measures of the same characteristic

as possible should be compared to increase the validity of the results.

The second function of the inventories is to facilitate identification of the relationships that are most important to the forecast and evaluation (this is discussed in the next section). The
assessor can then begin to make logical informed judgments about the
type and magnitude of the social impacts that are likely to occur
and to focus attention on the key factors and relationships.

The third function of the inventories is comparative. From the
organized inventories, comparisons can be made between the communities in the study area in terms of existing resources, social
organization, and indicators of well-being and in terms of the baseline and project inputs that will affect them. These comparisons
can be used to highlight similarities and differences between communities and the alternatives. These comparisons are particularly
illustrative when carried through the forecasting process and summarized in the technical report.

Organize and Systematize the Analysis:
Work Through the Social Organization Model

Identify and Analyze Direct Effects at the Community Level

Once the information has been organized as described in the
previous section, the forecasting process can begin. In most cases,
the forecasts are made for each affected community or subarea individually, with the results then compiled for the entire study area.
If there are large differences in the magnitude or characteristics
of the direct project inputs at the peak temporary and long-term
permanent periods, it is recommended that the impacts for each of
these time periods be forecast separately. One way this can be done
is by preparing graphic representations similar to those shown in
Figure 10-1. In any case, the temporal aspects of the impacts must
be clearly addressed, although it is rare for social forecasts to be
made on an annual basis.

To analyze this complex and interrelated information, a method
that helps simplify, organize, and systematize the analysis is
needed. Since the assessment of social impacts is based largely on
the estimation of qualitative changes and involves comparisons (the
future with the action to the future without the action, one alternative to another), it is particularly important that an approach be
used which ensures that all alternatives are analyzed using the same
methods and analytic framework.

A variety of different approaches can be used. The social organization model is suggested as an effective basis for organizing
the analysis. As indicated in the social organization model,
changes in community resources, social organization, and well-being
occur both directly from the introduction of baseline or direct
project inputs, and indirectly as these initial changes cause response and adjustment throughout the social system. In preparing to

Figure 10-1

Graphs Representing Population and Employment Change

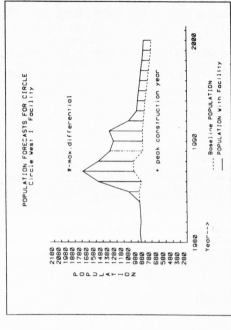

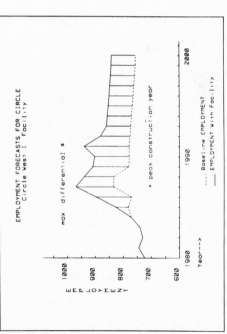

Source: Mountain West Research, Inc., 1981.

analyze the consequences of baseline changes or a proposed project, it is helpful to proceed systematically. After preparing the summary of information, it is recommended that you next work through each of the direct baseline and project inputs to determine which are pertinent to the assessment in terms of potential to cause changes in the social environment directly. A review of chapters 8 and 9 may assist this process. Depending upon the type of action being assessed, it may be that one or two baseline or direct project inputs can be identified as the key factors influencing the type and magnitude of the changes that would occur under baseline or with-project conditions.[1] If this is the case, it is helpful to organize the forecasting effort (and comparisons among alternatives) around this (or these few) inputs, using the others for refinement.

One way to start this analysis is to review the matrix developed in Chapter 8, shown again as Figure 10-2, which identifies all possible combinations of inputs and community characteristics. Based on the information compiled in chapters 8 and 9, which has just been reviewed and summarized, the task of the analysis/forecast is to answer the following questions for each combination: (1) How will the type of inputs that have been forecast affect this characteristic for each of the forecast periods, and (2) How will this characteristic affect the community's, group's, or individual's response to this input. The purpose of this technique is to organize and systematize the analytic process to ensure that no important direct effects are overlooked and to focus the remaining analysis by identifying the input/community/group interactions that have the potential to result in significant social change. Although the guide has attempted to provide some information about likely consequences of the interaction between particular baseline or direct project inputs and community social characteristics (see chapters 8 and 9) the basis for making these judgments should be a review of the pertinent literature, case studies that apply to the particular assessment you are conducting, and careful examination of the consequences of similar events in the study area or other areas with similar characteristics.

Once the cells in the matrix that identify the areas where baseline and direct project inputs could cause direct, consequential social change have been delineated, attention can be focused on forecasting the form and magnitude these changes would take. In making such forecasts, you will have to apply your knowledge of past trends in the community, the effects of similar interactions in other communities or in this community at some time previously, and of applicable research data and theory. It is important to be thorough in your analysis, and to examine your conclusions for logic and internal consistency.

---

[1]For example, in some cases when assessing the impacts of large-scale energy projects, population change can serve as such a key factor. For assessments of proposed modifications of grazing regulations, changes in income and in resources are often the key factors; little population or job changes are usually anticipated.

Figure 10-2

Matrix to Identify Major Relationships

COMMUNITY _____
ALTERNATIVE _____
PHASE _____

	DIRECT PROJECT INPUTS					
	People	Jobs	Income	Resources	Organizations/ Regulations	Health & Safety
COMMUNITY RESOURCES						
•Historical Experience						
•Culture						
•Demography						
•Occupations (Livelihood) Labor Force						
•Employment and Income						
•Facilities/Services/Fiscal						
•Organizations and Regulations						
•Leadership						
•Attitudes and Perceptions						
SOCIAL ORGANIZATION PROCESSES						
•Diversity/Complexity						
•Outside Linkages						
•Distribution of Resources/Power						
•Coordination and Cooperation						
•Personal Interaction						
WELL-BEING INDICATORS						
•Behaviors						
•Access to Resources						
•Perceptions						

Identify and Analyze Direct Effects and Their Consequences for Each Social Group

After the community level analysis has been completed, attention should be directed to an analysis of the direct consequences of the forecast baseline and direct project inputs for each of the social groups in the community and of the secondary effects of these changes. This analysis should follow the general sequence:

1) Review the profile information gathered in Chapter 8 concerning the type, characteristics, and relationships of the social groups in the community at the time of the study. The profile characteristics include:
   -- ethnicity/race
   -- language
   -- religion
   -- livelihood/occupation
   -- income/wealth
   -- property ownership
   -- residential location
   -- length of residence
   -- age/sex
   -- special interests/political positions
2) Forecast the distribution of baseline and direct project inputs among the social groups, being alert to the possibility that one or more new groups may be created by these inputs.
3) Determine how this distribution of inputs will affect each group's profile, including the size of each group.
4) Analyze how the distribution of inputs and changes in group profiles will affect group interactions, with special attention to those that would affect the group's role in the community.
5) Analyze how the distributive process, the distribution of effects, and group response to this process and its outcome (or anticipated outcome) will affect each group's participation in the community.
6) Analyze what these changes (1-5 above) mean in terms of community resources, social organizations, and well-being.

As throughout the assessment, your ability to perform this analysis will depend upon your understanding of the resources, social organization and well-being of the community, the accuracy and completeness of your information about baseline and direct project inputs, and your knowledge (based on previous research, theory, and experience) of social change processes. The discussions in chapters 8 and 9 specify the types of questions that need to be answered in order to complete this analysis.

Analyze the Consequences of These Changes for Community Resources, Social Organization, and Well-being

The next step in your analysis is to synthesize the conclusions you have reached thus far. The key to this synthesis is to identify and "sum-up" the factors or forces that would promote or inhibit change in each of the various aspects of the community included in the social organization model (resources, organization, and well-being). This summary must incorporate not only the direct effects of the baseline or project inputs but also the secondary or indirect effects of these changes. Given the complexity of social systems, it is impossible to trace all the ramifications of these initial changes, but by working through the social organization model and using the information obtained from the analysis of effects on social groups, it should be possible to identify these which will significantly affect the outcome.

As you proceed through this analysis, it is useful to consider whether each of the groups that would be affected by the change would consider it positive (and seek to enhance or ensure it's occurrence) or negative (and seek to prevent or modify it). It is also important to take into account the temporal sequence in which the various forces for change will occur. This summing up will allow you to estimate the direction and relative magnitude of the force for change exerted on each of the community and well-being characteristics for the baseline and each of the with-project alternatives being assessed. This information is necessary for both of the next two steps: (1) estimating the magnitude and direction of change that these forces will produce, and (2) evaluating its meaning.

Once the forces for change have been estimated (or while these estimates are being made), the ability and willingness of the community to increase, modify, resist, or prevent these changes should be evaluated, and the likelihood of intervention by outside actors (the state or federal agencies) in problem areas should be assessed. Based on this analysis, the magnitude of the changes that are likely to occur for each pertinent community characteristic and aspect of well-being should then be forecast. This process needs to be repeated for each of the alternatives being evaluated, with the conclusions noted in a way that will facilitate comparison between them. It is sometimes helpful to compare the conditions forecast for the community with those in another community that has received similar social impacts from other projects. (For example, you may be able to say that the study community will change to become similar to community X.) The next step is to make the comparisons between the with-project and baseline forecasts and determine the magnitude of the changes, or impacts, that can be attributed to the proposed action.

At this point, it is wise to reexamine the analysis to make sure that it is internally consistent, that all important relationships

and interactions have been taken into account, and that the decisions and conclusions follow logically from the data. It is important to provide some measure of your confidence in and strength of
the conclusions and to note the areas of uncertainty, assessing
their potential to alter the magnitude or direction of the change.
These conclusions can be recorded using the major elements in the
social organization model as an outline, although it should be noted
that the discussion should include only those inputs, community
characteristics, and impacts that have been found pertinent to the
particular assessment being conducted.

Evaluate the Meaning of the Action-related Change (Impacts) to the Community Residents

Once the existing, baseline, and with-action conditions have
been estimated and the portion attributable to the proposed action
has been identified, the social meaning of the impacts can be addressed. Two aspects of impacts must be evaluated. The first
involves changes that affect the basic structure and processes of
the community -- these affect how the community will deal with its
future. The second involves the importance of the changes to current and new residents of the study area. The basis for making
these evaluations is the data on attitudes and perceptions gathered
as part of the description of the existing environment, plus any
similar information on the newcomers that would be entering the community, the analysis of the effects on each social group, and the
relationships identified in the social organization model. Social
theory may be called upon to help assess the importance and meaning
of forecast change in the basic structure and processes of the community.

To the extent possible, this evaluation should be made for each
of the major groups in the community since the changes are likely to
have significantly different meanings to different groups. However,
where appropriate, it is also important to evaluate the changes from
the perspective of the community as a social unit. To guide this
evaluation, several questions can be asked:

1) How will the changes affect the way people (and each group)
   relate to or participate in the community during and after
   impact?
2) How will residents (and each group) feel about living in the
   community during and after impact? How will they feel about
   having the community as their home during this period?
3) How will residents (and each group) feel about sharing the
   community and its resources with the others, both current
   and new members?

Once the forecasts and evaluations have been made, the results
can be summarized in a format similar to that shown in Figure 10-3
to facilitate comparison of the alternatives. It may be worthwhile
to discuss your forecasts and evaluations with other members of the
assessment team, with knowledgeable persons in the study area, and

with other colleagues to make sure that nothing has been missed and to check the validity and logic of the argument.

It should be recognized that these determinations involve judgments and decisions. There is no way to avoid this aspect of assessment. Because the discussion of the meaning of the changes deals with values, it is particularly important that it be based on the data and that this be clearly evident from the process and documentation of the analysis. It is recommended that any available, valid material on the outcome and interpretations of similar projects/programs be reviewed, that as much exposure to field conditions in both pre- and post-impact areas as possible be acquired, and that a rigorous, analytic, and logical process be applied in the assessment.

10.3 Documenting and Presenting the Results

At this point, the results of the social assessment can be prepared for presentation to the decision maker and the public. Before starting this task, procedural and administrative issues such as schedules, desired length of the report, format specifications, and bibliographic requirements should be reconfirmed. The report should be tailored to the expressed needs of the decision maker and the assessment. The social assessment is usually only one of many components that will constitute the final technical report and environmental assessment. For this reason, conformance to established outlines and procedures is particularly important.

If time permits, it is recommended that a draft working paper, much more inclusive than the final report, be developed before you prepare the final report. The draft report would incorporate all the pertinent data/information that has been collected and analyzed. This draft can either incorporate the entire existing environment report or abstract portions from it. The objective is to develop a report that presents the impacts and a discussion of their meaning in a convincing and logical manner. It may be useful to summarize the findings in tabular form, similar to that shown in Figure 10-3.

When the draft report is completed, you may want to circulate it to others who are knowledgeable about the study area. These would include other team members (especially the economist, the facilities/services analyst) and other social scientists. Their review and comments should be taken seriously and the draft should be revised if necessary.

It should then be relatively easy to revise the draft report into the form desired for the final report, eliminating or condensing discussions that were not particularly pertinent. If the results are to be included in an EIS, the technical report will have to be drastically reduced in length and should include only those aspects genuinely important to describe and explain the impacts. Given the severe space restrictions imposed on each section of an EIS, it is especially critical that the material be presented clearly in a logical and straightforward manner. In some cases, additional analysis or discussion papers may also be required.

Figure 10-3

Comparison of Alternatives

ALTERNATIVE	SUMMARY OF SOCIAL IMPACTS		
	Community Resources	Social Organization	Well-being
Baseline	MAJOR OTHER		
Alternative 1	MAJOR OTHER		
Alternative 2	MAJOR OTHER		
Alternative 3	MAJOR OTHER		

The draft report and your field notes should be kept as documentation and backup: others may want to read them; they can provide a point of reference for monitoring the impacts that actually occur; and they can be used for other assessments, either in the same community or elsewhere.

10.4 References

References pertinent to this chapter can be found in the reference sections of chapters 8 and 13, and in Appendix A where bibliographic material has been consolidated to reduce duplication.

11. Mitigation, Monitoring, and Plan Selection

11.1 Introduction

One of the valuable uses of social assessment is to develop mitigation measures that can minimize a proposed plan's or action's negative effects and maximize its positive effects. Development of mitigation strategies, development and implementation of monitoring programs, and plan selection are generally team efforts to which the social assessor can contribute. As with the formulation of alternatives discussed in Chapter 7, identification and evaluation of mitigation/enhancement measures and monitoring programs depend upon an understanding of the mechanisms by which the adverse and positive effects are caused and how the affected parties are likely to respond. The assessment procedures described in the preceding chapters should help you develop this understanding. This chapter describes how social information can be used to contribute to the development of effective and implementable mitigation/enhancement measures and monitoring programs that can in turn contribute to the plan selection process. As throughout the assessment, the role of the organization conducting the assessment must be borne in mind. It may be that implementation of mitigation measures is beyond the authority and/or resources of the assessment team or the organization. In these cases, the focus of attention regarding mitigation may be on identifying effective mitigation approaches and presenting them in a manner that facilitates their adoption by those who do possess this authority.

11.2 Development and Evaluation of Mitigation/Enhancement Measures

The Changing Role of Mitigation/Enhancement Measures

Adverse social effects can often be mitigated and positive effects enhanced by modifying the characteristics of the project inputs or by increasing the communities' ability to respond. It is important that the opportunity to enhance positive effects not be overlooked by focusing entirely upon the mitigation of problems.

209

In addressing issues of mitigation, it is essential to understand both (1) the need for and benefits of clear, analytic examination of mitigation/enhancement opportunities and (2) the manner in which mitigation/enhancement is to be addressed in the particular assessment. In some cases, the position of your organization may be that mitigation/enhancement activities should not be identified, discussed, or recommended unless the organization has the authority and willingness to require that they be implemented. In others, the approach may be to identify possible mitigation/enhancement measures and evaluate their effectiveness in reducing the adverse impacts or increasing the benefits of the various alternatives, regardless of where responsibility for implementation would lie. In still others, only "committed" mitigation/enhancement measures are addressed, and the "mitigated effects" of the proposed action become the final evaluation of the likely impacts upon which decisions are based.

As more experience is gained in managing development projects, the approach to mitigation will undoubtedly continue to change. However, whenever participating in a mitigation or monitoring effort, it is important to remember that project- and site-specific characteristics must be taken into account. To be maximally effective, mitigation and monitoring programs need to be designed on a case-by-case basis, with careful attention to need and implementability.

Social assessment can contribute information that is very useful in identifying and evaluating mitigation/enhancement opportunities. Since experience has shown that many of the adverse effects of development projects can be substantially reduced by effective mitigation measures, it is important that the social assessor be prepared to develop this information and participate in the discussion and evaluation of mitigation/enhancement strategies.

A Framework for Identifying Mitigation/Enhancement Measures

The Approach

The principal problems in identifying mitigation/enhancement measures are to identify what could be changed to mitigate/enhance the effects of a proposed action and to determine how these changes could be made. There are two ways to affect the social impacts of a proposed action -- change the characteristics of the project inputs or change the characteristics of the impacted communities. The social organization model utilized throughout the guide provides a framework for identifying what could be changed in these two areas to alter the social outcome.

The process described in Chapter 10 for identifying and analyzing the major relationships between direct project inputs and community characteristics can also be used to identify and evaluate mitigation/enhancement measures. Here, the focus is on (1) identifying aspects of the project inputs (including uncertainty) or the community that could be changed to increase the community's ability to respond and therefore reduce the adverse or enhance the positive effects and (2) determining the mechanisms by which those changes could be made.

To determine how the desired changes could be made, it is necessary to consider which organizations have the ability to affect
either direct project inputs or community characteristics and what
types of actions could be taken to implement the desired change.
For most large-scale development activities, the principal organizations with this ability are the following:

1) Federal agencies that control the resources or regulate the
   activities
2) Companies or agencies that implement the development
3) State governments
4) Local governments and organizations
5) Union representatives

The principal actions available to these organizations include
the following:

1) Imposition of conditions under which the proposed action can
   be taken
2) Imposition of legislative requirements or restrictions
3) Negotiation
4) Technical assistance and/or provision of information
5) Voluntary decisions
6) Public and political pressure

Examples of Mitigation/Enhancement Measures

One of the problems in identifying opportunities for mitigation/
enhancement is knowing what kinds of alternatives to consider.
Mitigation/enhancement measures and needs vary greatly by situation,
as should be evident from consideration of the social organization
model. The following descriptions of possible mitigation/
enhancement measures should therefore be utilized as examples of the
types of options that could be identified. The examples are organized according to the components of the social organization
model, although other organizing criteria could be used. Further
discussion of mitigation/enhancement measures that have been applied
in communities experiencing large-scale development is provided in
some of the sources identified at the end of Chapter 8.

Direct Project Inputs

One effective way to alter a project's effects is to modify the
characteristics of the proposed action, and hence the direct project
inputs, in a manner that reduces adverse and enhances positive effects. Some of the problems that are amenable to this type of approach are created by the following:

1) **Uncertainty.** It is not at all unusual for it to take
   three, five, or even ten years for a project to move from
   its initial conception to the beginning of construction.
   During most of this period, everybody involved with the

project -- federal agency, sponsor, community -- is uncertain whether the project will actually happen. If the project is small, this may create few problems, except for those
directly impacted. But if the project is large, the uncertainty itself begins to create social effects. The biggest
problem is that it becomes very difficult to plan and prepare. For example, the housing developer doesn't know
whether the demand for housing will be large or small. The
school administrators don't know whether to add classrooms.
The city doesn't know whether to expand sewer facilities,
water hookups, etc. Entrepreneurs don't know whether to
expand their businesses. If facilities are built in anticipation of the project and it doesn't come or is delayed, the
people in the community have to pay for the facilities.
Once a project becomes certain, there often is insufficient
time to provide needed facilities before construction begins, with the result that the community suffers adverse
impacts during the construction period.

This uncertainty may be one of the most significant social effects of proposing a large-scale project. Some of
the effects of uncertainty occur whether or not the project
is ever implemented. Consequently, one aspect of modifying
direct project inputs is to reduce the degree of uncertainty
about the magnitude, schedule, and manner of their occurrence. This could be accomplished by:

-- Specifying early-on the type and magnitude of mitigation
   measures that affect direct project inputs. An important
   mitigation measure can be the establishment of a collaborative working relationship between the company or agency
   that will implement the action and the affected communities from the earliest stages of the planning or
   decision-making process. This collaborative effort can
   begin long before mitigation measures must be specified
   for an EIS, and the EIS can summarize agreements that
   have been developed through discussions and negotiations
   between the community and implementors over a period of
   months or years. Developing this collaborative relationship requires coordination and cooperation among all the
   important actors. The community may need technical
   assistance or support to ensure that it is in a position
   to participate as an equal in the negotiations. The
   implementor will need to be forthcoming with its plans,
   keeping residents thoroughly informed and resolving
   problems with the community in an open and visible manner, even if this becomes cumbersome or frustrating. The
   community will have to develop leadership, and a consensus behind the leadership, that permits it to be represented in an informed and effective manner.

-- Requiring that contingency plans be developed, with a
   fixed timetable for their implementation and clear delineation of responsibilites for costs incurred if the project does not proceed on its established schedule.

-- Specifying that a monitoring program be implemented in
   which project inputs are controlled or adjusted to

respond to emerging problems, or that other measures are taken to mitigate unanticipated problems.

2) **Sharp peaks and/or valleys in the entry/exit of people into the community.** Possible mitigation through modification of project inputs could include:
   -- Reducing the total number of workers utilized on the project.
   -- Reorganizing the construction schedule to minimize the peaks and valleys.
   -- Utilizing off-site construction techniques, in which components are fabricated elsewhere, trucked in, and assembled, thereby reducing the number of workers needed on-site.
   -- Providing convenient (and possibly subsidized) transportation to the job site, an approach especially appropriate if there is a regional center or larger town within about 100 miles of the site.
   -- Instituting local hiring policies to reduce the number of newcomers entering the community.
   -- Restricting mobile homes and subdivision development, which would limit the number of housing units that could be built in the community and therefore the influx of population.

3) **The distribution of employment or income among longtime residents and newcomers.** Possible mitigation through modification of project inputs could include:
   -- Developing training programs for local residents in advance of the project to provide them with the skills needed to obtain jobs, especially the higher-paying ones. Special effort could be made to increase the opportunities of community residents who are otherwise unlikely to be effective competitors.
   -- Developing on-the-job training programs to assist residents in upgrading their skills and to encourage local residents to qualify for permanent, well-paying positions.
   -- Establishing special hiring policies to encourage local hiring. For union jobs, this would require the cooperation of the union.
   -- Establishing a "buy local" policy, and assisting local businesses in acquiring the information and marketing skills that would enable them to compete for contracts to provide supplies and services.
   -- Adjusting the schedule to increase the work force more gradually in order to moderate excess demand, reduce local inflationary effects, and allow local businesses and workers time to respond.

4) **Additional resources provided by the project are insufficient to meet the additional demands.** Mitigative actions involving project inputs could include:
   -- Reducing the levels of demand by reducing the population increase (see (2) above).
   -- Providing or subsidizing the facilities/services for which there is excess demand. This may affect income

distribution and could be done by the implementor or other agency (e.g., the state).

-- Increasing or rescheduling the project's tax payments or payments made in lieu of taxes, either by changing local or state government tax schedules or by having the implementor make payments voluntarily.

-- Underwriting bonds for the provision of community services related to the project.

5) **Introduction of new organizations or regulations that reduce local autonomy and ability to respond.** Examples of mitigative measures affecting project inputs could include:

-- Having new organizations take "noninterventionist" or collaborative positions.

-- Providing technical assistance to local governments, businesses, and organziations on how to deal with the new regulations.

-- Establishing countervailing linkages with local organizations/government to offset the effects of new organizations or regulations.

Community Characteristics

The other effective way to alter project effects is to alter the characteristics and response of the community in a way which increases the ability of the community to respond, to reduce adverse effects, to maximize positive effects, and to adapt to change. Problems that could be addressed by modification of community characteristics include:

1) **Uncertainty.** Changes in the community that could affect this factor include:

-- Developing a clear set of community goals and objectives and consensus about actions that could be taken by the community to move toward those goals or to prevent movement from them.

-- Developing contingency plans for the community that identify alternatives, the response that would/could be made, and the likely consequences.

-- Developing overall planning and administrative capabilities in the community that shorten the lead time for responding.

-- Developing and pursuing strategies to diversify the economic base and reduce dependence on a single sector.

2) **Jurisdictional mismatch of funds and demand for services.** Changes in the community that could moderate this problem (and enhance the benefits from project revenues) include:

-- Establishing joint powers boards which enable the application of resources to the areas of greatest need. This may require state legislation as well as technical assistance and encouragement to local governmental bodies.

-- Modifying jurisdictional boundaries; for example, through annexation.

-- City-county consolidation.

3) **Inability of the local government to plan for or control development.** Mechanisms for moderating this type of problem include:

-- Establishing more formal procedures for dealing with growth issues, including the preparation of community development plans, zoning ordinances, and land use plans. This could be encouraged by federal and state agencies, by regulation, or by the provision of technical assistance.

-- Preparing contingency plans for all major affected services (schools, sewers, water, fire, police) to ensure the optimal use of existing or expected resources. This can also be encouraged by assistance from federal and state agencies or the implementor of the project.

-- Conducting community-sponsored workshops, public meetings, etc., to identify community concerns and positions, to establish plans for addressing them, and to develop a unified community position.

4) **Inability to respond to increased demand for services and facilities, including housing.** Mechanisms for response include:

-- Establishing policies that require developers to "pay as they go" in terms of utility hook-ups and that restrict additional residential growth to the desired areas through zoning and provision of utility hook-ups.

-- Developing strategies to increase the financing capability of the community and local businesses/developers through cooperation with local financial institutions, modifications of bonding limits, sale of bonds, etc.

-- Establishing outside linkages that can be used to obtain funds and technical assistance.

5) **Inequitable distribution of benefits and costs among residents.** This could be moderated by:

-- Designing training programs and support facilities that would ensure that groups otherwise not likely to obtain jobs or resources could do so. This could include such things as organizing and supporting transportation, child care, etc.

-- Developing programs to subsidize costs of development-inflated facilities and services for the needy (for example, rent supplements or construction of housing for the elderly or teachers), and ensuring that newcomers pay their way.

-- Establishing policies and procedures that limit the ability of the powerful to take advantage of opportunities to the disadvantage of others in the community.

-- Establishing zoning and tax laws that protect rural lands from excessive development pressure and increased taxes.

6) **Poor relationships between newcomers and longtime residents.** This could be modified through:

-- Encouraging civic and church groups to make active efforts to increase tolerance of the increased social diversity and to develop programs to make newcomers feel

welcome and more familiar (for example, Welcome Wagon, school open houses, etc.).
-- Encouraging project employees to take an active and responsible role in community life, making efforts to limit problems like traffic (by staggering shifts), and instituting hiring policies that discourage disruptive behavior by project-related workers.
-- Making efforts to decrease the turnover among newcomers.

Presentation of Mitigation/Enhancement Recommendations

The identification of mitigation alternatives is likely to involve both discussion and written presentation of results. Decision makers will expect the discussion of mitigation alternatives to address the issues of effectiveness and need -- which of the mitigation/enhancement measures that have been identified are likely to be most effective in reducing problems (at reasonable cost), and which effects really warrant mitigative efforts. Consequently, as part of this process, the analytic framework utilized to identify the mitigation/enhancement measures should also be used to work through a preliminary evaluation of their effectiveness. It would probably be useful to (1) prioritize the options first in terms of types of problems to be mitigated or areas to enhance and then in terms of the recommended approach and (2) identify who is responsible for effecting the mitigative actions.

Evaluation of Mitigated Alternatives

In some assessments, mitigation measures will be formally incorporated as part of the description of the proposed action, and the effects of the mitigated alternatives will be assessed as the basis for selecting the preferred alternative. If this is the case, the appropriate modifications should be made to the direct project inputs (and the community characteristics, if necessary), and the procedures described in Chapter 10 should be worked through for these modifications. The importance and meaning of the remaining social effects must be determined. As described in Chapter 10, it is recommended that the forecasts and interpretations be field-checked, if possible, and reviewed with other team members.

11.3 Design of Monitoring Programs

The Purpose of Monitoring Programs

It is increasingly common for projects with the potential to cause adverse effects to be monitored throughout the implementation period by one or more of the involved entities to ensure that unexpected adverse effects do not occur and that the expected benefits result. Federal agencies are generally directly involved only in monitoring programs for which they have implementation authority, or perhaps for those in which they have long-term policy interests.

State agencies and companies are more likely to have direct
involvement in the monitoring effort. The increased emphasis on
monitoring as an appropriate follow-on to impact assessment has
increased the value of the information acquired throughout the assessment process. This makes it increasingly likely that those
responsible for social assessment will be asked to participate in or
advise on the design of monitoring programs. However, as with the
formulation of alternatives discussed in Chapter 7, this step will
not necessarily be included in every assessment.

There are numerous factors, often outside the control of any of
the actors involved, that can alter a project's actual effects on a
community -- for example, the number and timing of workers can
change due to strikes, weather conditions, capital availability,
design or supply problems, or market factors. In addition, because
of the complex interactions that occur between the project inputs
and community characteristics, the project's effects (and the mitigation programs) are often not exactly what were anticipated. Since
these problems are frequently combined with unanticipated changes in
the baseline conditions (especially in the small towns with relatively undifferentiated economies), the level of uncertainty is such
that all actors -- federal agencies, implementors, local communities, and state governments -- have an interest in monitoring actual
outcomes and providing mechanisms for intervention to respond to
unexpected problems.

The basic objectives in designing monitoring programs is to establish agreement about how to identify and measure problems that
may emerge and how to allocate responsibility for responding to
them. The design of monitoring programs must therefore address the
following:

1) What variables should be monitored? How often?
2) How can the appropriate information be collected, compiled,
   or generated?
3) Who is responsible for providing what information?
4) Who is responsible for analyzing the information?
5) How is responsibility for intervention determined?
6) What sanctions are to be imposed if intervention does not
   occur or is ineffective?

In most cases, the principal negotiations take place between the
community and the implementor, although other federal and state
agencies may have roles as regulators, arbitrators, and facilitators.

The following example illustrates how this might work. An implementor and a community were badly divided over two issues: compensation to the town for road damage caused by heavy project trucks
and the need for additional housing. In the case of road damage,
the implementor and the community could not agree how much road
damage was likely to be caused by trucks related to the project and
how much would be due to timber trucks hauling logs over the same
roads. In designing the monitoring program, they agreed that during
the construction period an individual would be posted at a key
intersection to keep a tally of timber trucks and project trucks.
Using a mutually acceptable formula, the implementor agreed to then
reimburse the town based on the actual count. The implementor also

agreed to pay for the cost of keeping the tally. (This brings up an important limitation on monitoring -- sometimes the costs of monitoring are greater than simply agreeing to someone else's estimates.) In the case of housing, the implementator agreed to pay for a housing census to be conducted at the beginning of construction and at periodic intervals thereafter. Based on an established formula, the implementator would provide alternative forms of housing (e.g., camper hookups, trailer parks) or worker transportation from surrounding communities, if necessary.

Obviously, it must be possible to make the responses which have been agreed upon within the time frame available. For example, a housing census would have to be able to predict housing problems far enough in advance that temporary housing or transportation could be provided by the time it was needed.

While there are limitations to monitoring in areas undergoing large changes, such as the major energy-impacted areas of the West, periodic monitoring may be an alternative to conducting expensive studies of project effects that could more reliably be measured as they are happening.

Guidelines for Designing Monitoring Programs

There are several guidelines that should be observed in the design of monitoring programs. These include the following:

1) **Objectives and issues must be clearly defined.** Monitoring programs should only be developed for areas of significant need or likely impact, as documented by the assessment. They should not be used as "research for research's sake," nor should they be used when there is a simpler, more direct solution upon which people can agree.

2) **Measurements must match objectives.** A major problem in developing monitoring programs is getting agreement on what measures accurately portray the effect being measured. The things which can be measured are usually very specific and concrete, while the social effects that are occurring are often relatively intangible. How do you measure a loss of the sense of knowing and being known by others in the community? Care must be taken to ensure that the thing being measured in fact measures the characteristic or effect people are concerned about. Does, for example, a "housing shortage" mean a very low vacancy rate, which is comparatively easy to measure, or does it include numerous other issues such as cost of housing, living in housing less satisfactory than previous housing, changes in the types of housing (being forced to live in multiple-unit housing when one would prefer a single family residence) and so on. If the other factors matter, then the measures must take them into account.

3) **Availability of data.** The problems of creating a monitoring program that really measures what it is supposed to measure are created largely by the desire to use existing data. It is usually expensive to generate primary data, so

there is a tendency to use an indicator that is available, even if it doesn't really solve the problem. However, if the available data can serve as an adequate proxy, they should be used to reduce the costs and time delays often associated with primary data collection.

4) **Timeliness of data.** Data which could be used for monitoring are often generated and compiled by existing agencies. A potential problem may be that the data are not available in a timely enough fashion to be useful for monitoring purposes. If, for example, population size is to be monitored, it cannot be based on Regional Economic Information Service Data (REIS), which has a time lag of eighteen to twenty-four months, too great to be useful in measuring what is actually happening in the community. In this case, a method of population estimation that could be done rather quickly and inexpensively would need to be used. Before committing to the use of any existing data source, it is important that its availability and timeliness be checked. Much of the pertinent published data for measuring social effects have at least a two-year lag.

5) **Reporting frequency.** Even if primary sources of information -- such as a housing survey -- are used, they must be repeated at appropriate intervals to be useful. If it takes six months to respond to housing problems, then the problems must be identified early enough to permit effective response. If the time between monitoring is too long, the effects may be discovered only after they are serious and can no longer be prevented.

6) **Specifying authority for implementation.** A monitoring effort is much more effective if there is clear agreement about what is to be done if problems are discovered. To accomplish this requires not only agreement among the parties involved, but also some institutional analysis to ensure that the program is implementable. An area that should be clearly defined in advance is who is responsible for interpreting the monitoring data and who has the authority to trigger action.

7) **Community "ownership."** The monitoring program need not be established by imposition; it is usually more effective if it results from negotiations between the stakeholders so that several parties or organizations have the responsibility, or a sense of ownership, for the program.

In most cases, federal agencies do not have the power to impose a monitoring program, but can accomplish the same effect by encouraging negotiations between the stakeholders.

11.4 Participation in Plan Selection

The role of the social assessor during plan selection varies considerably based on the decision-making process and the relationship the assessor has built with the assessment team leader and/or decision maker. At a minimum, once mitigation plans have been

finalized for each plan, the assessor will develop a final statement
of probable social effects for each. Preferably the assessor will
have the opportunity to participate in the trade-off discussions or
other kinds of decision-making meetings in which social information
may be important.

During plan selection, the basic tasks include the following:

1) In conjunction with the public involvement staff, identify
   the reactions of the various stakeholder groups to the mitigation alternatives. (This task may have been completed as
   part of the work discussed in Section 11.2.)

2) Assist in ensuring that a negotiation process takes place
   that leads to a mitigation plan which is acceptable to the
   federal agencies, implementor, communities, and state
   governments involved.

3) Review the institutional arrangements for the final mitiga-
   tion/enhancement plans to make sure they are feasible.

4) Present the final statement of social effects for each alternative, based on the final mitigation plans (developed in
   Section 11.2), in which the anticipated social effects are
   described and evaluated and the reactions of stakeholder
   groups to mitigated alternatives are summarized.

5) Attend trade-off or other decision-making meetings to explain the social effects projections or to portray the concerns of the stakeholder groups.

Determine Stakeholder Reactions

Social effects are caused by perceptions as well as by actual
events. For this reason, it is important to know how the stakeholder groups evaluate the proposed mitigation/enhancement measures and
monitoring programs. The acceptability of the plans is an important
component of their social effectiveness. In determining acceptability, you are often in a position to serve as a conveyor of information because of your previous contact with community residents and
stakeholder groups. In many cases, this task will involve not just
information concerning social mitigation, but that concerning mitigation of effects on the natural environment as well.

Conveying this information and identifying the positions of the
stakeholder groups is a role likely to be shared with public involvement staff. Consultation between the various team members is
often necessary to ensure that there is not an unnecessary duplication of effort and that the efforts complement and reinforce one
another.

Participate in Establishing a Process of Negotiation, if Appropriate and Possible

One of the things that may not be adequately covered in EIS procedures is specification of the process by which final commitments
are made on mitigation. It appears that a process of negotiation
that includes the affected communities and companies is more

effective than mitigation imposed solely by an outside agency. If
mitigation commitments are determined without the participation of
the affected communities and companies, residents' feelings of losing control over decisions affecting their future can be aggravated,
and company officials may take the role of uncooperative outsiders.
Participation in this process encourages a better understanding of
the possible effects and the mechanisms by which they are caused,
thus allowing more effective response and the reduction of adverse
consequences.

It is often not entirely clear whose responsibility it is to
establish such a negotiation process, although it is evident that it
cannot be initiated without the approval and support of the agency
responsible for making the decision to allow or deny the proposed
action. The agency personnel most likely to be concerned about the
negotiation process are the decision makers, the social assessors,
and the public involvement staff, both because they have some sense
of responsibility for such issues and, in the case of the social
assessor and public involvement staff, because they are in regular
contact with the community and (hopefully) have professional training which can be helpful in establishing or facilitating such a process.

One responsibility that is shared by the social assessor and the
public involvement staff is to identify the need for such a process
and communicate that need to the decision maker. Neither the assessor nor the public involvement staff can initiate such a process
without the decision maker's approval. Once the decision has been
made to establish such a process, the assessor and the public involvement staff can work together to identify alternative approaches
and to recommend a course of action.

Quite obviously, establishing such a negotiation process requires the cooperation of all the important actors. If the relationship among them is antagonistic, some party may be unwilling to
participate. To the extent that the agency conducting the assessment is in a decision-making or regulatory position (i.e., has the
power to grant or deny a permit), it is in a position to apply its
leverage to encourage such cooperation.

Review Institutional Arrangements

Typically, mitigation plans will involve the cooperation of
several community institutions or governmental entities. Cooperation may be needed for things like changes in tax rates, establishment of joint boards, agreement to operate a facility, and so on.
This is true to some extent with environmental mitigation, but it is
particularly true for social mitigation, where efforts are needed
from a number of different institutions and actors in order to be
effective.

However, the responsibility within the agency for exploring the
institutional feasibility and commitment to mitigation programs is
not always clear. Although there is no specific authority for the
social assessor to be the person who does an institutional analysis,
you are likely to be the person in the organization with the most
information about the institutions and the skills to perform the

analysis. Whether or not you take on this responsibility should be decided in consultation with the assessment team leader or decision maker.

Prepare Final Summary of Effects

Once final mitigation plans have been developed and agreed upon, you are in a position to assess the probable social effects of each mitigated alternative, as described in Section 11.2. Although a number of variables and complex interactions must be considered, it is important that effects be summarized for easy review, with back-up materials available as needed.

One caution is to avoid stating social data in quantitative terms just because it makes them easier to summarize. Much social information is inherently qualitative and is distorted when stated solely in quantitative terms. It is better to develop a short verbal statement with reference to back-up material for this type of information than to distort it by inappropriate quantification. However, where quantification is possible and meaningful, it can be particularly effective. The purpose of the summary -- to accurately and succinctly present the conclusions of the assessment -- should serve as the principal guide to presentation format.

Although the community residents and other interested parties have probably seen preliminary estimates of effects, it is only after final mitigation plans have been determined and a final appraisal of effects has been made that they will have a chance to see a final assessment of probable social effects. As a result, a final review of stakeholder reactions is needed to determine what effects the proposed mitigation plans have on acceptability. Coordination among team members is particularly important at this step. The information obtained about the acceptability of the various mitigated alternatives to various stakeholder groups should be included in the summary, with back-up materials explaining why the stakeholder groups take the positions they do.

Participate in Trade-off Meetings

Participation in trade-off meetings or other discussions regarding plan selection is often an effective means to insure that social data is understood and that the possible reactions of the stakeholder groups are taken into account. In order to be a welcome participant at such meetings, you must remember that while it is appropriate to make clear the significance of the social effects, it is not your role to judge the relative importance of social effects in relationship to economic or environmental effects. That responsibility remains with the decision maker.

11.5 References

There are relatively few published documents that specifically address the issues of mitigation and enhancement. The literature on needs assessment may be helpful to those involved in designing monitoring and mitigation programs. These references are provided at the end of Chapter 8.

Section III:
Methods and Techniques

12. Organizing and Conducting a Field Trip

12.1 Introduction

This chapter provides guidance on planning and conducting field work. Although some of the suggestions included in this chapter may appear obvious, a review of the basic steps involved in planning a field trip and working in the field can be useful even for those with substantial field experience.

12.2 Define the Purpose of the Field Work

One of the most important aspects of preparing for field trips is to clearly define why the trip is being conducted and what it is to accomplish. Field trips can serve a wide variety of functions, from familiarizing yourself with the general characteristics and appearance of an area to providing specific information.

Several factors influence the purpose of a field trip. These include the following:

1) **The objective of the overall assessment effort.** This influences the type of information required for the social assessor to meet the needs of the decision maker.

2) **The role of this field trip within the social assessment process.** During the scoping phase of an assessment effort, the purpose of a field trip is usually to gather general information about the size, location, and appearance of study area communities and to identify major stakeholder groups, social groups, and community issues. During later phases, the purpose is likely to be to gather more specific information or to verify data or analyses.

3) **The information requirements of this particular social assessment.** Although it is useful to field check conclusions reached from secondary data, the field trip should focus on obtaining information about community characteristics that could be important to the assessment. It is easy to become sidetracked in the field, and although curiousity about how the communities work and what is happening in them

227

can be beneficial, it needs to be controlled in order to maintain focus on the pertinent aspects of the community.

4) **The availability of information from other sources, including other team members.** A field trip should not be used to collect information that is already available from secondary sources or from other team members. Field time is valuable and should be used to acquire information not otherwise available.

5) **Other team members' needs for information.** Social assessment requires familiarity with the study area communities. Since gathering much of the information required by the social assessment involves observing how the community functions and talking with community residents, you are likely to need first-hand exposure to the communities. In some cases, you can gather field information for other team members who have less need for this exposure to the community.

In order to define the specific purposes of a field trip, other available materials need to be collected and reviewed. These are described below.

12.3 Review Available Materials

There are a number of documents or materials -- "secondary sources," as they are called -- that can profitably be reviewed before visiting the study area. Reviewing these materials prior to the field trip allows you to determine what information is already available (and therefore does not need to be collected in the field) and to become better informed about the area. This advance preparation permits collection of better information by identifying important issues or questions that should be covered in the field work. It also helps build credibility for the assessment effort and enhances your ability to initiate interviews in the study area communities. As the work proceeds in the community, new sources of information will be found. It should be kept in mind that utilization of secondary sources is a continuing activity, not simply advance work. Specific guidance on data analysis and the use of secondary sources is provided in chapters 13 and 14.

Particularly in areas where previous large-scale development has been proposed, a great number of lengthy reports have often been prepared. An incredible amount of time can be consumed if those reports are read in detail instead of scanned for information relevant to social concerns. Consequently, a useful skill to develop is the ability to scan documents and abstract the pertinent information without getting bogged down in extraneous details.

As has been indicated, the range of possible secondary sources is wide and varies from site to site. Among the most useful types of secondary sources are:

1) **County comprehensive plans.** Many counties have prepared comprehensive plans that provide valuable background information about the area, the institutional structure, and the expectations and preparations that have been made for the

future. These plans are generally available in the local library or from the area planning board.

2) **Census data.** Data from recent U.S. censuses can provide a good indication of the type of change that has occurred in the area over the last several decades. It is useful to obtain any special census data that have been compiled for communities or counties in the study area. These data are generally available in local libraries or at libraries serving as federal depositories.

3) **Research reports and community case studies.** If previous research has been conducted in the area, it is likely that research reports and articles have been prepared. These can be a very valuable source of data and theory on social change.

4) **Environmental impact statements/socioeconomic studies.** In many cases, other state or federal agencies or private companies have prepared environmental impact statements or other socioeconomic studies as part of their proposed activities in the same geographic area. These often provide background information about the area.

5) **Local histories.** Local authors frequently have written and published histories of the area. These documents can be helpful, but it is important to remember that they have often been written by people with a particular point to make (such as demonstrating the importance of their own family in local history) or by people who need to maintain peace with their neighbors. Care in their use must be taken because some of the more controversial community events or issues may be distorted or downplayed.

6) **Maps.** Accurate maps of the towns and counties included in the potential study area should be examined and kept handy for reference.

7) **Lists of public officials.** Developing a list of local elected and appointed officials, major agency directors, and their principal functions can prevent unnecessary social errors and enhance understanding of the institutional structure of the area. Usually preliminary lists can be compiled from materials available from state agencies, the local chamber of commerce, or city or county administrative offices. Back issues of these documents can also be useful.

8) **Local newspapers.** Scanning local newspapers and/or conducting content analyses is one good way to identify social groups, key stakeholder groups, major controversies, and how the community deals with issues. Long-standing or unusual levels of conflict between groups or jurisdictions, for example, will usually show up in some form in the local newspaper. Normally it is useful to review at least two or three weeks worth of recent newspapers and the most recent annual edition of the newspaper before beginning field work. Local newspapers are usually available at local libraries or at the newspaper office itself. Newspapers, especially the editorials, can often provide additional information and a different perspective on the important issues/events identified in local histories.

Given the wide array of potential secondary sources, the first step in this task is to gather the available materials, review them, and prepare a bibliography, noting additional studies or reports that should be obtained for review. By checking with the person responsible for report format to make sure that the information included in your bibliographic references and lists of personal communications is complete and properly arranged, you can save considerable inconvenience later on.

Once agreements have been made with other team members and available secondary sources have been reviewed, the field trip can be planned and scheduled. In some cases, considerable coordination with other team members will be required, so scheduling of the trip should be done well in advance.

12.4 Plan the Field Trip

The major steps that need to be taken to prepare for a field trip include:

1) Review the area maps and familiarize yourself with the geography of the proposed study area, noting particularly transportation links, distances between towns, and the location of county seats and regional governmental offices, if pertinent.

2) Make sure you understand how the agencies that either provide or regulate the important services in the area are organized, where the offices with jurisdiction in the study area are located, and where the jurisdictional boundaries are located.

3) Think through the assessment process. Identify for yourself the important attributes of the proposed types of alternatives, given the study area characteristics. Based on the review of secondary sources, note characteristics of the study area as well as data gaps and questions that seem important and require additional information or field-checking. (See chapters 6 and 8 for additional discussion of this process.)

4) Review the list of public officials and identify those who should be notified about the study and those who should be interviewed.

5) Determine who else from the assessment team will be in the field and whether a joint trip should be planned. Make sure coordination with other team members is working, set a schedule for your trip, and make travel arrangements. The duration of the trip will depend on the size of the study area and the number of communities that need to be visited. Remember that a staggering amount of information can be obtained each day on a well-organized field trip and that to be useful, this information must be recorded and analyzed. Several shorter trips, separated by office time to document the field work and prepare for the next step, are preferable to fewer long ones.

6) Determine the appropriate sampling and surveying methods for the field work (see Chapter 13). If informal interviews are to be used, prepare a set of interview guides and become sufficiently familiar with them so that interviews can be conducted fluently in a conversational, rather than "questionnaire," format. Prepare bibliographic forms for referencing personal communications.

7) Check with people you know to see if they have any good contacts in the study area communities. Although they must be used with caution, mutual acquaintances can help to break the ice in unfamiliar communities and can often provide access to people who would otherwise be difficult to interview.

8) Notify local officials of your visit and set up initial appointments. This can and should be done in advance. Notification of officials can be used as an opportunity to set up the initial appointments in a community (a good way to force yourself into those difficult first interviews). If you do this, make sure to allow ample time between interviews. Nothing is more frustrating than having an interview reach a critical point when you must leave to meet with someone else. If you really plan to conduct an interview, not just pay a courtesy call or pick up some data, allow at least an hour between interviews, preferably somewhat more.

9) Organize the materials you will take along. If available, a small cassette tape recorder can be very useful for recording field interviews and observations. Make sure you have sufficient forms and interviewer guides and clear instructions about the information you are to gather for others. Know and follow the administrative procedures regarding travel and travel expenses. (Make sure that you have sufficient money for the trip. Smaller restaurants and stores in rural areas often do not accept checks or credit cards.)

12.5 Notify Local Officials

The manner in which initial contacts in the local community are made influences the professional credibility of the assessment effort. It is important to be well informed before going into the field. It is also important to observe protocol by notifying appropriate local officials that researchers will be working in the community or study area. In a rural area in particular, outsiders are very visible. Promptly and clearly notifying local officials about the nature of the work underway can often avert suspicion and damaging rumors. Extending courtesy to local officials also helps you establish yourself as a professional who knows how to do his or her job. It also validates your function and reason to be in the community. In rural areas in particular, establishing this legitimacy can save considerable time and effort by creating an atmosphere that encourages people to come forward and volunteer information.

The persons who should usually be notified in advance about the field work include the following:

1) **County commissioners.** In western states, each county is governed by county commissioners or, in some areas, a board of supervisors. Typically this is one of the most powerful political entities in the area. Sensible protocol dictates that county commissioners be notified before beginning work in the area. Usually a phone call will suffice. If the community in which work is to be done lies solely within the electoral district of one commissioner, he or she would be the person to notify. If multiple districts are involved, the chairman of the county commission should be notified. If there is a county administrator, it is advisable to notify him or her in addition to the commissioners.

2) **City administrators.** City or town officials should also be notified. It is best to notify both an elected official and city staff.

3) **Agency directors.** Depending on the community, directors of state or federal agencies or local service agencies may need to be notified. Be sure to know and follow the protocol of your own organization regarding notification of officials in field offices of your presence and work.

4) **Law enforcement officials.** While not mandatory, it is often helpful to advise the local police chief or county sheriff when working in an area.

12.6 Prepare Interview Guides and Field Instruments

When the purpose of the field trip has been established and the available information reviewed, instruments or forms for obtaining and recording information in the field can be prepared. The purpose of these guides and forms is to organize the collection and analysis of the information. An incredible amount of information can be obtained in an intensive day of work in the field. Documentation of this information is important. Particularly in assessments that cover a number of different communities, a systematic method for organizing data collection and recording is critical.

Guidance on identifying the information needed about the existing environment in each community is provided in chapters 6 and 8. Chapter 13 discusses the selection of sampling procedures and survey methods as well as the preparation and use of interview guides and questionnaires. If the field work is to include the supervision or implementation of a survey (either the dropoff and pickup or face-to-face type), this task needs to be scheduled into both the field time and the time allotted for reviewing and analyzing the information.

12.7 Conduct the Field Work

Typically, most of the field work will consist of a series of interviews with local officials, influential citizens, and other knowledgeable community residents along with continual observation. It frequently starts with interviews of people holding key positions (a list of whom was prepared prior to the field trip) and leads to interviews with other people in the community who were mentioned in previous discussions as being influential or well informed. It is also possible to set up informal group meetings, such as coffee klatches or kitchen meetings (where a few neighbors get together) or interviews with high school students, to participate in formal workshops, or even to conduct mini-surveys (small random sample surveys).

It is often difficult to determine how to initiate the field work once you arrive in the community. Several specific things can be done to get started. These include the following:

1) **Drive through the community.** Upon arrival, it is often helpful to drive through the community until you develop a sense of geographic and visual familiarity. This will help make you feel more comfortable and "at home." Familiarity with the area can contribute greatly to your ability to appear well prepared and well informed about the area. Driving through a community will often provoke ideas or questions about how the community is organized and may suggest alternative methods for obtaining information or prompt you to think of other questions to ask or other groups or individuals to interview.

2) **Interview local officials.** The process of notifying local officials provides an opportunity to schedule interviews with these people and/or to solicit suggestions about who should be interviewed. (After all, it is the political lifeblood of an elected official to know who the influential people in the area are.) It is wise to schedule the first one or two days of interviews in advance of the field trip. This not only prevents wasted time trying to set up interviews in the field, it is also an effective way to force yourself into those first difficult interviews.

3) **Visit the local library.** A visit to the local library will usually be required to review newspapers and locate local histories, as suggested earlier. While there, it is useful to explain the assessment effort to the local librarian. Librarians often pride themselves on being helpful in locating source materials and, if he or she understands what the social assessor is trying to accomplish, can be an invaluable guide to the materials in the library. Not infrequently, the local librarian has been a part of the local community for a number of years and may be personally acquainted with much of the history of the area, even if it is not in written form. The library is also often a good place to go to write up interview notes.

4) **Visit public service agencies.** Local public agencies are accustomed to receiving inquiries from people outside the community and can be very helpful in providing or finding the needed information. Public service staff can often empathize with the problem of being a stranger in town and may therefore be good subjects for the first interviews in the community. People who are often particularly helpful include the director of the local chamber of commerce, the local agricultural extension agent, the mental health director, and the director of the social welfare department.

5) **Contact retired officials.** Some of the most valuable in-
   formants are often residents who formerly held public positions in the community; for example, retired judges, former
   newspaper editors, former county commissioners, and former
   city council representatives. The review of the local newspaper may turn up a few names of such individuals, and other
   suggestions will be made during interviews.

The reason for making specific suggestions about what to do when
first entering the community is that the first interviews are often
hard to initiate. Driving around the community and gaining a sense
of "knowing" it can heighten confidence and make the first contacts
easier. Having made firm commitments for specific interviews
beforehand also helps avoid delaying tactics. Feeling reluctant to
initiate interviewing is one of several problems that frequently
occur. Being prepared to recognize and deal with the following
problems can make field work more productive and less anxiety-
provoking.

1) **Talking too much or too little.** When people are nervous
   or anxious, they have a tendency to either talk to relieve
   their anxiety or to become very quiet. However, the essential art of interviewing is to be a good listener while
   simultaneously guiding the interview onto the topics that
   need to be covered. Being sensitive to the need to monitor
   your participation in the interview and being prepared to
   adjust your approach will make your interviewing much more
   effective.
2) **Supporting a particular position.** Good assessment requires objective data collection and objective analysis.
   This means that you must put aside your personal preferences
   to the extent possible and make every effort to give all
   points of view a fair hearing. The assessment process is
   inherently very political, and you may be encouraged (sometimes pressured) to take sides in your analysis or presentations. Once you are perceived as having abandoned your objective position, your professional credibility will be
   seriously jeopardized. Consequently, while in the field it
   is best to keep personal positions to yourself; they have no
   place in the discussions. Your assessment is to be based on
   the information you are trying to gather, not on your own
   views. Be careful to make clear that you will maintain your
   personal integrity in using and interpreting the information
   you receive.
3) **Making too many commitments.** There is a tendency early in
   a study to make commitments that can be difficult to meet;
   for example, to share copies of findings, to include particular information in reports, or to interview people again
   later in the study. Even if these commitments are made with
   the best of intentions, they often can't be kept. Changes
   in time frame and budgets within the agency may limit your
   ability to keep these commitments, or they may even redirect
   the entire thrust of the study. Your appraisal of what
   issues are significant may change as the study progresses,

making earlier commitments inappropriate. As much as possible, it is preferable to avoid making these types of commitments.

4) **Forgetting you are under observation.** In small, rural
communities, any outsider is under observation twenty-four
hours a day. No distinction is made between on-duty and
off-duty time. One needs to be very circumspect about con-
versations and behavior at all times while in the field.

12.8 Document the Field Work

Upon completion of the field work, the data obtained in the
field must be recorded and stored so that they will be easily
accessible in the future. Specific tasks that need to be carried
out include the following:

1) Record and file field notes, interview notes, and all other
data collected in the field.
2) List all follow-up letters and phone calls that need to be
made, such as thank-yous, requests for information, and responses to requests.
3) Write a trip report that covers all major activities and
events in the order they occurred. (Keep in mind issues of
confidentiality if the reports are to be shared with others.)
4) Prepare a list (including bibliographic information) of the
material that was obtained and personal contacts that were
made.

Once this documentation is completed, it is a good time to
analyze what has been done, what was most productive, and what
follow-up tasks are needed in order to determine what revisions need
to be made in the social assessment plan and perhaps to start planning the next field trip.

12.9 References

A number of pertinent references are included in chapters 8 and
13. It is important that you become knowledgeable enough about secondary data collection and analysis, interviewing, and critical sociological observation techniques that you feel prepared to conduct
your field work. Review of some of the materials referenced in
these two chapters may be helpful if you do not feel confident of
your skills in these areas.

13. Sampling, Surveying, Interviewing, Questionnaire Design, and Data Analysis

13.1 Introduction

Much of the information for a social assessment will usually be obtained by talking to people in the community. Community leaders, representatives of stakeholder groups, staff of service-providing agencies, and residents of the community all have information and perceptions that are important to the assessment. The purpose of this chapter is to provide guidance on how to determine which people to interview (sampling), what method to use to collect the information (survey approach), how to prepare for and conduct effective interviews (interviewing), and how to analyze and use the information (data analysis, report preparation). Since most of these areas are well documented in the social science literature, the focus of this chapter is on highlighting the important considerations and identifying pertinent references for each topic. Because specific terminology has been developed to describe sampling and questionnaire design that may not be familiar to all users, a glossary of commonly used terms is provided in Figure 13-1.

It should always be kept in mind that the purpose of the assessment is to provide usable, valid information at an appropriate level of detail. The purpose of the assessment must be understood before decisions regarding sampling, surveying, and interviewing can be made.

13.2 Define the Objectives of the Primary Data Collection Effort

Before the technical issues of sampling, survey method, interviewing techniques, and questionnaire design can be addressed effectively, the purpose of the data collection effort must be defined and the type of information being sought must be identified. This requires carrying out a process similar to that described in Chapter 12 for defining the purpose of the field work, although at a somewhat greater level of specificity. Survey and other primary data collection is an activity that must be planned and designed. Four basic questions influence all sampling and survey decisions:

Figure 13-1

Glossary

Call-back. An attempt to contact a potential respondent who was not contacted on earlier tries. This includes returning to the residence or calling until the respondent is contacted or dropped from the sample.

Item Nonresponse Rate. The number of times a particular question in a survey was not answered by a respondent divided by the number of completed questionnaires containing the questions.

Nonprobability Sampling. Sampling techniques in which the probability of a unit or person being selected is unknown. Generally refers to sampling techniques that are not guided by probability sampling.

Population. All persons or units with attributes that meet the critieria specified by the researcher.

Primary Data. Data that is compiled or collected specifically for the project.

Probability Sampling. Sampling techniques in which the probability of each person or unit being selected is known before the sample is drawn.

Response Rate. The number of completed interviews divided by the sample size. This can be refined somewhat by subtracting the number of respondents who could not be contacted from the denominator. Refusals should be kept in the denominator, however.

Sample. A proportion, or subset, of the population of interest that is selected to be interviewed or sent questionnaires.

Sampling Frame. The test, schedule, or definition of the population from which the sample is drawn.

Sample Size. The total number of persons or units to be interviewed or sent questionnaires.

Snowball Sampling. A sampling technique in which an initial set of respondents are asked to name others who should be interviewed, those named are interviewed and asked to name others and so on.

Structured Questionnaire. A questionnaire in which all the questions are preset before the interview and are asked exactly the same way in each interview.

Unit of Analysis. The level of types (such as households, individuals, etc.) in terms of which the sample is drawn and data are analyzed and discussed.

1) What information is needed?
2) Who has the information?
3) How can the information best be obtained?
4) How should it be analyzed to provide the information in the most useful format?

Before proceeding with design of the data collection, it is essential that the first two questions be answered carefully (based on the information provided in chapters 6 through 12) since specification of the information requirements and sources defines the objective of the sampling and the interviews/surveys. It also determines many of the technical decisions. Without a clear delineation and understanding of the information requirements and who it is who can provide such information, it is not possible to design an appropriate sampling or survey procedure or to develop useful interview guides or questionnaires.

The procedures described in chapters 6 through 11 were designed to help you determine what information you need and to suggest secondary materials that could provide some of it. But secondary materials are rarely sufficient. In most cases, adequate information about resources, social organization, and attitudes/perceptions will not be available from secondary sources. In addition, you may be conducting interviews or surveys in other communities in order to obtain information about project inputs or the social effects of similar projects that can provide a firmer basis for your analysis and forecasts.

Based on your analysis of information needs and potential sources of information, two principal questions must be answered before proceeding with the design of the primary data collection effort. First, you must determine whether the information you are seeking is best obtained through informal or semistructured interviews or whether it is best obtained from the administration of formal, structured questionnaires. The preferred methods should be determined by the functions they are to serve. Second, you must determine whether your organization or the practicalities of the assessment effort preclude particular data gathering methods.

Although standardized surveys and large samples have come to dominate much of social science investigation, unstructured or semistructured survey methods have a long history in the social sciences and are very legitimate techniques. Unstructured or semistructured interviews are likely to be superior to standardized questionnaires for obtaining much of the information needed in social assessment. Standardized questionnaires are not sufficiently flexible to be good for exploratory data gathering or for addressing the complexity of many aspects of community response and social organization. Standardized questionnaires are specifically tailored, however, for gathering data to describe population characteristics and to quantify the distribution of attributes within a given population. In many cases, the ideal solution would be to utilize both unstructured/semistructured interviews and standardized questionnaires, each applied to the type of information for which it was most effective. Practical constraints, however, frequently limit the options available for primary data collection.

Federal agencies are constrained by Office of Management and Budget (OMB) restrictions on surveys. According to OMB Circular A-40, a questionnaire in which ten or more persons are asked identical questions cannot be used by representatives of a federal agency without prior clearance by the OMB. In the past, obtaining such clearance has been a laborious and time-consuming process. The restriction is limited to the application of identical questions, however, and does not apply to the use of unstructured or semistructured interviews based on "topical guides" -- outlines of topics to be covered or general questions to be answered that do not specify wording. Time, budget, or organizational policies may impose other constraints on the alternatives you have for collecting primary data. In designing your approach, therefore, your task is to determine the best methods; minimize organizational obstacles to their implementation; and apply those that, within organizational constraints, best serve the data collection functions of your particular assessment.

13.3 Sampling

The process used to determine who should be interviewed is called "sampling." Sampling procedures can be divided into two main types: (1) probability sampling and (2) nonprobability sampling. As with the selection of unstructured/semistructured interviews versus structured questionnaires, the selection of sampling procedures depends upon the purpose of the surveys, what type of information is being sought, and who the best source of that information is.

Probability Sampling

Probability sampling procedures are used when it is important to make inferences from the sample to the population. Probability sampling is necessary when the purpose is to determine (or estimate) the characteristics of the population or to determine the effects of particular characteristics, programs, or situations (through statistical hypothesis testing). Probability sampling procedures are sometimes called "scientific" procedures because they are designed to address the issues of representativeness. Because probability sampling procedures are systematic, they provide a basis for replicating the survey to verify results or to compare one sample or population with another.

The main purposes of probability sampling in social assessment are the following:

1) To compare the characteristics and responses of different groups
2) To identify characteristics that are associated with differences in response
3) To estimate characteristics of the total population (including the distribution of characteristics within the population)

4) To provide a basis for comparing the characteristics of groups or the total population at two or more different time periods

In general, one can make stronger statements about the implications of data obtained from probability samples than of data obtained from nonprobability samples. A great deal of work has been devoted to the development and analysis of various sampling procedures, and there are a number of excellent books and articles that explain the theory, mechanics, and implications of various probabilistic sampling procedures. It is useful to understand and feel comfortable with the fundamentals of probability sampling, since this provides a good basis for most of the sampling problems that will be encountered in a typical assessment.

Unless you have a good deal of training in sampling and surveying, it is recommended that the assistance or advice of a specialist be sought if the purposes of the assessment indicate a need for a survey that will estimate total population characteristics. Large scale surveys are very expensive. The cost of preparing, conducting, and analyzing telephone and mail surveys can range from $15 to $25 per interview, while surveys utilizing face-to-face interviews can easily cost $50 to $150 per interview. There are well-established procedures for sample selection and data analysis and it is important that they be followed correctly if this approach is selected.

Probability Sampling Procedures

If it is necessary to gather information from a representative sample of the general population of the community or of particular groups in an area, a probability sample will need to be drawn. Several steps are involved in drawing a probability sample:

1) Define the population from which the sample is to be drawn
2) Determine the appropriate unit of analysis (e.g., individuals, households, organizations)
3) Establish a sampling frame (a listing of the population from which respondents can be drawn)
4) Select a sampling technique (e.g., simple random, stratified, cluster)
5) Determine the sample size
6) Draw the sample

Define the Population

The first thing that must be done is to identify the population of interest by specifying the criteria and boundaries that define the population. This is necessary for two reasons: (1) to clearly identify the population the sample represents (e.g., all adult residents of the county, members of the industrial association) and (2) to determine who qualifies for inclusion in the sample and who does not. The definition of the population must be consistent with the unit of analysis and sampling frame that are utilized. In some cases, the population is defined in terms of the sampling frame (for example, all residents of the county with a telephone). Obviously, it is important to make sure that the population is appropriate for the purposes of the assessment and that an accurate description of the population is prepared.

Determine the Appropriate Unit of Analysis

Selection of the appropriate unit of analysis requires consideration of the purpose of the information being gathered along with the cost and time required to develop a sample frame for this unit. The units of analysis most commonly used in assessment work are individuals (usually adults), households, and organizations. It is important to think through what you want to be able to say as a result of the survey or interview and then to determine the unit of analysis that would provide the information needed for that purpose. In some cases information may be needed for two different units of analysis -- individual adults and households, for example. In these cases, it is especially important to be clear about the sampling technique (for example, sampling households and then sampling from the adults in the households, as opposed to sampling adults from a list of all qualified adults) and to make sure that the questions are asked and analyzed in a consistent manner. For example, if the household is the unit of sampling and analysis, but information is gathered about individuals within the household, this information must somehow be aggregated to the household level in order to be analyzed. Appropriate qualifications need to be applied when utilizing an individual's attitudes in a survey where the sampling and analytic unit is the household or organization.

Establish a Sampling Frame

In order to draw a sample, one must establish a sampling frame which lists or delineates the entire population the sample is to represent. Developing a good sampling frame is often one of the most difficult tasks of the sampling process. A sample can only be as representative and reliable as the sampling frame from which it is drawn. Some common sampling frames include the following:

1) Published telephone directories
2) City directories
3) Voter registration lists
4) Platted maps or tax rolls identifying properties
5) Directories of organizations
6) Lists of public utility customers
7) Aerial photographs
8) Concise definitions of the population (i.e., all elected officials)

Every sampling frame should be evaluated in terms of its correspondence with the defined boundaries of the population, its

comprehensiveness, and its currency. Sudman (1976) provides an excellent discussion that is highly recommended for those developing
or using sampling frames. The complete reference is provided in
Section 13.7.

Select a Sampling Technique

Three sampling techniques are commonly used to draw a probability sample from a sampling frame. Simple random sampling involves
selecting each respondent at random from the entire population.
Cluster sampling involves a two-step process. In the first step,
clusters (such as census blocks) are selected at random from the
population. Next, respondents are randomly selected from within the
clusters. This technique is used frequently in face-to-face surveys, for which costs can be substantially reduced by clustering
respondents geographically. Stratified sampling involves organizing
the sampling frame to group the population with characteristics of
particular importance or interest into different "strata." Each
stratum is then sampled separately. This technique is often used to
ensure that a sufficient number of respondents with a particular
characteristic, such as race, sex, or occupation, are included in
the sample to support the desired analysis. If knowledge of the
characteristics of a small group is particularly important, this
technique can be modified to sample each of the "strata" as if it
were a separate population.

Once the sampling technique has been decided upon, the size of
the sample that needs to be drawn can be calculated. Different
sampling techniques will generally require different sample sizes.

There are a variety of other, more specialized probability
sampling procedures that can be used. In general, these more elaborate procedures are used to lower costs and to improve the efficiency of the survey effort. The steps for the other sampling
procedures are similar to those described above.

Several good references on sampling techniques and the analysis
of data obtained from samples drawn using different techniques are
identified in Section 13.7.

Determine the Sample Size and Sampling Fraction

The appropriate sample size is determined by the sampling technique (simple random, stratified) in conjuction with considerations
of the purpose of the interview/survey, the characteristics of the
population (size, variability), and the time and resources available
for the work. There is no one "correct" sample size; it is a com-
promise among all these important factors.

There are formulas which can be used to estimate sample size.
Sudman (1976), referenced in Section 13.7, provides a clear and concise discussion of the methods used to determine sample size. It
should be kept firmly in mind that the process of sampling should
serve the purposes of the assessment, not the other way around. It
is important to be familiar enough with the procedures to select the

one that is most efficient and effective for the assessment and to utilize the data correctly and effectively once it has been gathered.

Draw the Sample

After the sampling frame, the sampling technique, and the sample size have been determined, drawing the sample is generally a straightforward task, but one that may be time consuming. As with other aspects of the assessment process, it is recommended that the process be thought out in advance and that the procedures be carefully organized and documented. Throughout the process, it is important to remember that sampling is a tool to be used to ensure that the appropriate information will be collected and is not an end in itself.

Nonprobability Sampling

Nonprobability sampling differs from probability sampling in both purpose and technique. Nonprobability sampling is appropriate when precise representation or estimation of the characteristics of the total population is not necessary, when the data will be used to inform the investigator rather than to conduct statistical tests of hypotheses, or when the effort is exploratory. Nonprobability sampling is particularly appropriate when the purpose of the investigation is to obtain specific information that is known by only some members of the community. Nonprobability sampling techniques range from those that are highly unstructured (use of available respondents, for example) to those with a substantial degree of structure (theoretical sampling, "snowball" techniques). The technique chosen depends to a great extent upon the type of information being sought and the level of effort that can be expended.

Many of the needs of social assessment are often best met by using "theoretical" sampling, a form of nonprobability sampling. It is therefore recommended that this technique be understood and utilized when appropriate.

Theoretical Sampling

Theoretical sampling is a procedure that can be utilized to insure that the full range of opinions or issues are identified and that information is obtained about the pertinent characteristics of the area. Effective use of theoretical sampling depends upon clear formulation of the objectives of the assessment and upon continual review and analysis of information as it is being obtained. With this approach, people are included in the sample because of who they are and the information they can provide. The purpose of this approach is to attain a complete understanding of the topic and the range of perspectives, not to make a statement about the statistical representativeness of characteristics or opinions. Theoretical sampling is an open-ended process -- investigation and sampling continue until no additional information is needed or until no new information is being gained from additional interviews. Consequently, in theoretical sampling, the sample is not established in its entirety at the beginning of the process, as in most sampling procedures, but on a continuing basis as the result of previous data gathering and analysis.

Theoretical sampling is an analytic process. It requires sufficient understanding of the social organization model or other analytic or theoretical framework to determine what information is pertinent to the assessment and what characteristics could cause particular people or groups in the communities to differ in terms of opinion, perspective, or knowledgeability about the topics of interest. This understanding is used to select the initial sample of persons to be interviewed. Unstructured or semistructured interviews with this initial sample are used to identify additional interviewees and to determine additional questions to pursue. The process seeks to ensure that persons with the maximum divergence of opinion and/or positions are included in the sample and that the important issues or information are identified and pursued.

Theoretical sampling can be an extremely useful technique in social assessment. Those unfamiliar with its application are encouraged to read the book by Glaser and Strauss (1967).

Sampling Procedures to Identify Community Leadership Characteristics

The principal information needs for social assessment often include the identification and description of the community leadership and the delineation of community history, social organization processes, and service provision. This information can often be gathered most effectively by identifying those in the community who are most knowledgeable about these topics and conducting in-depth interviews with them, rather than by interviewing a random sample of residents. Respondents capable of providing this type of information are community leaders and are most frequently identified and selected by one of two approaches.

The first, called the positional approach, involves preparation of a list of persons who are holding or have held formal leadership positions (or positions that make them likely to be knowledgeable about the type of information being sought). If the questions being addressed involved leadership, the list would include persons in elected or appointed positions of leadership such as the mayor; city council representatives; county commissioners; state government officials; the city attorney; the school superintendent; law enforcement administrators; directors of planning agencies; and officers in voluntary associations such as unions, fraternal lodges, church organizations, or action groups.

Once the list has been prepared, a procedure must be determined for selecting the interview sample from those on the list. A number of alternatives can be used:

1) Everyone on the list can be interviewed
2) One or a number of persons can be selected at random from each leadership category
3) The categories can be weighted by drawing more respondents from some categories than from others
4) Respondents can be drawn randomly from the entire list
5) Respondents can be selected from the entire list based on some criterion to ensure representation of the divergent perspectives, attitudes, or positions present among members of the list

The most appropriate procedure will vary according to the particular purpose of the data collection effort and the information requirements.

A criticism of the positional approach is that it can miss excellent sources by excluding those not in formal positions. The reputational approach is designed to alleviate this problem. The reputational approach is similar to the positional approach, but it is based on the development of a list of persons with a reputation for knowledgeability or influence in the area being investigated.

With this approach, the list is compiled by contacting a person in the community who is known to be knowledgeable or influential, explaining the purpose of the procedure, and asking him/her to identify others in the community who would be appropriate respondents ("Who in the community knows most about...?" "Who are the leaders in the community?"). The names are recorded, and each person identified in this way is then contacted in a similar manner and asked to identify other persons who would be appropriate respondents. The process can be terminated when no new names are suggested or after a specified number of contacts have been made.

Once the list has been completed, a sampling procedure must be developed to select persons from the list to be interviewed. The alternatives include the following:

1) Interview everyone on the list (this is feasible only if the number is quite limited)
2) Determine the maximum number of interviews that can be conducted and choose that number of people, starting with those whose names were mentioned most frequently and working toward those mentioned less frequently
3) Select a random sample of persons on the list
4) Select a sample of the persons on the list based on some specific criterion such as membership in a particular group

In general, the reputational approach will provide a more diverse sample than the positional approach, although in small communities it is common for the positional and reputational approaches to give very similar results. It should be noted that the sampling frame for both the positional and reputational approaches provides useful information about the community that should be incorporated into the analysis.

13.4 Data Collection Methods
General Issues

Once it has been determined what information is needed, who has the desired information, and how an appropriate sample of respondents can be drawn, the next decision is to select the appropriate methods for collecting the data. There are three major methods for obtaining information from respondents:

1) Face-to-face interviews
2) Telephone interviews
3) Mailout (or dropoff and pickup) surveys

Knowledge of sampling and survey methods is important for implementing the assessment process described in the guide. Whether one needs to interview only a few community leaders or to do more extensive interviews with a larger random sample, decisions must be made about who is to be contacted and how the information is to be obtained. To be most effective and to best utilize the time and resources available, serious consideration should be given to utilizing a combination of sampling and surveying methods. It is likely that face-to-face interviews with some community members will be necessary. Telephone interviews may be appropriate for gathering other types of information or for clarifying information already gathered in face-to-face interviews. The question which the assessor must ask when designing the primary data collection effort is: What survey methods will provide the best information at the lowest cost?

The Three Methods

Face-to-Face Interviews

Face-to-face interviewing is a method that has been commonly used in social assessment work. With this method, the assessor (or interviewer) meets personally with the respondent and asks the necessary questions. The interviewer can utilize an unstructured or semistructured guide or a formal, structured questionnaire. When unstructured interviews are being conducted, the nature of the interview is often conversational rather than interrogatory.

Face-to-face interviewing has many strengths. High response rates can usually be obtained with this method. Most people will agree to be interviewed and will provide the requested information. One reason for this is that many respondents appreciate having an opportunity to talk with someone about such high interest topics as development, especially if they feel their thoughts and opinions will be brought to the attention of the decision maker.

An additional advantage of the face-to-face method is that it provides the assessor an opportunity to observe the respondent and to look for indications that questions were not understood, that the respondent was uncomfortable answering the question, or that he or she didn't really know the answer. These visual clues can be very helpful and are very important in assessing the validity of the response and the intensity of feelings on controversial issues. Face-to-face interviews also provide the assessor with an opportunity to observe the physical environment in which the respondent lives or works. Observations on housing or office type and location, type and quality of interior furnishings, awards or pictures hung on walls, available magazines and books, etc. can provide additional information and insight about the respondent and the community.

A further advantage of the face-to-face method is that complex issues can be addressed using this method. Interviews lasting several hours can be conducted, although the normal time span for face-to-face interviews is from forty-five to ninety minutes. In addition, if desired, additional questions can be asked at the conclusion of a formal questionnaire to pursue issues that are better clarified through unstructured discussion.

The major disadvantage of the face-to-face survey method is cost; it is the most costly of all the survey methods. Included in the cost of this method are travel time for the interviewer, per diem expenses, low productivity (i.e., fewer interviews per time period), and high call-back costs.

A second disadvantage is that people are becoming more reluctant to open their doors to strangers, regardless of whom the stranger claims to represent. This is causing a decline in the response rate and a raising of costs. This is particularly true in urban areas, but given national trends, it may soon begin to occur even in rural areas.

One other disadvantage of this method is that it is time-consuming. The assessor is often a "staff of one," which means that his/her time must be used judiciously. Even though this method can be used to establish rapport with community residents, gain legitimacy in the community, and become familiar with community patterns, for many assessments it is unrealistic to plan to conduct numerous face-to-face interviews in each community. As will be discussed below, serious consideration should be given to the use of a combination of survey methods.

Arranging a face-to-face interview is a process in itself. Unless there are unusual circumstances, an appointment for the interview should always be made. This is particularly true if the interview will take more than a few minutes. The appointment should preferably be made a day or two in advance. There are two general methods for making the initial contact. In the first, which is used particularly for surveys involving probability samples, an advance letter is sent to prospective respondents informing them that they have been chosen for interviewing and that a call will follow to schedule the interview. A sample letter is included in Figure 13-2. In the second, an approach more appropriate for informal interviewing, the letter is bypassed and the appointment is made by calling the respondent directly. The drawback of the direct call method is that the prospective respondent may be caught off guard and fail to fully understand the purpose of the interview, who the assessor is, or who he or she represents. They may therefore decline to be interviewed. As a general rule, an advance letter helps prepare the prospective respondent for the call and the interview. The reasons for calling ahead are (1) courtesy, (2) to schedule

Figure 13-2

Sample Letter Requesting a Face-to-face Interview

October 14, 1980

Dear

We are requesting your participation in a study we are conducting to gather public information that will be useful in the Mount St. Helen Regional Environmental Impact Statement. We are particularly interested in your concerns regarding potential future tourist development in this area.

The results of this study will be helpful in suggesting areas that may need further examination, as well as being available to decision makers to aid them in this important process.

Yours is one of a relatively small number of randomly selected households being asked to assist us. Your candid help is crucial to the success of the study and the accuracy of the results. One of our team members will be calling you shortly to arrange a convenient time for a brief interview; either you or your spouse (if you are married) may take part. Your participation is, of course, entirely voluntary, and your comments are confidential. Please be assured that we will come prepared to listen to all of your comments.

We shall be happy to answer any questions you might have. Please don't hesitate to call the project manager, Joe Black, or myself at (XXX) XXX-XXXX.

Sincerely,

SOCIOLOGIST
STATE DEPARTMENT OF COMMERCE AND DEVELOPMENT

appointments and reduce call-back requirements, (3) to allow the prospective respondent to be prepared for the interview, and (4) to initiate contact and establish rapport that can make the interview more productive.

Telephone Interviews

As a consequence of the increasing costs and declining response rates for face-to-face interviews, telephone survey techniques have been refined and successfully applied to an increasing range of survey situations over the past decade. This method deserves serious consideration for use in obtaining information for social assessments. The two major advantages of telephone surveys are lower costs and higher speed. Compared to face-to-face interviews, telephone surveys are inexpensive (the major expenses are telephone toll charges, with very low call-back costs) and substantially less time-consuming, since travel time is eliminated. This means that a greater number of interviews can be conducted for the same amount of time and money.

It is true that some sampling bias is generated if published telephone books are used as sampling frames. However, in most rural towns the bias is not large. Most households now have telephones, and most have listed phone numbers, especially in rural areas. In large urban areas, where there are more unlisted numbers, and in areas growing very rapidly, where there is such rapid population change that phone books quickly become outdated and many residents are without telephone service, the problems of bias are somewhat greater. Although this bias can be reduced by using random digit dialing techniques, these techniques have drawbacks of their own and are generally not recommended for assessment work. Considering the uses of the data, the bias created by using phone books as sampling frames in telephone interviews are generally not serious enough to preclude their use.[1]

Research has shown that telephone interviews do not have to be limited to a very few questions with specified responses. A well-designed and administered telephone survey may last for twenty minutes or more. This is especially true when the survey addresses a controversial issue such as development, a topic that interests respondents and about which they frequently have opinions they would like heard.

When conducting telephone surveys, it is suggested that an advance letter be sent to the potential respondent. This letter should indicate briefly what the survey is about, approximately how long the interview will be, and that it will be conducted by telephone. Such advance letters significantly increase response rates and may allow longer interviews to be conducted, since the respondent has some idea of the topic and how long the interview will take. An example of an advance letter for a telephone survey is shown in Figure 13-3.

---

[1]This also applies to the use of telephone books as sampling frames for face-to-face or mail surveys.

Figure 13-3
Sample Letter Requesting a Telephone Interview

January 28, 1981

Dear

Within a week or so we will be calling you as part of a study we are conducting concerning potential future changes in federal regulations regarding public access to federal lands in the Crazy Mountains. We are particularly interested in your opinions about future private development in this area. The information will be useful for the Crazy Mountain Regional Environmental Impact Statement and helpful in suggesting areas that may need further examination. Also, it will be made available to decision makers to aid them in their important decisions concerning possible development in this area.

We are writing to you in advance of our telephone call because we have found that many people appreciate being advised that a study is in process and that they will be asked to participate. Altogether the interview should only take about fifteen minutes. If by chance we should happen to call you at an inconvenient time, please tell the interviewer and he or she will be happy to call back later.

You are one of a relatively small number of local residents being asked to participate in this study. Your candid help is crucial to the success of the study and the accuracy of the results. We will greatly appreciate your assistance. Your participation is, of course, entirely voluntary and your comments will be confidential.

If you have any questions, please don't hesitate to call me or Jane Black, who is conducting the study, at (XXX) XXX-XXXX.

Sincerely,

Project Manager
EIS Team
U.S. Department of ...

Both face-to-face and telephone survey methods can be used with structured or unstructured interviews. There is no inherent reason that either of these methods cannot be used for unstructured interviews in which all of the questions are open-ended. However, because of the difference in the medium, the two methods require some differences in the way the questions are asked. References to sources that provide guidance on construction of questionnaires for telephone surveys are included in Section 13.7.

Mailout Surveys

The mailout (or dropoff and pickup) survey method is appropriate only for formal standardized questionnaires. The format, wording, and response categories of mailout questionnaires need to be designed specifically to facilitate completion by the respondent. Consequently, mailout and face-to-face questionnaires addressing the same subject will differ in these characteristics. Caution is advised when attempting to utilize questionnaires developed for another survey method -- major modifications are usually necessary.

The main advantage of mailout questionnaires is cost. This method has the lowest overall cost of the three survey methods for large, geographically dispersed samples. It also has the advantage of reducing the effects of the interviewer on response patterns. However, the relatively extensive administrative requirements of mailout survey procedures and the cost of printing and sending questionnaires and follow-up materials can make mailout surveys comparable in cost to telephone surveys for medium-sized samples.

In addition to the restrictions associated with utilizing a standardized questionnaire, mailout questionnaires have several additional drawbacks. The most important may be the length of time required to complete the survey process. In order to achieve an acceptable response rate, up to three follow-up mailings may be necessary. This can extend the time necessary to complete the survey to over two months. Additional drawbacks of mailout surveys for assessment work include generally lower response rates, inability to ensure that the designated household member completed the form, and high item nonresponse rates. These drawbacks make the mailout survey method somewhat less desirable for assessment work than the other alternatives.

13.5 Questionnaire Design and Interviewing Techniques

An important element in gaining useful and valid data is the development of good interview guides or questionnaires and good interviewing techniques. As with sampling and survey techniques, there is a well-established literature on questionnaire design and interviewing. The assessor is strongly encouraged to become familiar with the literature cited at the end of this chapter and to develop and practice good questionnaire construction and interviewing skills.

Questionnaire design and interviewing involve two principal tasks: (1) formulating and asking questions and (2) obtaining and recording responses.

Formulating and Asking Questions

An effective interview or questionnaire results when the questions asked of the respondent are:

1) Pertinent to the assessment
2) Appropriate for the respondent, which means that the respondent has the information that is being sought
3) Stated clearly, so that the respondent understands them
4) Presented in a manner that encourages accurate and complete response

Formulating Questions Pertinent to the Assessment

Throughout the assessment process, the assessor must constantly strive to identify and formulate questions that will yield the information needed to forecast and evaluate the effects of the proposed action. If a structured questionnaire is to be used, the questions must all be formulated well in advance of the interview or the mailing of the survey. It cannot be stressed enough that the questions to be asked must result from careful analysis of the assessment purpose and the available information and that they must serve a specific analytic purpose. When developing interview guides or questionnaires, it is essential that careful attention be given to the analysis and utilization of the responses. It is especially important that questions be asked for a specific purpose, and that you know how you want to use the information you are seeking. Unless these issues are thought through during the design stage, you are likely to collect information that you will never use, or find that you need somewhat different information for your analysis than you have obtained.

When informal interviews are being conducted, there is an opportunity to formulate questions based on the information being provided in the interview. Topics will arise in an interview that should be pursued. Formulating pertinent questions in these circumstances requires quick thinking and good interpersonal communication skills. Good interviewing requires thought, both in preparing for the interview and in conducting it. Examples of fairly detailed topical guides for informal interviewing are shown in figures 13-4 and 13-5.

Ensuring that the Questions Are Appropriate for the Respondent

In designing a questionnaire or conducting an interview, it is important to ascertain (and monitor, if possible) the respondent's ability to provide the information being requested. Persistently asking respondents questions about which they have no knowledge or

Figure 13-4

Example Interview Guide:
Service Agency Interviews for
a Community Impacted by
Energy Development

Schools
1) Introduce yourself and explain the purpose of your visit --
    you want to know how the community addressed each of the
    needs that occurred during the period of rapid growth (or
    last five years).
2) Review population data and causes of growth.
3) Review data on school district characterisitics --
    enrollment by grade, personnel, facilities, budget (have
    copy ready for them). Make any corrections/additions, add
    comments. If data are not available locally, find out where
    they would be.
4) How has demand changed (especially during the energy growth
    period)? Why? (Cover both qualitative and quantitative
    changes.)
5) Has classroom space been adequate and available when needed
    to meet demand? If not, when was the problem period? Why
    did the problem occur? How was it resolved or why did it
    remain unresolved?
6) What important changes have occurred in the areas of ....?
    Was that a problem? How were problems addressed? What are
    concerns for the future?
    -- curriculum/educational approach
    -- staff (morale, reactions to staff level changes)
    -- student behavior and characteristics -- probe especially
        for transiency and student conflict (check availability
        of data on turnover rates)
    -- administrative procedures
        - general description
        - any changes due to growth (ask as general question,
            then follow-up)
        - any special programs for newcomers
        - any special problems created by newcomers (esp.
            disorientation or mental health problems among student
            body)
    -- financing
        - bond issues (did they pass)
        - financial issues or problems
        - consequences to district of financial characteristics

(Figure 13-4 cont'd.)

7) What school-related changes or issues have there been that drew public interest or participation (e.g., consolidation, new school construction, etc.)? The point is to articulate public decision-making process. What were the concerns? How were they resolved? When?
   -- who, when, what, how, why; who were the parties involved
   -- who was not involved that logically should have been
   -- if there were factions, what were the issues; how recurrent were they; what are the names of the prime actors on each side
   -- was there a point when problems started being addressed in a new way; when; why

8) At the beginning of the growth period (or 10 years ago), who were the influentials in the community?
   -- how has that changed; what was the projects' role; who were key decision makers for the community during the growth period

9) Check for changes in extralocal linkages (source of funds, contacts, source of teachers, etc.).

10) In their opinion, were there groups in the community that have been (or would be) affected differently by the growth and energy development?
    -- both positive and negative
    -- who, how and why; seek mechanism and understanding of change and community structure that distributes effects/opportunities; prompt for employment, housing, services, schools, way-of-life

11) What are the major social groups and major characteristics of social differentiation?
    -- try to get a description of criteria for social differentiation (in pregrowth period if there was one) and of each of the major groups (size, ethnicity/race, language, religion, income, property ownership, residential location, length of residence, age/sex, political positions/special interests, relationships among groups); how has that changed (criteria, groups or group characteristics). The purpose is twofold: (1) to describe structural/organization characteristics of community and (2) to identify attributes of groups that could influence distribution of project effects. Get names of group representatives. (The ability of respondent to answer provides good evidence of his/her familiarity with different strata).

12) What are the demographic characteristics of respondent?
    -- position and history of employment
    -- length of residence in community
    -- where from (why did respondent come to this community)
    -- family and personal characteristics (age, sex, religion, ethnicity, language, occupation, property ownership, residential location, political position)
    -- relationship to energy development

(Figure 13-4 cont'd.)

Law Enforcement

1) Introduction.
2) Review growth data.
3) Review Part 1 and Part 2 crime data and service provision data over at least the past five years.
   -- reported crime
   -- calls for service
   -- budget
   -- uniformed officers and personnel
   -- cars
   -- facilities
   -- relationship between city and county
4) Did crime and/or calls for service increase during growth period? What are expectations for future growth?
   -- what types of crime(s)
   -- who were (will be) perpetrators
   -- who were (will be) victims; did (will) crime occur in particular neighborhoods/areas
   -- what do they think was (or will be) reason for change
   -- what about specific non-metro county problems -- trespass, poaching, cattle rustling, etc.; what is county people's view
5) What happened to service provision?
   -- were (will) personnel and equipment (be) adequate; if not, when was it inadequate; why was it inadequate
   -- what important changes have occurred (or are anticipated) in their department;
     - staff and facilities
     - administrative procedures
     - manner of enforcement
     - source of financing
6) What law enforcement changes (or issues) have there been that drew public interest or participation (e.g., new jail, consolidation of enforcement)? The object is to articulate public decision making, and to discuss the sequence of response by the community and its leaders regarding energy-related demands.
7) At the beginning of the growth period, who were the influentials? How (and when) did that change? What was the role of energy development?
8) Check for changes in extralocal linkage.
9) Ask about groups and distribution of growth effects to different groups. Check especially for relationships among groups. Ask if they know representatives from each group that could be interviewed.
10) If appropriate, ask personal interview questions. At least get demographic characteristics
    -- position and history of employment
    -- length of residence in community
    -- where they are from
    -- family and personal characteristics
    -- relationships to energy development

(Figure 13-4 cont'd.)

Social Service/Public Assistance and Mental Health

1) Introduction.
2) Review growth pattern and causes.
3) Review agency data, structure of agency.
   -- by type of assistance
      - total annual expenditures
      - expenditures per 1,000 population
      - case loads
      - staff levels
4) How has demand for service changed? Why? What has been the change in use patterns by longtime residents? Why? Are there different use patterns by newcomers? Why? How are these reflected in the data?
5) Have staff and resources been adequate and available when needed to meet demand? If not, when was problem period? Why was there a problem? How was it resolved? Have they received adequate support from the state? From the county? From the community?
6) What important changes have occurred (or are anticipated) in the areas of ....? What is their view on the sources of change? Is data available on
   -- child abuse and neglect
   -- marital discord, spouse abuse, divorce
   -- alcoholism
   -- mental health problems
7) What public service/assistance-related changes or issues have there been that drew public interest or participation? Describe these issues, when they occurred, who played what roles, what was outcome, how does that fit into overall de-cision-making pattern in community? Was there a point (in growth period) when decisions started being made in a new way or by different people?
8) Who were influentials at the beginning of the growth peri-od? How has that changed? What was the energy project's role? Get names of key individuals regarding community actions.
9) What distinquishable groups are there in the community? What are the criteria for social differentiation? What are distinctive attributes of each group? How would one char-acterize relationships between groups? What about prior to growth? (Are there particular neighborhoods in the commun-ity? What are their characteristics?) Get names of people who could discuss each group.
10) Have groups been affected differently by growth, especially energy development? What about inflation? How have effects of energy development been distributed among groups? How has that occurred? What evidence can they offer?
11) What are the social characteristics of the respondent?
   -- position and history of employment
   -- length of residence in community
   -- where are they from and why did they come
   -- family and personal characteristics
   -- relationship to energy development

Figure 13-5

Example Interview Guide:
Group Representatives/General Population Interviews for a Community Impacted by Energy Development

1) Introduction -- describe purpose of study and area of interest.
2) Background (family, where they lived; family and personal characteristics).
3) When did they come to this community?
4) What is their educational history?
5) Describe their occupational history, esp. during last ten years.
   -- occupational mobility/immobility
   -- energy-related employment
      how did (would) they get it; if they are entrepreneurs, ask about financing, business style changes and expansions; did it create particular benefits or problems
6) What are the characteristics of their housing? (Price and/or availability; any problems, good points.)
7) Family history.
   -- family and employment history of spouse
   -- school experience of children
8) What happened to service provision? Any problems? How do they evaluate/compare predevelopment conditions with current conditions?
9) What recreational/social activities are available and used; compare predevelopment (or future) with now.
10) Who are their friends? What are their friends' occupations'? Length of residence? Where do they live? How did they become friends? Have their friendships changed during the study period?
11) Who are their children's friends?
12) How were friends affected by development?
13) How about others in the community? What other groups do they see? Were any affected differently? How?
14) Have newcomers been accepted as part of the community? Get examples of interaction between longtime residents and newcomers; between various groups.
15) How do they feel they personally have been (or anticipate being) affected?
16) How do they feel their neighborhood has been (or anticipate its being) affected?
17) If their parents are in the community, how have they been (or are they anticipate to be) affected?

(Figure 13-5 cont'd.)

18) What changes have occurred (or are anticipate) in the community? What effects have there been (or are anticipated) from energy development? Probe child abuse, mental health, social conflict, community participation and the relationship between these changes and
    -- change in decision making
    -- change in orientation/focus
    -- sense of vitality
    -- sense of community purpose
19) What is their general satisfaction with past and expected changes?
20) What do they like and dislike about the community? What community characteristics are most important to them? How has that changed? Do they like community better now or before? Why?
21) If the respondent is a good spokesperson for his/her group, get a
    -- profile of group prior to development
      - ethnicity/race
      - language
      - religion
      - livelihood/occupation
      - income/wealth
      - property ownership (including location)
      - residential location
      - length of residence
      - demographic characteristics
      - special needs, interests, or political positions
      - intergroup relationships
      - position in community and relationship with other groups
    -- distribution of effects from previous development
      - employment, income, and occupation
      - size of group
      - demographic and cultural characteristics (age/sex, language, religion, ethnicity)
      - housing
      - facilities/services
      - decision making
      - relationship with others
    -- profile of the group now
      - (same characteristics as identified in predevelopment)

information not only wastes time and resources and generates useless data, it can annoy, bore, or frustrate the respondent and jeopardize the effectiveness of the entire questionnaire or interview. For structured surveys, sampling procedures should be coordinated carefully with questionnaire design to prevent the selection of inappropriate respondents or the inclusion of a long series of questions that may be appropriate for only a portion of the respondents. Indeed, designing questions that are applicable and understandable to all members of the sample is one of the biggest challenges of questionnaire construction. The development of topical guides for unstructured interviews is somewhat less difficult, since some responsibility can be placed on the interviewer to select the appropriate topics and frame the questions to be pertinent for the interviewee. In unstructured interviews, the interviewer must be sensitive to clues that the questions or topics are not appropriate and be prepared to adjust the focus of the questions accordingly. (The fact that a respondent does not have information that he/she was expected to have can be revealing and should be noted.) In these circumstances, it is often useful to summarize the type of information being sought to determine which topics (if any) are pertinent and to solicit suggestions from the respondent about where the other information could be obtained.

Stating Questions so They Are Clearly Understood

In order to obtain a valid response, questions must be accurately communicated to the respondent. This means that the questions must be formulated and worded clearly, using concepts and terminology familiar to the respondent. The difficulty of this task should not be underestimated, and it is one reason that sufficient time and effort must be allocated to the development and pretesting of the questionnaire or interview guide.[1] Particularly difficult questions (regarding community social organization, for example) may need to be formulated in several alternative ways. While interviewing, the interviewer should be alert for indications that the question has not been understood so that clarification can be made (or the response can be interpreted accordingly).

Questions often need to be formulated differently for the different survey methods. Jargon and technical language should be avoided. Each question should be as short as possible, and should ask only one question. Questions should be direct and unambiguous. In telephone and face-to-face interviews, the interviewer should speak clearly and loudly enough to be heard easily. A need to repeat questions can detract from the interview and result in invalid responses and should be taken as an indication that the formulation or presentation of the questions needs be modified. The layout and appearance of the questionnaire should facilitate its completion.

---

[1] It is useful to go over the questionnaire with some of those participating in the pretest (after they have finished) to obtain their comments and to ensure that they interpreted the questions as they were intended.

One question should flow into the next in a logical and systematic order.

Designing the Questionnaire and Conducting the Interview to Encourage Accurate and Complete Responses

The manner in which an interview is conducted and the way questions are formulated and presented can have great influence on the respondent's willingness and ability to provide accurate and complete information. Biased questioning produces biased information. It is very important to analyze the wording, sequence, and intonation of questions to guard against the introduction of unintentional bias and to be alert for questions that lead the respondent to a particular answer or that are likely to elicit a socially desirable response. It is helpful to examine each question from the perspective of the respondent to determine whether it is confusing, ambiguous, or "requires" or leads to a particular response. Questions that are biased, misleading, or ambiguous will yield little helpful information, may adversely effect the willingness of the respondent to participate and should either be dropped or reformulated.

Even with the best questions, interactions between the interviewer and the respondent can affect the respondent's ability or willingness to answer accurately and completely. The interviewer needs to be sensitive to the effects of age, sex, education, and organizational affiliation on the interview. Although these effects cannot be completely eliminated, they can be minimized by the manner in which the interview is conducted. To be effective, an interviewer needs to be continually sensitive to the perspective of the respondent and to his or her own ability to shape the responses by the wording of questions or the emphasis on certain topics.

Obtaining and Recording Responses

Obtaining accurate and complete information from questionnaires and interviews requires not only that questions be asked clearly, but that the respondent's answers be correctly recorded. Questions may be asked in an "open-ended" or "fixed-response" format. With the open-ended format, respondents must formulate their own responses with no guidance or direction provided in the questionnaire or by the interviewer. With fixed-response questions, respondents must select their answer from a set of alternatives provided by the questionnaire or interviewer. The choice of format depends upon several considerations. Fixed-response questions, though harder to formulate, are easier and quicker to answer (and code) because the range of answers is constrained to those provided. For the same reason, fixed-response questions help ensure that all respondents have considered the same alternatives when making their response (for example, in ranking questions) and that they are all applying a similar scale to the question (i.e., strongly agree, agree, neutral, disagree, strongly disagree). The major disadvantage of fixed-response questions is that they can result in an oversimplification of either the question or the response and force respondents to choose an answer that may not reflect or express their true beliefs. The major problems with open-ended questions are that they place a heavy demand upon the respondent (especially in mailout surveys), they are difficult and time-consuming to code, and they frequently produce such a wide range of answers that it is difficult to identify clear trends in responses or to interpret the results. The open-ended format is required for exploratory questions as well as for questions which seek to determine how the respondents define the response alternatives when given no prompting.

In selecting the response format, it is important to determine whether enough is known about the survey population that an appropriate set of responses can be developed. It is also important to plan the data analysis before finalizing the question and response format to determine what type of response categories are needed and what format would be most efficient.

Interviewing requires good listening skills. The interviewer must listen to what is said; not to what is expected to be said. This is hard work and requires that the interviewers be well prepared, since it is particularly difficult to listen carefully when distracted by the need to figure out the next question or to record the response. Careful listening serves three important functions. First, it ensures that the response made to the question is accurately understood. This is of obvious importance. Second, it encourages the respondent to answer carefully and completely by conveying that their response is being taken seriously. Third, in unstructured interviews, it allows the interviewer to identify and pursue information about important topics that have not previously been raised.

Recording responses and documenting interview results is an important part of the interviewing process. Responses need to be recorded in sufficient detail to ensure accurate representation of the respondent's answer for later analysis. It is important to guard against bias or selectivity in the response categories or in recording the responses from open-ended questions. It is frequently very instructive to occasionally double up on interviews, having two people record the responses from the same interview and then comparing notes and perceptions afterward.

An interviewer is always placed in somewhat of a dilemma. The need to listen carefully, create a comfortable interviewing climate, and maintain eye contact (in face-to-face interviews) conflicts with the need to record the response thoroughly and accurately. Experienced interviewers generally follow one of two strategies.

One technique is to prepare an interview guide/questionnaire that facilitates the recording of brief notes (stressing the key points made about each topic) during the interview and that can also be used to either record a more complete discussion or serve as an outline for the preparation of a detailed conversation report. It is important that a complete record be prepared as soon after the interview as possible, preferably before the next interview is conducted. Time must be allowed in the interviewing schedule for this task. In face-to-face interviews, interviews are sometimes tape recorded in their entirety. This approach is somewhat problematic because it (1) can create a strained atmosphere for respondents not accustomed to being interviewed, (2) tends to inhibit respondents

from making candid evaluations of controversial issues like leadership and community coordination, and (3) generates an unwieldly
amount of information that is costly and time-consuming to put into
a usable form. Its great advantage is that it provides a complete,
accurate record of the interview.

The other strategy, which works well but often is not feasible
for budgetary reasons, is to have two people involved in the interview, with one person asking the questions and the other recording
the responses. For really key interviews where a lot of information
is obtained, this approach, (or tape-recording) can be very helpful.

Especially on federal projects where information may be subject
to disclosure though the Freedom of Information Act, the interviewer
should be cautious in extending guarantees of confidentiality to
respondents and should be circumspect in documenting interview results.

13.6 Data Analysis

At some time in the assessment process, the need will arise to
analyze the data that has been obtained either from the primary data
collection effort or from secondary sources. As has been emphasized
throughout this chapter, this need must be anticipated early in the
process -- the entire information collection and analysis effort
must be carefully thought out before the data collection effort is
designed and initiated.

The design and execution of an appropriate analytic approach
involves five general steps, each of which is discussed below.

1) Clarifying the purpose and use of the data -- what do you
   want to be able to say, and to whom?
2) Reviewing of the data collection procedures and assessing
   the quality and limitations of the data -- what can be
   said, given the type of data?
3) Preparing the information/data for analysis.
4) Analyzing the data.
5) Interpreting and presenting the results.

Although these five steps apply to the analysis of all types of
data, the remainder of the discussion focuses on the analysis of
survey or interview data.

Clarifying the Purpose and Use of the Data

In order for the sampling procedure, survey method, question-
naires/interview guides, and analysis to be designed effectively,
information needs must be clearly stated and understood. This requires the assessor to work through the assessment process and
determine what information is needed and how it will be used. As
discussed previously in this chapter, this preliminary work must be
very specific if it is decided that a probabilistic sample and a
structured questionnaire are to be used. In this case, a very specific plan for the use of each piece of information to be obtained

from the survey must accompany the design of the questionnaire itself. If not, it is very likely that some of the information
collected will not be used, and that important information will be
omitted or obtained in a less than optimal form. The same requirements hold for the compilation and analysis of secondary data.

Informal interviewing based on theoretical sampling has equally
rigorous, but sequentially different, requirements. With theoretical sampling, the objectives of the research must be clearly understood at the outset, but the data is analyzed as it is obtained to
inform the research effort. In this process, each interview is
carefully analyzed after it is completed to answer several questions, such as: (1) Did the interview provide any new information?
(2) Did it raise new questions that should be asked to subsequent
respondents? (3) Did it suggest some other new people or groups to
talk to? Answers to those questions will inform and direct the next
stages of the data gathering process.

The appropriate research design and analytic (data analysis)
approach are determined by the questions that are to be answered by
the information. If the questions are primarily descriptive (e.g.,
What are existing patterns and recent trends?), the appropriate
analytic approach will be primarily descriptive and will be likely
to focus on frequencies (the number and percentage of respondents
with each characteristic or expressing each view) and cross-tabula-
tions (calculation of the number and percentage of respondents having a particular combination of characteristics). If the questions
are primarily analytic (e.g., Do two different groups of respondents
differ? Why?), the analysis will focus on tests of relationships
and differences.

To date, the purposes of data analysis in impact assessment,
have tended to be primarily descriptive, associated with description
of the existing environment and recent trends. Those intending to
test hypotheses or analyze their data for other purposes are encouraged to read Davis (1971), or a good general statistics book as
referenced in Section 13.7. The discussion here will focus on analysis of primary or secondary data for use in the assessment effort
itself.

Reviewing Data Collection Procedures and Data Quality

The analysis of data is guided by the quality of the data itself. Indeed, examination of the data to determine its quality is
often considered part of the analytic process. There is little
point in conducting an analysis that "goes beyond" the data. The
quality of data can be affected by the sampling procedures utilized
to select respondents, by the collection procedures utilized to obtain the data, and by the coding procedures utilized to transform
the data into usable categories for analysis. Sample size can also
affect the usefulness of the data for some types of analysis. Small
sample sizes (or large samples that are divided into numerous subgroups that have been asked a variety of different questions) can
limit the types of analysis that are appropriate. For the generally
small sample sizes and highly variable topics that frequently result
from informal interviewing (particularly from theoretical sampling)

and for the purposes of most assessment work, relatively straightforward analytic techniques are generally the most appropriate.
During this step it is useful to consider what can be said about
population characteristics, given the sampling procedures and types
of questions. Unless the necessary procedures have been followed,
generalization about the population will not be possible. Understanding this limitation can influence the decisions regarding the
design of the analysis as well as use of the data.

Preparing the Information/Data for Analysis

In most cases the information available from secondary as well
as primary sources will require compilation and manipulation before
it can be analyzed. This generally involves development of a format
and procedure for organizing the information and reducing it to a
set of numbers or categories that can be analyzed.

For primary data, this requires the development and implementation of a coding scheme; the process by which information (for example, responses to a question) are evaluated and placed into an
appropriate category. The preparation of the response categories
for fixed-response questions anticipates this requirement, and generally follows the procedures described below. Coding reduces the
data to a manageable and standard form so that the responses from
one interview or source can be compared to those from another.
Quite obviously, it is important that the coding scheme effectively
reduces the information to a usable form without distorting or biasing it in the process.

The first step in developing an effective code is to determine a
set of response categories that would cover the range of responses
that could or have been made. Codes must be designed so that each
response can be placed in one and only one response category. The
response categories must be appropriate for the data -- they must
reflect the range and nature of the responses or they will distort
the information. The third step is to evaluate the use of the data
to determine how the response categories can best be organized or
grouped. The response categories, or code, must be appropriate for
the purposes of the analysis.

When formal questionnaires are used, many of the questions incorporate the code into the statement of the question (so-called
fixed-response or closed-ended questions). This process occurs before the data are collected, which places an additional burden on
the designer of the questionnaire to ensure that the response categories allow respondents to accurately express their views. When
informal interviews are conducted, most questions are "open-ended"
in that no response categories are suggested. In this case, the
code must be derived from the responses themselves.

One particularly appropriate method for coding information from
informal interviews, public involvement records, or newspapers is
called content analysis. Content analysis provides an objective and
systematic method for abstracting information from interview or
other narrative data. To conduct a content analysis, a sample of
interviews (or all interviews or materials being analyzed, if the
number is not large) are read carefully to familiarize the code

developer with the nature and range of topics and responses that
have been covered. Following this, a coding scheme which provides a
set of response categories for each topic, is developed. An essential feature of content analysis is that the data inform the analysis. The appropriate portions of the interviews are then coded and
thus reduced into a form that can be examined and analyzed.

Once the data have been coded, they can be either entered into a
computer file for analysis or utilized for hand compilation or calculation.

Analyzing the Data

For impact assessment, a major purpose of the analysis will be
to provide descriptive information about existing conditions and
attitudes and to describe trends. In many cases, the analysis will
also focus on comparisons (this group compared to that group, this
community compared to another, this year compared to last). For
this type of purpose, some form of percentage analysis is frequently
the most appropriate.

Percentage analysis, when presented in conjunction with the actual numbers to demonstrate sample size, standardizes results so they
are directly comparable. An additional advantage of percentage
analysis is that it is understandable to a wide audience, something
that is often not true of the more sophisticated analytic techniques. Zeisel (1968) presents a good discussion of percentage analysis.

If the available data or the assessment's purpose allow more
extensive data analysis, the opportunity should not be wasted if it
will contribute to a more informed forecast and interpretation of
the probable social impacts. It should be recognized, however, that
complex analysis is both time-consuming and expensive and that it
must be carefully thought through to ensure that both the data and
the information needs warrant the analytic effort. A wide variety
of references discuss all aspects of quantative analysis (see Section 13.7).

Interpreting and Presenting the Results

The final step in the analytic process is to interpret the information, identifying patterns and characteristics that describe
existing conditions or that clarify the social consequences of similar activities in other communities. These results must be incorporated into the forecasts of social impacts. If the data are being
presented, it is essential that they be accompanied by a discussion
of their limitations and meaning. The basic question that must be
addressed in this discussion is: What types of inferences can be
made from the data?

If the data are from secondary sources or from interviews of
persons selected on a nonprobability basis, inferences can generally
be made only at the level of the data and not generalized further.
It is at this point that comparison between different data sources

(triangulation) can be used to increase the generalizability of the conclusions.

In presenting the results of a survey using either (or both) nonprobability sampling procedures or topical guides, it is very important that these methods and limitations and the appropriate use of the data be explained clearly and explicitly. Great care must be taken in the presentation of the results; the wording of the presentation is critical. A misunderstanding of the results or their implications can jeopardize the credibility and defensibility of the assessment.

13.7 References

General Survey Research Methods

Social science methodology textbooks can provide a good place to start. These textbooks usually have chapters on sampling, survey techniques, interviewing, and questionnaire construction. Some recommended textbooks include the following:

Chadwick, Bruce, Howard Bahr, and Stan Albrecht
1984   Social Science Research Methods. Englewood Cliffs, N.J.: Prentice-Hall.
        This new book discusses a variety of research methods including participant observation.

Denzin, Norman K.
1970   The Research Act. Chicago: Aldine Press.
        This book discusses a variety of research methods, many of which are applicable to assessment work.

Goode, William J., and Paul K. Hatt
1952   Methods in Social Research. New York: McGraw Hill.
        A little "old," but still a classic in the field of methods with a lot of good information.

Galtung, Johan
1969   Theory and Methods of Social Research. New York: Columbia University Press.
        At times this book gets a little difficult to read, but it can provide some valuable insights that make it worth the effort.

Kerlinger, Fred
1973   Foundations of Behavioral Research. 2nd ed. New York: Holt, Rinehart, and Winston.
        Perhaps one of the best methodology textbooks. Well written, a good place to start.

Selltiz, Clare, Lawrence S. Wrightswan, and Stuart W. Cook
1976   Research Methods in Social Relations. 3rd ed. New York: Holt, Rinehart, and Winston.
        Another good and well written methodology textbook.

Survey Research

There are many books that concentrate strictly on survey research. Recommended ones include the following:

Alwin, Duane F.
1978   Survey Design and Analysis: Current Issues. Beverly Hills, Calif.: Sage.
A collection of papers on different aspects of survey research. Chapter 1 is very good.

Babbie, Earl R.
1973   Survey Research Methods. Belmont, Calif.: Wadsworth.
An excellent introduction to the field of survey research. Comprehensive without being overly technical.

Backstrom, Charles H., and Gerald Hursch
1963   Survey Research. Chicago: Northwestern University Press.
A short introductory book, not as comprehensive as Babbie.

Hyman, Herbert H.
1955   Survey Design and Analysis: Principles, Cases, and Procedures. Glencoe, Ill.: The Free Press.
A classic in the field.

Moser, C.A., and G. Kalton
1972   Survey Methods in Social Investigation. 2nd ed. New York: Basic Books.
A good handbook for reference with a helpful discussion on the design of surveys.

Sampling

There are several books on sampling, but few on nonprobability sampling. A few references for both are included below:

Cochrane, William G.
1977   Sampling Techniques. 3rd ed. New York: Wiley.
Deals with probability sampling of various designs. Assumes a good background in algebra.

Glaser, Barney G., and Anselm L. Strauss
1967   The Discovery of Grounded Theory. Chicago: Aldine Press.
Chapter 2 of this book discusses "theoretical" sampling, a good nonprobability sampling technique. This whole book could be profitably be read by anyone doing social assessment.

Mendenhall, William, Lyman Ott, and Richard L. Schaeffer
    1971   Elementary Survey Sampling. Belmont, Calif.: Duxbury.
            This book covers probability sampling at a slightly
            less technical level than Cochran. Chapters 1-3
            provide a good introduction to sampling procedures and
            concepts.

Schuesller, Karl
            Sampling in Social Research. Englewood Cliffs, N.J.:
            Prentice-Hall.
            A good, rather nontechnical introduction to sampling
            that covers most of the important topics.

Sudman, Seymour
    1976   Applied Sampling. New York: Academic Press.
            An excellent practitioner's book on sampling. Chap-
            ters 1-3 are particularly recommended.

Telephone and Mail Surveys

There are two recent and useful books on mail and telephone surveys.

Dillman, Don A.
    1978   Mail and Telephone Surveys: The Total Design Method.
            New York: Wiley.
            An excellent book all around, it has an especially
            good bibliography on the issues regarding use of these
            two survey methods.

Groves, Robert M., and Robert Kahn
    1979   Surveys By Telephone. New York: Academic Press.
            Compares responses to telephone interviews using ran-
            dom digit dialing and personal interviews.

Inteviewing and Questionnaire Design

There is a large literature on interviewing and questionnaire
construction. In addition to the information provided in the general methodology books, good discussions are included in the following:

Cannell, Charles F., and Robert L. Kahn
    1968   Interviewing. In Handbook of Social Psychology, Vol.
            II, 2nd ed. G. Lindsey and E. Aronson, eds., pp
            526-595. Reading, Mass.: Addison-Wesley.

Hyman, Herbert, et al.
    1954   Interviewing in Social Research. Chicago: University
            of Chicago Press.

Richardson, Stephen A., Barbara S. Dohrenwend, and D. Klein
  1965   Interviewing, its Form and Functions. New York:
            Basic Books.

Sudman, Seymour and Norman M. Bradburn
  1982   Asking Questions: A Practical Guide to Questionnaire
            Design. San Francisco: Jossey-Bass.

Schuman, Howard and Stanley Presser
  1981   Questions and Answers in Attitude Surveys. New York:
            Academic Press.

Methods to Identify Community Leaders

Procedures for locating community leaders have been discussed
extensively in the literature. Some helpful references include:

Aiken, Michael, and Paul E. Mott, eds.
  1970   The Structure of Community Power. New York: Random
            House.
            Has chapters that present and critique the different
            ways to locate community leaders.

Hawley, Willis D., and Frederick M. Wirt, eds.
  1968   The Search for Community Power. Englewood Cliffs,
            N.J.: Prentice-Hall.
            Contains some articles on locating leaders. Especial-
            ly interesting is the article by Freeman, et al.

Lawmann, Edward O., and Franz U. Pappi
  1973   New Directions in the Study of Community Elites.
            American Sociological Review 38: 212-30.
            Demonstrates a useful method of finding community
            leaders. These two authors also published a book en-
            titled Networks of Collection Action (New York: Aca-
            demic Press, 1976) that provides a good understanding
            of community decision making and influence.

Data Analysis

At some time, the data that has been collected will have to be
analyzed. Since much of the data will often be in the form of responses to open-ended questions, the best method is content analysis. Two good books with good bibliographies are the following:

Holsti, Ole R.
  1969   Content Analysis for the Social Sciences and Humani-
            ties. Reading, Mass.: Addison-Wesley.

Krippendorff, Klaus
  1980   Content Analysis: An Introduction to Its Methodol-
            ogy. Beverly Hills, Calif.: Sage.

If the assessor has quantitative data from secondary sources or from standardized questionnaires, a useful discussion of methods for data analysis methods can be found in the following:

Blalock, Hubert M., Jr.
1979   Social Statistics. Revised 2nd ed. New York: McGraw-Hill.

Davis, James A.
1971   Elementary Survey Analysis. Englewood Cliffs, N.J.: Prentice-Hall.

Zeisel, Hans
1968   Say It With Figures. 5th ed. New York: Harper and Row.
         A good book on percentage data analysis and presentation.

14. Use of Secondary Data and Sources

14.1 Introduction

Research information is generally divided into two categories: primary data and secondary data. Primary data is information that is generated and compiled for a particular project, such as survey data as described in the last chapter. Other types of primary information are obtained from observation (including participant observation) and various types of unobtrusive measures (such as traffic counts). Secondary data is data that has been collected for another purpose. Social assessments utilize both types of information. This chapter identifies and discusses some of the major secondary sources and how they may be used in a social assessment. Secondary data can be used to supplement and validate primary data and to cover topics for which it is not feasible to collect primary data. Secondary data can often be used to help focus the assessment by narrowing the questions that need to be asked. It can also help answer many important questions, thereby reducing the requirements for primary data collection and enhancing the validity of the analysis.

14.2 How Secondary Data and Sources Can Be Used

Secondary data can be used in two principal ways: descriptively and analytically. Secondary sources can often help describe the characteristics of the existing environment by providing information about historical trends and present conditions. Census data or attitude surveys from previous assessments, for example, can be used to develop a profile of important community or area characteristics. Comparison of data collected at different times (for example, the decennial censuses for 1960, 1970, 1980) can provide information about the stability or variability of community characteristics in the recent past and about the patterns of changes that have occurred (trends).

Census data, environmental impact statements, agricultural experiment station bulletins, state reports, and local newspapers and histories can be very valuable sources of descriptive information. These, plus any other pertinent studies that have been conducted, can provide information about the community, the area, past development, and such things as particular controversies or issues, that broaden your perspective on the study area communities and aid in the assessment effort.

The second use of secondary data is analytic. Secondary sources can be used to analyze what type of information is likely to be important, what types and magnitude of social impacts are likely to occur, and what meaning they might have for the community and its residents. Sources such as previous environmental impact statements, community case studies, professional papers and articles, local newspapers, and statistical records can provide information about the characteristics of direct project inputs and the changes that have (and have not) occurred in other affected communities. This information can not only help focus the assessment, it can also provide an empirical basis and analytic framework for forecasting the direct project inputs and the social impacts they would cause. The experience of previously affected communities (and the analysis of that experience that is provided in some research reports) can help identify and clarify the major relationships between project inputs and community characteristics that determine the social impacts. It can also provide evidence to support analysis of the type, magnitude, and meaning of the social changes likely to occur.

Throughout the assessment process, information from secondary sources should be used to check and inform the analysis. In other words, it should be used not only to validate the information obtained through interviews and observations, but also to provide insight and direction. An excellent article on how to use secondary sources in social impact assessment is by Shields (1977).

14.3 Useful Sources of Secondary Data

In social assessment, the primary information requirements center around the four major steps of the assessment process:

1) Describing the existing environment
2) Forecasting the baseline and direct project inputs
3) Forecasting and evaluating the social impacts
4) Developing mitigation measures and evaluating the mitigated alternatives

Many of the sources pertinent to each of these steps have been identified in chapters 8 through 11. Some sources are sufficiently useful to warrant separate discussion.

The United States Census

The decennial census of the population is a rich source of demographic, employment, occupational, and income data. Data readily available at the county level (and sometimes at the community level) that might be useful include:

1) Population size
2) Age and sex distribution
3) Educational characteristics
4) Migration data
5) Occupational distribution (by sex)
6) Employment by industry (by sex)
7) Family characteristics
8) Income distribution

In counties with substantial minority populations (such as blacks or persons with Spanish surnames), these data are broken out for the separate groups. There is also a decennial census of housing that provides information about housing type, facilities (e.g., bathrooms, running water), ownership patterns, and cost. These data are often available, but less readily, for subcounty areas such as incorporated communities (minor civil divisions) and census tracts. It is also not unusual for a special or interim census to be conducted in communities experiencing rapid growth or decline. It is worth checking to see if this has been done in the study area.

For years ending in 2 and 7 (1967, 1972, 1977), the Bureau of the Census publishes the City and County Data Book, which contains useful summaries of economic, demographic, and governmental services data for counties and cities with populations greater than 25,000. Other census publications that can be useful are the censuses of agriculture, mining and manufacturing, and businesses. In addition, the Bureau of the Census publishes numerous special reports and technical papers that can be pertinent.

Although most of the readily available census materials break information out only to the county level, information for minor civil divisions, tracts, or blocks can be requested and obtained from the Bureau of the Census. However, turnaround time is often slow. Since there are usually few communities in western counties, county level data is frequently adequate to describe the community for assessment purposes. If a more specific breakout is necessary, the subcounty data can be requested or the available data can be extrapolated to the community level, either on a mathematical, statistical, or judgmental basis. In sparsely populated areas with unincorporated or very small communities, even subcounty data may cover more than one community and require extrapolation to estimate community characteristics. The Bureau of the Census also publishes estimates of population and per capita income for intercensal years (in the P-25 and P-26 series), which can be helpful in updating the decennial census data and determining intercensal trends in population change.

A common problem with census data is that it is frequently badly out of date, since it is collected only once every ten years. Even if an interim census has been conducted, the infrequency of collection can impose serious limitations on the applicability of the data, especially in rapidly changing communities. However, even in these circumstances, census data is often the best alternative available. By using the most recent census data as a comparison point, community residents can often identify the general type and magnitude of the changes that have occurred. This approach is also often helpful for estimating community characteristics from the county level data.

One aspect of experience is knowing where and how information is available. Since familiarity with the various types of census data can increase the efficiency and quality of the assessment, it is well worth the effort required.

State Publications

State governments compile a good deal of information on schools, taxation, and social services that can be useful in assessment work. This data is usually gathered on the county level, although it can in some instances be collected for separate communities. These data are often available only from individual state agencies, so their acquisition can require some research and effort.

One of the most usable state documents is the annual vital statistics report. These reports usually contain statistics on marriages, divorces, county populations, infant mortality, and so on. If the agency has not already conducted an analysis of trends, this information can be developed by comparing the statistics for different years.

Crime statistics can normally be obtained from the state's attorney general or justice department. Annual reports of Part I (major) crimes are usually published broken out to at least the county level. The FBI Uniform Crime Reports, which are widely available, are useful to provide data at the state and national level.

Many states are now making their own population projections. These are made either by a state agency or by a department of one of the state universities, usually at the county level. Local development activities and migration are often taken into account in these projections, which are therefore often more useful than U.S. Census projections. Nevertheless, particular attention must be paid to the validity of the assumptions that underlie the projection techniques, as well as the assumed levels of development and migration for the study area.

State agencies also publish economic data (e.g., employment/ unemployment figures) and studies that can be useful. In addition, state agencies may have conducted studies of separate communities, especially those which have been or are likely to be impacted, that can provide valuable information.

Federal Government Publications

The federal government, and separately its many bureaus and agencies, publishes an enormous amount of information, some of which can be useful in social assessment. In addition to the Bureau of the Census publications described above, other federal agencies that may provide pertinent information include the Environmental Protection Agency, the Bureau of Labor Statistics, the Department of Energy, the Department of Housing and Urban Development, the Department

of the Interior, the Department of Health and Human Services, and
the Department of Education. Since some of these documents are not
published by the U.S. Government Printing Office, and thus are not
listed in its catalog, active searching may be required to identify
and obtain those pertinent to your work. Many of the publications
or information of interest can be obtained by calling offices in
these departments or agencies and inquiring about what new materials
are available.

College and University Publications

College and university publications can be good sources of
data. Some particularly likely sources are departments of sociology, social work, economics, and business. Faculty and/or students
in these departments may have conducted specialized studies in the
community or areas of interest. Also, there may be pertinent theses
or dissertations on the community or area. It can also be helpful
to talk to some of the faculty, since they may know of other sources
of information on the community or area.

Another potentially valuable source is agricultural experiment
station research bulletins or reports. Many community studies are
published by experiment stations, and they often address issues of
interest to the social assessment.

College and university libraries are also good information resources. Some are depositories for federal and state documents and
reports, and many attempt to collect all reports and studies done in
the state, whether prepared by public or private organizations.

Professional Papers and Journal Articles

A great deal of information about social impacts is contained in
papers that are published in journals or presented at conferences,
workshops, symposia, or other types of professional meetings. Such
meetings can cover a particular topic, such as human services in
impact areas, or they can cover the whole spectrum of social assessment issues. Usually these meetings are announced well in advance,
but it may be difficult to identify and obtain the papers presented
at earlier meetings.

Professional journals also contain articles that will be of interest to the assessor. Articles may deal with theoretical perspectives on social assessment, reviews of literature, community
case studies, or comparative analyses of several communities and
areas.

"Fugitive" Documents

Outside of the census data, perhaps the richest source of information is contained in "fugitive" documents. These are studies that
were conducted for internal use by companies or state, regional, or
federal agencies or that were written as working or conference
papers by persons interested and active in social assessment. Many

are "back-up" documents prepared by the agency staff or consultants as part of the work necessary to prepare a published report.

The essential feature of this material is that it is difficult to identify and hard to obtain. The best approach is continual inquiry -- be persistent in asking if anyone knows of any good material on the topics of interest. Once identified, the material can frequently be obtained from the author or, failing that, from the person who provided the reference. It is often necessary to pay reproduction costs and postage to obtain these documents, which are frequently unpublished or out-of-print.

A general rule to follow at the start of each assessment is to telephone colleagues to ask who has been working either in the study area or on the topics of interest. Then contact the persons identified to solicit materials and additional references. The literature review prepared for the Bureau of Land Managements Social Effects Project (Thompson and Branch 1981) and the book by Murdock and Leistritz (1979) provide a place to start on this search. The complete references for these and other documents are provided at the end of Chapter 8.

Appendixes

Appendix A:
Demographic Projections

A.1 Introduction

The population projection is frequently the basic material from which the social assessment is made. Consequently, the projection of population change is of fundamental importance to many social impact assessments, particularly those addressing large-scale development projects.

This appendix discusses population projections. The major types of population projections are presented and briefly discussed. The purpose of the appendix is to familiarize you with the major types of projection methods, along with their uses and limitations. Following this, some guidance on population projections in general are offered. Since the specific formulas used in population projections are readily available from the references given at the end of the appendix, they are not included in the text.

Before discussing particular projection methods it is useful to distinguish between population estimates and population projections or forecasts. Population estimates deal with the current size, and perhaps structure (e.g. age-sex distribution), of the population of some area (city, county, state, nation) or the size of the population at some point in the past, usually some intercensal year. Methods of population estimation are not considered in the appendix, but for the convenience of the reader, a few references on estimation are provided in Section A.6.

A population projection is a calculation of the future size, and perhaps structure, of a population, based on a set of assumptions. A projection is therefore a calculation of expected future population. Generally, the terms "population projection" and "population forecast" are used interchangeably.

The process of assessing the demographic impacts of a large-scale project requires projection of the demographic change that would occur without the development, projection of the demographic change that would occur with the project, and analysis of the differences between the two. The steps involved in this process are similar to those of the overall assessment process:

1) Describe the existing environment
2) Forecast baseline conditions

3) Describe the pertinent characteristics of the proposed action
4) Forecast conditions with the proposed action
5) Analyze the project effects

It should be noted that population projections can be developed to project population segments such as school age population, race/ethnic composition, labor force characteristics, urban/rural residence. However, these are specialized projection techniques and will not be discussed here. They are sometimes broken out in economic-demographic models, such as described in Section A.4. The books by Bogue (1979) and Shryock and Siegel (1975) cover these types of projections.

Prior to beginning serious work on population projections or population phenomena in general, familiarity with the basic terminology of demography and the importance and interpretation of age-sex structure is recommended. A working knowledge of basic demographic concepts will enhance one's ability to think and communicate intelligibly in the field of demography. The significance of these and similar factors for social phenomena are clearly described in a number of standard demographic references including Shryock and Siegel (1972), Pittenger (1976), Irwin (1977), Bogue (1969), Petersen (1975), Matras (1977), and Smith and Zoph (1976). The work by Matras is especially helpful because of its sociological emphasis.

These authors emphasize several general principles of population projections, including the fact that a population projection is only as accurate as the assumptions on which it is based and that assumptions (and projections) are generally more accurate if performed:

1) For an entire nation or large geographic region rather than for a small component area or subregion;
2) For total populations rather than for subpopulations or population subgroups;
3) With series using data directly related to population change (births, deaths, and migration data) rather than those using data that provide indirect or symptomatic indicators of population change (automobile registration, housing counts, etc.);
4) For shorter rather than longer periods of time;
5) For areas in which past trends are more likely to continue than new patterns to arise; and
6) For areas undergoing slow rather than rapid change.

Obviously, the areas and circumstances under consideration in social impact assessment are not very congruent with factors that allow accurate forecasting. This requires the assessor to pay close attention to the population projection and how it is done. It also requires appropriate caution in the interpretation of population projections for rapidly changing small areas.

Population projection methods can be conveniently divided into two broad categories: those that project the size of the total population and those that project the population by age-sex structure. The two methods differ significantly. Irwin (1977a)

provides an excellent brief description of the major projection
techniques.

A.2 Methods of Total Population Projection

The methods of total population projection can be subdivided
into two types. The first are methods based on mathematical functions and may be called mathematical methods or models. These are
direct methods of population projection. The second are indirect
and are termed ratio or share methods.

The mathematical methods of total population projection are
relatively easy to do and the data they require is generally readily
available. One advantage of the mathematical methods is that they
can be used at the community level. Generally the necessary data
are available at that level. On the other hand, the drawbacks and
limitations of these methods, discussed below, make them less than
attractive. Underlying all of the total population methods is the
assumption that population growth (or decline) will follow a smooth
curve that is defined by a particular mathematical function. More-
over, the methods are based on functions derived from past population growth, which may not be particularly relevant to future change.

In social impact assessment, use of the mathematical models
should be limited to situations in which little or moderate population growth is anticipated, the projection period does not extend
very far into the future (e.g., not more than ten years), and interest is limited to the size of the total population. If it is anticipated that there will be large population changes, these methods
are inappropriate for two reasons. First, large population changes
are not historically characteristic of many areas that are impacted,
and second, these methods do not project the age-sex structure of
the population, which is crucial for assessing the social consequences of large population change.

Mathematical Methods

Although there are a number of different mathematical models for
projecting total population size, only a few -- the most widely
known and used -- are discussed here. The basic idea behind mathematical methods of population projection is to extend a population
pattern of the past into the future. (Although, as will be seen, it
is possible to introduce a new growth rate into some of the models.)

The methods described in this section are called noncomponent
methods because they do not take into separate account the three
components of population change: births, deaths, and migration. In
the methods presented, only the total population is projected, and
it is not possible to state whether the change in population size is
due to changes in births, deaths, or net migration, or some combination of the three. Since many of the impacts on a community are
related to changes in the age-sex structure of the population and
not just to change in the size of the total population, the methods
discussed are useful in social impact assessment only under conditions where little population change is expected to occur and where

the main force for social impact is something other than population change.

The Logistic Curve

Perhaps the most famous and widely used of the mathematical methods is the logistic curve developed by Pearl and Reed (Pittenger 1976). Although the logistic curve has, at times in the past, been successful in predicting the size of the total population for the U.S. and other countries, the claim by Pearl and Reed that it is a law of population has not been substantiated (Dorn 1950). The logistic curve requires more data than some of the other mathematical techniques, but can be used to project population further into the future (Shryock and Siegel 1975).

Two features of the logistic curve should be noted. First, it sets an upper limit (or asymptote) above which the size of the population cannot grow. That is, the logistic curve does not project population of unlimited size in the future. This is helpful since it is safe to assume that any population will not increase to an unlimited number. A second feature of the logistic curve is that it can be used only for conditions of increasing population. If the population of the study area has been decreasing, or is expected to decrease, a logistic curve cannot be used.

The Exponential and Geometric Curves

Two other commonly used mathematical models are the exponential and the geometric curves. These are similar in form and nature, the difference being that the exponential model is used to forecast continuous data, whereas the geometric model is used to make forecasts for discrete intervals, e.g. ten-year periods.

Both of these methods can be applied with little data on the past population, but the projection can be made for only a short period into the future. It is possible to use these models to examine the potential size of the future population using new growth rates rather than those that have occurred in the past. That is, from other, "exogenous" sources the forecaster may determine (or assume) that the population will grow by 1.5 percent per year for three years and then grow by 1 percent per year for the remainder of the forecast period. These growth rates can be used directly, along with the size of the population at the beginning of the forecast period, to project the future population. These methods can be used with either increasing or decreasing populations. However, they have the capacity to yield unreasonably large, small, or even negative population totals.

Regression Techniques

Regression techniques forecast the size of the future population as a function of one or more independent variables such as registered vehicles, population density, or similar population-related

variables. They require a large amount of data on both past population size as well on the independent variables.

In their pure form these techniques assume that the form and
nature of the relationship that existed between the independent
variables and total population size in the past holds, without
change, into the future. Under the impact conditions, this generally is not a very safe assumption and limits the situations in which
these methods are appropriate.

Polynomial Projections

The final mathematical model to be considered is that of poly-
nomial projection, in which past population is plotted and a curve
is fitted to the data. The formula defining the curve of past population size is then used to project future population. Although
this approach may be effective for forecasting baseline conditions
(if no major change agents are anticipated) it is clearly inadequate
for areas expecting large, atypical population change as a result of
the proposed action.

Share and Ratio Methods

Two types of indirect methods of projecting the size of the
total population will be briefly examined here. Again, the assessor
should study the methods in more detail from the references in Section A.6 if it is decided that they can be used. These methods are
indirect in the sense that they do not use rates of growth directly,
but derive the population projections on the basis of its relationship to some other population.

The Share Method

The share method relates the population of the area of interest
to a larger area in which the area of interest is located, a common
example being a small town and the county in which it is located.
In this approach, the historical pattern of the share of the smaller
area to the larger is examined, the population of the larger area is
projected, and the size of the smaller area is extrapolated from
that projection, based on the historical pattern. The logic behind
the share method is that the growth rate of the smaller area may not
be known but that it will remain at a constant ratio to that of the
larger area.

Under impact conditions, however, the population share of an
impacted area is likely to change with respect to the larger area.
Indeed, identification of such change is one of the principal objectives of population forecasting in impact assessments. For this
reason the historical pattern is often not very relevant to the
problem except for forecasting baseline population levels. This
limits the usefulness of this approach for assessments addressing
activities that will drive population change in a manner dissimilar
to the historic activities of the area.

The Ratio Methods

The basic idea behind the ratio methods is that one can establish population ratios for factors that can be forecast -- employment or housing stock, for example -- and use these ratios to
project population. Thus, if one knows or can project the future
labor force size, the population can be forecast by applying the
appropriate ratios (or multipliers, as they are sometimes called) to
these projections. Because of area/community specific factors which
influence such ratios, these methods have not been very accurate.

There are several other types of share or ratio methods that
have been proposed and/or used. These include a population density
method, a ratio-correlation method, and a housing stock method.
Overall, these methods have not been all that productive and are
generally not pertinent to population projection associated with
large-scale development.

Both mathematical and share and ratio methods have been extensively used in population projections, but as Pittenger (1976) notes
they have not been all that useful. These methods should be used
when more complete data on the population to be projected is not
available or when a short-term projection of the total population is
all that is needed. In the latter case the mathematical methods
would be the more appropriate. All these methods are inadequate
when major population changes are anticipated.

Indeed the limitations of the mathematical and share and ratio
methods have led to their general abandonment for almost any serious
population projection efforts. They have been replaced by component
methods which use the process of births, deaths, and migration and
which project population by age and sex.

A.3 Component Methods of Population Projection

The Cohort-Component Method

There are two principle types of component population projection
techniques: cohort-survival and cohort-component. The only difference between the two is that the former does not take migration
into account since its purpose is to project a closed population.
Both techniques use birth and death information. These methods are
almost never used to make projections directly at the community
level; community projections are derived from the allocation of
county or regional (constituted by two or more counties) level projections. This is because the necessary population data (birth
rates, migration rates) are not availale at the community level,
particularly for rural communities. This discussion concentrates on
the cohort-component technique since migration is usually a very
important consideration for impact assessment.

These methods generally project population by five-year age
groups, by sex, at five-year intervals, although this does not have
to be the case. The exact procedures by which projections are made
using these methods are quite detailed. Since they are readily

available in the references cited at the end of this section, they are not specified here. Rather, the discussion focuses on the kinds of assumptions that need to be made about mortality, fertility, and migration when using these techniques.

The population projection made by the cohort-component method is driven by the assumptions made about the levels, or rates, of mortality, births, and migration (which includes in-migration and out-migration). The rates used in the projection are age-specfic rates. The age interval for the rates must be the same as the age interval for the projection. (For example, if the age structure is broken down into five-year intervals and one of those intervals is 26-30, data on age-specific mortality rates for males and females must be available for these same intervals). Age-specific birth rates for females in the child-bearing years (generally considered to be 15-44, although 15-49 is also sometimes used), must also be available.

The assumptions about how these rates will behave in the future determine the outcome of the projections. It is therefore imperative that the person making the forecasts pay close attention to the assumptions that are made about these rates and how they change over time.

Mortality Rates

Data on mortality rates are generally fairly easy to obtain and are not particularly controversial.[1] Mortality rates in the United States have stabilized and are not expected to decline significantly in the near future, unless there is some major medical breakthrough on heart disease or cancer. For this reason, mortality rates derived from the state or national population can generally be used and the age-specific mortality rates found in state or national life tables can be used directly. Mortality rates are given by age and sex for the total population and by race. The rates that are used need to conform to the projection. For example, if the population is being projected without regard to race, then the mortality rates for all males and all females (not separated by race) for the respective age groups should be used.

Many component models employ an assumption that the mortality ratio will fall to a hypothesized minimum level at some fixed rate. This assumption is probably unnecessary, since mortality rates have generally stabilized and the hypothetical minimum for each age-sex group is not significantly lower than the present level. (This does not apply, however, to developing countries where mortality is still declining.) Thus, for the United States, one may use current age-specific mortality levels as constants in the projection and be on safe ground (Pittenger 1976).

---

[1]In actuality, survivorship rates (one minus the mortality rate) are used in the projections. However, the convention is to speak of mortality rates.

Birth Rates

Assumptions about birth rates are not as easy to make as those about mortality rates. Decisions must be made about which rates to utilize and how they should be modified over time. National, state, and county age-specific birth rate data are generally available. The principal reason not to use national rates is the confounding influence of urban/rural and regional differences.

If the assessor wishes to derive age-specific birth rates from state or county data, the information found in Pittenger (1976), Shryock and Siegel (1975), and Tarver and Black (1966) is useful. Unlike mortality rates, birth rates should usually not be kept constant through the projection period. How to trend the fertility rates is a judgmental decision. Some of the factors to take into consideration are national fertility trends, local (state and/or county) trends, very recent upswings or downturns in fertility levels, and so on. There are no hard and fast rules to guide these decisions other than that they should be reasonable and accord with present and past data, and, of course, be such that they do not lead to outlandish projections.

Migration

In many situations involving social impact assessment, migration is the population component from which almost all of the population change will come. Therefore, particular attention needs to be given to assumptions about the rate of migration for different age and sex cohorts.

Migration rates for impact assessment forecasts are typically derived through analysis of labor market demand. It is assumed in these projections that workers (both primary and secondary) will come in to fill jobs that the local labor market cannot fill. This makes for an economic/demographic model that links the labor force and economic conditions to the more demographic phenomena of mortality and fertility. The crucial assumptions that need to be carefully worked out are the rates of in-migration by age (the scheduling, when the peak will occur) and subsequent rates of out-migration.

If a labor market demand model is not used for the migration portion of the model, it might be best to use the age-specific migration experience of other places that have experienced projects similar to the one under consideration.

Allocation of the Population to Communities

As was mentioned earlier, the cohort-component techniques do not project populations of communities per se, but of counties or regions. This raises the problem of how to allocate the projection to the relevant communities. This problem occurs with the projection of both the baseline and the with-project population.

There are several techniques to allocate the population with respect to the baseline projection; the share method discussed earlier is probably the most reasonable. Allocation of the project population projection is more problematic. Gravity models have been extensively used, but have been shown not to be all that useful in rural or sparsely populated areas (Murdock, Wieland, and Leistritz 1978). Judgmental approaches have also been suggested and may have some validity (Leistritz and Murdock 1981, Mountain West Research 1979). Informed judgment is best based on careful examination of the experience of similar areas that have experienced development to find out the how the incoming population distributed itself throughout the area, and of the housing stock likely to be available in each community. In this process it is important to consider the plans and capabilities of the local communities in terms of zoning, land use control, housing development and facilities/services provision. Population growth through migration is an interactive process between the incoming migrants and the communities.

The problem of the allocation of the population is crucial. Only through the allocation will the assessor be able to determine which communities will be impacted and in what magnitude. There are no clear-cut rules or guidelines for making the decision on how to allocate the population. Like so many other aspects of population projections, good judgment, knowledge of community characteristics, and reasonableness are the key to good projections.

A.4   Economic/Demographic Models

Overview

Recently, impacts asessments have made increased use of methods that combine economic-based and cohort-component techniques, with a corresponding decrease in the use of the population-to-employment ratios that dominated earlier impact projections. Most economic-based techniques employ or are a combination of the economic projection methods (such as export base or input/output) to project labor requirements and a cohort survival method, in conjunction with a set of projected labor force participation rates, to project labor availability. Labor requirements are compared with labor availability to derive projections of in- or out-migrating labor These are converted to population projections through application of a set of assumed population characteristics (average family size, age, marital status, etc.).

In order to illustrate how all of these components contribute and interact in the population projection, a description of an economic/demographic model developed by Mountain West Research, Inc. for use in the assessment of large-scale projects is provided. This illustrates not only the data requirements for the projection, but the types of data one may expect from an impact assessment population projection model as well. Working through this model can help you become more familiar with projection models and facilitate more effective interaction with the economic/demographic analyst. A number of other models have also been developed for use in similar situations.

In addition, several manuals on economic/demographic projection methods have been prepared, and are referenced in Section A.6.

The economic/demographic simulation model used in this example analyzes the consequences of various assumptions and scenarios on the population, employment, and income of a region. The roots of this type of model can be traced to the Susquehanna River Basin Model, originally developed by Battelle, and similar models used in Wyoming, Arizona, and Utah.

The overall theoretical construction of these models is essentially the same; three submodels comprise the fundamental structure. A demographic submodel accounts for population characterisitics, such as births and deaths and the age/sex composition of an area. The supply of labor is determined from labor force participation rates and the "survived" population. An economic submodel determines labor demand utilizing an economic base approach to estimate total employment. A labor market submodel reconciles model estimates of labor supply and labor demand. Labor market imbalance triggers either in- or out-migration from the area. The process results in consistent levels of population, employment, and income for the area.

Although the structure of the example model follows this general approach, the three principal submodels have been refined extensively and three additional components have been added. The first additional component, the construction worker submodel, determines the geographic source (local/nonlocal) and the residential choice of construction workers related to large-scale development projects. A community allocation submodel has also been added to produce community-specific population projections and impacts. Finally, a project management submodel organizes project-related information and other user-supplied inputs that form the alternatives to be evaluated. The general flow of information in the model is summarized in Figure A-1.

Demographic Submodel

The demographic submodel serves as an accounting framework to keep track of the population characteristics of an area and, in particular, the components of population change that occur from year to year: migration, births, and deaths. The demographic submodel utilizes a process known as "cohort-survival" that separately estimates births and deaths based on age- and sex-specific vital rates. This allows the composition of the population to be considered in the determination of the births and deaths. In addition, any anticipated changes in fertility and survival patterns may be included. Finally, special subpopulations, such as large construction work forces or Native American populations, that may have demographic characterisitics that differ substantially from the general population are explicitly considered. Figure A-2 summarizes the cohort-survival process utilized in the model.

Economic Submodel

Current research in regional economic modeling, particularly that related to impact assessment, has revealed that there are

Figure A-1

Economic/Demographic Assessment Model
Overview

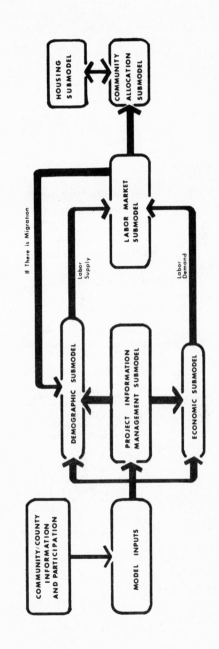

MOUNTAIN WEST RESEARCH, INC

Figure A-2
Economic/Demographic Assessment Model
Demographic Submodel

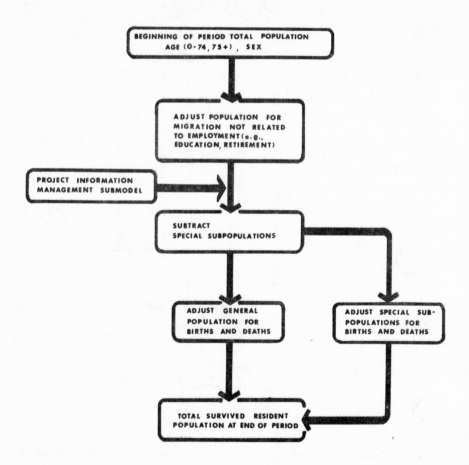

MOUNTAIN WEST RESEARCH, INC

strong similarities among properly specified input-output, econo-
metric, and export base models. The multipliers derived from the
three approaches have been demonstrated to be consistent, both
theoretically and empirically. Regional economic modeling, therefore, has become increasingly eclectic, often utilizing aspects of
all three techniques. In practice, the essential differences among
the methods concern the degree of sectoral disaggregation, the data
base from which they are estimated, and the ability of each to answer particular questions and incorporate and evaluate alternative
assumptions and options.

The economic submodel in this example is appropriately classi-
fied as an export base model that produces consistent forecasts of
employment and income. It postulates that total economic activity
is determined by basic labor income, nonbasic labor income, and nonlabor components of personal income. Basic labor and income is that
which is not dependent on the local population or income, but which
serves a larger (export) market, and which brings income into the
local area through the export of goods or services.

The general framework of the economic submodel is shown in
Figure A-3. Beginning with basic employment projections supplied by
the user, basic income is calculated by multiplying basic employment
by sector-specific annual wage rates. Basic income is used to estimate nonbasic employment and nonbasic income, which are then used to
calculate nonlabor income. Both the nonbasic income and the nonlabor income estimates are added to the basic income figure to
approximate total personal income. The calculations of nonbasic
employment and income and of nonlabor income are then repeated using
this new level of personal income. Since any change in personal
income is assumed to affect nonbasic employment and a change in nonbasic employment affects income, the iterative process is continued
until a consistent level of personal income and nonbasic employment
is established. It is this simultaneous determination of income and
nonbasic employment that distinguishes this technique. Since basic
income is determined through the basic employment projections supplied by the user, it is not affected by changes in the level of
personal income. Nonbasic employment, and hence nonbasic income,
and the nonlabor income components do change with changes in personal income and subsequently induce further changes in personal income.

The economic submodel has been structured to account for some of
the shortcomings of traditional simple export base formulations. In
particular:

-- Basic employment is weighted to reflect earnings differentials among sectors. It makes little sense to postulate
   that a change in relatively low-waged tourist-serving trade
   employment will have the same effect on the local economy as
   a change in heavy construction employment. The appeal of an
   income-driven base model is apparent.
-- Rigorous attention is paid to the split between basic and
   nonbasic employment. Even "ballpark accuracy" for multipliers demands this approach. Much of the a priori categoriza-
   tion of export base approaches is contrary to the observed
   experience of economic sectors in smaller counties.

Figure A-3

Economic/Demographic Assessment Model
Economic Submodel

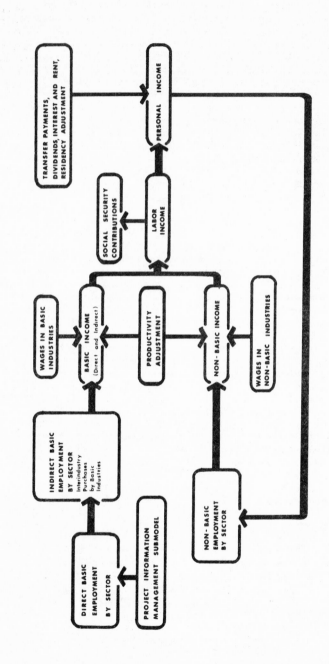

-- Trading relationships within the local impact area are explicitly examined because of the interdependencies of local economies. If one part of the local impact area is an important trade or service center, this raises different analytical problems than would be experienced if all parts of the impact area were economically homogeneous.

-- Finally, a simulation model is only as valid as its current information. The economic submodel is structured so that the user can "override" many of the model parameters, thereby incorporating more appropriate or more recent data as deemed necessary.

Labor Market Submodel

The labor market submodel evaluates the consistency between labor supply and labor demand. The basis for estimation of labor demand is the level of total employment produced by the economic submodel, adjusted for residency and multiple job holding. Labor supply is computed from the survived population in each age and sex cohort and the corresponding labor force participation rate (LFPR). If there is an excess of jobs relative to the size of the available labor force, it is assumed that the balance between the supply and demand for labor will be reestablished by in-migration or labor market entrants. If, on the other hand, there is an excess supply of labor, it is assumed that out-migration or reduced labor force participation will occur.

When the implied unemployment rate is outside a prespecified range, the model will calculate the number of labor force migrants required to achieve labor market balance. The labor force migrants are allocated to age and sex groups according to the industrial composition of the regional economy, and the appropriate number of dependents associated with labor force migrants is then calculated. From the new level of population (adjusted), the relationship between supply and demand for labor has to be reconsidered. These iterations continue until the implied unemployment rate is brought within the appropriate range. The general flow of information in the labor market submodel is presented in Figure A-4.

Community Allocation Submodel

The community allocation submodel is used to allocate the county-level population projections to specific communities in the study area. The allocation procedure addresses each of the components of population change individually. The community allocation routines are designed to take advantage of as much recent, user-supplied data as is practical, but they are, nonetheless, structured to make the allocation processes as straightforward as possible. The model contains four community distribution algorithms that may be used to distribute each of the components of population change. The user, however, has the option of entering additional distributions if desired.

Figure A-4

Economic/Demographic Assessment Model
Labor Market Submodel

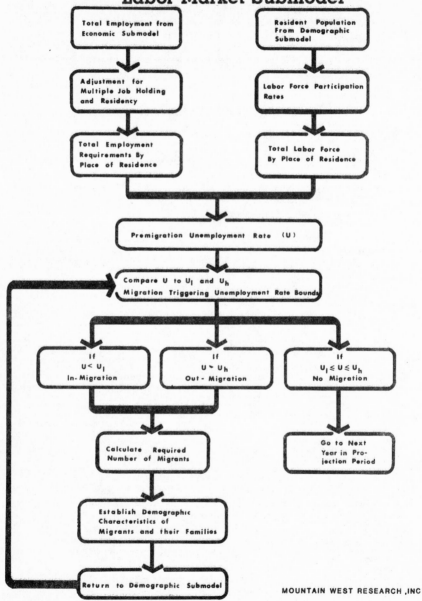

MOUNTAIN WEST RESEARCH ,INC

The first distribution generated by the model is based on each community's share of the county's population for the first forecast year. A second option is based on each community's share of the county's population for the previous year. The third distribution formula uses the growth experience of each community between the first census year and the first forecast year, relative to the overall growth of the county during that period. Nonlocal construction workers and their dependents are allocated on a project basis according to the allocation assumptions of the construction worker submodel or the allocations supplied by the user in the project management submodel.

Project Information System

The project information system is a data base program that keeps track of project-related information individually. For each identifiable project within the region, the system stores the following information:

-- Name and type of project
-- First and last year of project
-- Project employment by year
-- Average wages paid by year
-- Nonmover/mover proportions by year
-- Community distribution of nonmovers
-- Community choice of movers
-- Local purchases of materials and services by sector and year

The program has been designed to accept user input for these items and allows the user to update the information for a given project at any time. The project information system has been directly linked to the forecasting model so that the user can specify an alternative for a region by selecting which of the projects contained in the data base are to be included in each run. Thus, a set of projections can be made with one set of projects, and another projection run can be produced using a different combination of available projects. In addition, the system can be used to modify project data. An important use is to change project construction timetables and analyze the impacts associated with the change. Although this is a somewhat "typical" alternative futures procedure, the appeal of the project information system lies in the ease of combining projects, eliminating the major sources of human error associated with trying to keep track of what projects were used for each scenario. In addition, the project information system can be used to override the construction worker subroutine.

Construction Worker Submodel

An important use of the model is to analyze the economic and demographic implications of major construction projects. Critical to this analysis is the determination of the likely source of the

construction work force. If a large proportion of the workers are
from the local study area, the impact on the region will be less
than if the project caused the in-migration of a large number of
temporary construction workers. A related issue concerns the residency choices of the temporary work force that migrates to the area.

The construction worker submodel provides a systematic method
for determining the proportion of the construction work force that
will come from within commuting distance of the project (local workers) and the proportion that will migrate into the study area to
work on the project (nonlocal workers). In addition, the submodel
allocates the nonlocal workers to specific communities and areas
around the construction site according to the relative attractiveness of each community and the distance from the project site.

The construction worker submodel may be overridden by the user,
the necessary information to allocate local/nonlocal workers being
provided by the project management program.

A.5 Summary

Obviously, population projections using component methods and
interfacing economic and demographic factors is not something one
would want to do with a desk-top calculator, as was the case with
the mathematical model and share and ratio methods. The component
projections require both large data bases and large computer facilities, to which the assessor may not have access. To obtain
component projections, it may be necessary to contract out to organizations that have such capabilities.

If the decision is made to contract out for the population projection, there are several key factors that must be included in the
request for proposal (RFP). First, the type of projections that are
needed should be clearly stated. The RFP should state that a
cohort-component method is wanted, not just a population projection. The latter could include almost anything from a full-blown
population model to a rough guess. Second, it may be desirable to
specify what age categories are to be used and for how far into the
future the projection is to be made. Third, if the mortality,
birth, and migration rates are not already established, the RFP
should clearly state that the contractor will be responsible for
specifying the rates used in the model. This is extremely important. If the assumptions are not specific or are unknown, the assessor will not be able to judge the adequacy of the model. Keyfitz
(1972) gives some excellent guidelines on the importance of the underlying assumptions and how they should be stated. It would be a
good idea for the assessor to require that the assumptions be stated
in the format proposed by Keyfitz. Lastly, but importantly, the RFP
must clearly state what the population projection is needed for, the
dimensions of the project, and its starting time, duration, and
location.

Frequently, several population projections are needed, not just
one. For example, a population projection may be made with one
level of fertility, which may be considered "high," another projection with a level of fertility considered "medium," and a third one
with a fertility level considered "low." The three projections are

then compared and implications are derived. For impact assessment, a number of projections are often needed: one without the proposed action and one for each of the proposed alternatives. It is useful if the projections are presented in both tabular and graphic form.

Once the assessor has the population projections in hand, they should be seriously studied and evaluated before being used. Population projections cannot be used uncritically. Indeed, population projections are least effective if they are seen as strictly a mechanical process (Morrison 1977). Questions that need to be asked include: Are the projections reasonable? Do they match what is known about the project? In essence, the assessor should be completely familiar with the projections and what they imply before using them.

A final word of caution: population projections for small areas are prone to large errors, mostly due to the factor of migration. This problem is confounded in projections for impact assessment. For these reasons population projections should be used carefully and not be made for more than twenty years into the future (Shryock and Siegel 1975).

As stated at the beginning of this section, the population projection is of fundamental importance to the assessment process. It deserves the full attention and critical thinking of the assessor. It must be kept in mind that the assessment begins with the population projection. If these projections are in serious error, all subsequent results are jeopardized.

A.6 References

The references cited here are sufficient to introduce the assessor to population projections and to economic/demographic analysis. The book by Pittenger is especially recommended as an excellent introduction.

Argonne National Laboratory
 1976 A Framework for Projecting Employment and Population Changes Accompanying Energy Development. Argonne, Ill.: Argonne National Libraries.

Bogue, Donald
 1969 Principles of Demography. New York: Wiley.

 1974 Techniques for Making Population Projections: How to Make Age-Sex Projections by Electronic Computer. Chicago: Community and Family Study Center.

 1979 Techniques for Making Functional Population Projections. Chicago: Community and Family Study Center.

Booz, Allen, and Hamilton, Inc.
 1974 A Procedures Manual for Assessing the Socioeconomic Impact of the Construction and Operation of Coal Utilization Facilities in the Old West Region. Washington D.C.: Old West Regional Commission.

Dorn, Harold F.
    1950   Pitfalls in Population Forecasts and Projections. Jour-
            nal of the American Statistical Association 45: 311-334.

Irwin, Richard
    1977a   Guide for Local Area Population Projections. Bureau of
            the Census Technical Paper 39. Washington, D.C.: U.S.
            Government Printing Office.

    1977b   Methods and Data Sources for Population Projections of
            Small Areas. In Population Forecasting for Small Areas,
            pp 14-24. Oak Ridge, Tenn.: National Technical Infor-
            mation Service.

Keyfitz, Nathan
    1972   On Future Population. Journal of the American Statisti-
            cal Association 67: 347-363.

    1977   Applied Mathematical Demography. New York: Wiley.

    1981   The Limits of Population Forecasting. Population and
            Development Review 7: 579-593.

    1982   "Can Knowledge Improve Forecasts?" Population and Devel-
            opment Review 8: 729-751.

Leistritz, F. L., et al.
    1979   A Model for Projecting Localized Economic, Demographic,
            and Fiscal Impacts of Large-scale Projects. Western
            Journal of Agricultural Economics 4: 1-16.

Leistritz, F. Larry, and Steven H. Murdock
    1981   The Socioeconomic Impact of Resource Development: Meth-
            ods for Assessment. Boulder, Colo.: Westview.

Matras, Judah
    1977   Introduction to Population: A Sociological Approach.
            Englewood Cliffs, N.J.: Prentice-Hall.

Morrison, Peter A.
    1977   Overview of Forecasting for Small Areas. In Population
            Forecasting for Small Areas, pp 3-13. Oak Ridge Tenn.:
            National Technical Information Service.

Murdock, Steven H., F. Larry Leistritz, and Lonnie L. Jones
    1979   Interfacing Economic and Demographic Models for Rural
            Areas: Design and Methodological Considerations. South-
            ern Journal of Agricultural Economics 11: 139-144.

Murdock, Steven H., J.S. Wieland, and F. Larry Leistritz
    1978   An Assessment of the Validity of the Gravity Model for
            Predicting Community Settlement Patterns in Rural Energy-
            Impact Areas in the West. Land Economics 54: 461-471.

Petersen, William
   1975   Population. 3rd ed. New York: MacMillan.

Pittenger, Donald B.
   1976   Projecting State and Local Populations. Cambridge,
          Mass.: Ballinger.

Resources for the Future, Inc.
   1976   The Regional Economic and Fiscal Impacts of Energy Re-
          source Development: A Case Study of Northern Great
          Plains Coal. Washington, D.C.

Shryock, Henry S., and Jacobs Siegel
   1975   The Methods and Materials of Demography. Washington
          D.C.: U.S. Government Printing Office.

Smith, T. Lynn, and Paul E. Zoph, Jr.
   1975   Demography: Principles and Methods. New York: Alfred.

Tarver, James D., and Thiel R. Black
   1966   Making County Population Projections - A Detailed Expla-
          nation of a Three Component Method, Illustrated by Refer-
          ence to Utah Counties. Logan, Utah: Utah Agricultural
          Experiment Station Bulletin (Technical) 459.

Tiebout, Charles M.
   1962   The Community Economic Base Study. Committee for Econom-
          ic Development Supplementary Paper No. 16. New York:
          Council of Economic Development.

U. S. Department of Commerce
   1977   Population Forecasting for Small Areas. Oak Ridge,
          Tenn.: National Technical Information Service.

Population Estimation

California Office of Planning and Research
   1978   Economic Practices Manual. Sacramento, Calif.:
          California Office of Planning and Research.

Chalmers, J.A. and E. J. Anderson
   1977   Economic/Demographic Assessment Manual. Denver, Colo.:
          U.S. Bureau of Reclamation.

Lee, Everett S. and Harold F. Goldsmith, eds.
   1982   Population Estimates: Methods for Small Area Analysis.
          Beverly Hills, Calif.: Sage.

Morrison, Peter A.
   1971   Demographic Information for Cities: A Manual for Esti-
          mating and Projecting Local Population Characteristics.
          Report R-618-HUN. Santa Monica, Calif.: Rand Corpora-
          tion.

Mountain West Research, Inc.
1979   A Guide to Methods for Impact Assessment of Western
        Coal/Energy Development. Reston, Va.: U.S. Geological
        Survey (Missouri River Basin Commission).

Shryock, Henry S., and Jacobs Siegel
1975   The Methods and Materials of Demography. Washington,
        D.C.: U.S. Government Printing Office.

Smith, Stanley K., and Burt B. Lewis
1980   Some New Techniques for Applying the Housing Unit Method
        of Local Population Estimation. Demography 17: 329-339.

Appendix B:
Guide to Facilities/Services
and Fiscal Assessment

B.1   Introduction

Recently, analysis of effects on the provision of facilities and services in areas affected by large-scale projects has played an increasing role in EIS and site permitting processes. As a result, the methods for conducting the analysis to determine the facility/ service and net fiscal effects of a proposed project have increased dramatically in sophistication and complexity. Forecasts are now frequently made for capital and operating system requirements at a high level of disaggregation, with explicit attention to both annual and cumulative net (revenues minus expenditures) fiscal effects.

This appendix describes two approaches to the analysis of these impacts. One is a quick assessment method that is appropriate for evaluating alternatives that have not yet been specified in detail or for other "order of magnitude" assessments. The second is a comprehensive technique that will yield an analysis of the type and magnitude of the facilities/services impacts and the overall fiscal effects of a proposed action that is thorough enough to serve as the basis for specific planning and mitigation. In both, the purpose of the assessment is to determine what types of changes/response the proposed action will be required of the affected jurisdictions and to assess each jurisdiction's ability to respond. The quick approach focuses on service areas which have been shown to be the critical indicators of impacts on facilities and services, primarily because they require major capital investment as a consequence of population growth. This approach provides a reasonably good estimate of the magnitude of the facilities/services impacts, but does not address each aspect in detail. This approach is usually most appropriate for assessment of a primary or general nature that will be followed by more detailed site-specific assessments, or for the assessment of projects which have large uncertainties regarding work force schedules, location, and project value.

The more detailed technique provides information that is appropriate for planning and mitigation purposes. With this approach, all of the affected jurisdictions are identified, and the impacts assessed at a level of detail useful for site-specific planning and for detailed consideration of mitigation needs. The purpose of this appendix is to familiarize you with these two approaches and to

provide more detailed references for those who may need to conduct a
facilities/services/fiscal assessment. The appendix alone is not
intended to serve as a detailed facilities/services/fiscal manual.

B.2   The Purpose of
Facility/Service/Fiscal Assessment

The primary purpose of a facility/service/fiscal assessment is
to determine how the facilities and services available to local residents will be affected by the proposed action and how the changes
in service/facility demands and revenue sources will affect tax
levels and net fiscal balance. When viewed in its entirety, the
purpose of a facilities/services/fiscal assessment is twofold: (1)
to identify areas requiring planning, expansion, or modification to
meet changing needs, and (2) to assess the burden placed on local
jurisdictions and local residents, their ability to respond, the
potential consequences of inadequate response, and opportunities for
mitigation.

Since the effects of large scale projects are generally not distributed uniformly across time nor among different local jurisdictions, it is important that the methodology be sensitive to both
temporal and jurisdictional differences. The approach suggested
here is composed of five principal steps, which can be utilized for
either the quick or the comprehensive assessment effort.

1) Identify the local jurisdictions, area agencies, and state
   agencies active in the affected area that are either providing services or receiving revenues that would be affected by
   the proposed action, and delineate their responsibilities
   and relationships.

2) Inventory the existing facilities and services of these
   jurisdictions and agencies. This inventory should include
   description of mechanisms by which revenues are obtained
   (e.g., taxing powers, boundaries for ad valorem taxes, and
   revenue sharing strategies) and description of existing
   physical plants, staff characteristics, and staff requirements. When compiling this inventory, it is important that
   deficiencies and total capacities be noted, as this information is important in analyzing ability to respond.

3) Determine the pertinent project inputs and forecast the
   demand for facilities and services and the revenue flows,
   taking into account, where possible, particular needs
   created by rapid growth, temporary growth, and the likely
   characteristics of the new population (which, for example,
   may demand higher service levels or different services than
   the existing population).

4) Analyze the ability of the various jurisdictions and agencies to meet this demand. This analysis requires a combination of fiscal and organizational analysis, since the
   question is twofold: (1) Will the jurisdiction have sufficient funds to provide the service? and (2) Are the lead
   time and organizational characteristics such that problems
   and/or shortages can be avoided? Historical exposure to
   change, the presence of effective ordinances, the existing

structure, and attitudes toward meeting the increased demands are important indicators.

5) Assess the consequences and, if appropriate, delineate and evaluate mitigation measures to address the shortfalls. In the facilities/services/fiscal area (more clearly than most others), problems can be avoided if sufficiently aggressive mitigation measures are taken. Mitigative strategies can include grants, loans, loan guarantees, modification of ordinances, reorganization of governmental boundaries and/or relationships -- the alternatives are very broad.

As mentioned above, this appendix has been designed to provide guidance in addressing facilities/services/fiscal assessment at two levels -- one which estimates and evaluates the magnitude and consequences of the facilities/services impacts of a proposed action or set of actions in general terms and one which analyzes these effects in considerably greater detail. As throughout the guide, it is important that the level of detail of the facilities/services assessment be appropriate to the information available and to the overall assessment effort.

B.3   The Approach

Identify the Affected Jurisdictions and Agencies and Inventory Existing Facilities and Services

This step leads to the preparation of a description of the existing environment and requires an approach similar to that described in chapters 6 and 8 (i.e., it is important to know something about both the existing environment and the proposed action before starting this step in earnest). Here, the main questions to ask are the following:

1) Will the change in population or population characteristics be sufficient to cause an appreciable change in the demand for services? If yes, which ones? What jurisdictions, services, and facilities will be likely to be affected? Will they be able to respond adequately and in time? This requires that you determine the historical relationships between population and facility/service requirements. Some facilities and services are best calibrated on a per capita basis (for example hospital beds) while others are more effectively calibrated on a household basis.

2) Will the change in property values or tax revenues be sufficient to cause an appreciable change in the ability of any jurisdictions or agencies to provide adequate service? Would this provision necessitate changes in local tax rates that would adversely affect any group(s) of local residents (e.g., the elderly)? This step requires an understanding of the taxing mechanisms, the assessed valuation and production levels/valuation of the proposed project, and the costs associated with facility development and service provision.

Level One Approach: Estimating the Magnitude of the Problem

For the quick approach, the following steps and level of detail are recommended. First, list the counties that will be affected by the project, based on the population forecasts and the location of the project. For each of these counties, the boundaries of the municipalities, school districts, hospital districts (or facilities, if private), and significant water and sanitation districts need to be delineated. The following data then need to be compiled:

1) Inventory of key facilities, noting present capacity, local standards, major deficiencies, and unit costs.
   -- County jail
   -- County office building
   -- Municipal office building (usually including police and retention cells)
   -- School buildings
   -- Hospital(s)
   -- Major water treatment plants
   -- Major sewage treatment facilities
2) Inventory of personnel/personnel needs, focusing on personnel essential to service provision and identifying local standards and shortages.
   -- Law enforcement (sworn officers)
   -- Health care (physicians, dentists, nurses, public health nurses)
   -- Human services (mental health, alcohol and drug counselors, family crisis counselors)
   -- Education (teachers, counselors, support staff)
3) Estimates of operating costs that can be used to estimate cost per population (or household) ratios that are adequate for forecasting.
4) Delineation of revenue sources for the key services. At this stage, it is important to understand the overall taxing and revenue flow structure of the jurisdictions being examined. A particular problem in impact situations is that the additional revenues flow to a limited number of jurisdictions (frequently a county and a school district) while the demand for services is manifest in others (particularly municipalities and other school districts). Another frequent problem is that demand for services is manifest prior to the increase in tax revenues. When delineating revenue flows, it is important to be alert to these two types of problems.

Level Two Approach: Detailed Delineation for Comprehensive Assessment

This level of analysis addresses all affected public and quasi-public services. For this approach, considerably more effort is required to inventory the existing level of services and quality of facilities, to establish service standards and decision-rules regarding facility expansion, to delineate revenue flows, and to develop equations for translating baseline and direct project inputs into facility/service/fiscal requirements and net fiscal effects. As with the previous approach, the affected counties must first be identified, and for each affected county the boundaries and characteristics for all of the following districts/jurisdictions/agencies should be delineated:

1) Counties and municipalities
2) School districts
3) Hospital districts (or private hospitals)
4) Water districts
5) Sanitation districts
6) Fire districts
7) Library districts
8) Recreation districts
9) Public and quasi-public human service groups/agencies (mental health, alcohol and drug abuse, sheltered environments, day care, multi-county planning or service groups)

Once this is done, a facility inventory needs to be completed for each of these districts/jurisdictions/agencies which includes the following:

1) Inventory of present facilities, noting present capacity, local standards, and major deficiencies.
2) Inventory of present land holdings, with an assessment of the appropriateness of the land for public use (e.g., as a school site, an office/maintenance site, recreation area).
3) Description of plans to expand service, including expansion time frame, and evaluation of the probability that the project will actually be funded and developed.
4) Delineation of developer requirements and ordinances that require developers to carry the cost of providing facilities.[1] It is important to identify requirements since this means that the costs will be shifted from the jurisdiction to the developer (or purchaser of a home). Examples of developer requirements include:
   -- Land set aside for parks, open space, and schools
   -- Water lines
   -- Sewer lines
   -- Plant investment (water and sewage treatment)
   -- Utility lines
   -- Street improvement
   -- Acquisition of water rights

---

[1]Another important aspect of impact assessment is the analysis of impact on housing. This analysis is usually conducted by the economist/demographer, but may be treated as a separate component or allocated to the facilities/services analyst. Housing forecasts depend upon population forecasts, information about the current housing stock and capacity to develop new housing, housing preferences, and housing provision policies of the developer.

5) Delineation of facility and operational costs. For each of the jurisdictions included in the assessment, it is necessary to identify the costs associated with major capital outlays and with provision of manpower, maintenance, minor capital outlays, and other operational expenses. Based on these data, a coefficient of the relationship between operational and maintenance expenditures and population served can be developed for use in the forecasting steps. To enhance the reliability of the coefficient estimates, it may be useful to include data from other counties in the same state to increase the sample size and guard against biases introduced by a small number of observations.

6) Delineation of fiscal conditions. For each of the jurisdictions, the following characteristics need to be determined:
-- Present indebtedness
-- Debt service requirement
-- Bonding limitations
-- Revenue mechanisms and amounts (ad valorem taxes, sales and use taxes, revenue sharing, intergovernmental transfers, and other taxing authorities/powers)

This information must frequently be compiled from sources at both the state and local level.

Prepare the Existing Environment Report

In preparing the existing environment report, it is recommended that a separate study file be created for each jurisdiction and agency and that these disaggregated files be maintained throughout the assessment process. Aggregating well-documented information from separate files to summarize impacts is easier than trying to reconstruct disaggregated data if other combinations or separate jurisdictions need to be examined. The interviewing and secondary data collection techniques described in chapters 13 and 14 should be applied in obtaining the information necessary to describe the existing environment.

Describe Pertinent Project Inputs

Population Forecasts

Impacts on facilities and services are primarily a function of changes in the population served or of revenues available. In order to adequately assess the facilities/service effects of a project, it is necessary to have annual estimates of the baseline and with-project population. For the level one analysis, these estimates will need to be disaggregated by school-aged children (elementary, junior high, senior high) and by total population for impacted counties and municipalities. For the level two analysis, the estimates may need to be disaggregated into five-year age and sex categories for each of the jurisdictions or service areas. Separate forecasts by single year of age may be needed for detailed analysis of demands on school facilities.

The population data are used to forecast demand for facilities and services (although some demand may be more easily forecast from housing or household estimates). The disaggregated age/sex data are used for generating information about specific health and human services activities/programs.

Revenue Forecasts

In order to assess the effect of the proposed project on the balance between demand and supply, it is also necessary to determine the baseline and with-project revenues for each of the affected jurisdictions. The principal purpose of the revenue forecast is to determine whether forecasted revenues will meet or exceed the forecasted demand for expenditures.

The taxes (or revenue sources) to be forecast for each jurisdiction/agency include the following:

-- Ad valorem taxes
-- Sales and use taxes
-- Receipts from revenue sharing
-- Other local taxes

For the level one analysis, the focus is on determining the annual revenue flow for the entities that are being reviewed. Calculation of total baseline and project-related revenues are generally based on information from state and local service providers and from company estimates (either of actual tax payments or of total value/sales to which local tax rates/formulas can be applied).

Level two analysis requires development of annual revenue flows for each jurisdiction or agency over the study period. This requires thorough examination of local budget data because intergovernmental relationships and revenue flows are frequently complex and are not always evident from the available secondary data. In addition, in level two analysis, careful review with responsible personnel is important in order to obtain information about local policies and plans that will affect future revenue flows and expenditure patterns. Obviously, if numerous jurisdictions are involved, a level two analysis can be a major undertaking requiring substantial field time collecting and confirming the data and preparing the baseline forecasts, not to mention the impact analysis and its confirmation.

It is important to realize that mechanisms which affect flow of funds vary from state to state and from county to county. Consequently, it will be necessary to review the laws, policies, and precedents involving the following:

1) Revenue sharing among local jurisdictions
2) Definitions and effects of home rule
3) Taxing powers of different entities
4) The availability of state impact funds, severance taxes, or conversion taxes

5) The distribution (and timing) of sales and use taxes, if any exist
6) Consolidation, annexation, or boundary change requirements
7) Other laws affecting local taxing powers or funds flows, with particular attention to those dependent upon local initiative/leadership.

Where local governments have considerable flexibility in matters of taxation or revenue sharing, and there are precedents regarding collaboration between jurisdictions, it is more likely that a method can be found to cause funds to flow to the jurisdictions/agencies with the greatest needs than where such flexibility is limited and few precedents exist. It is not at all uncommon in areas impacted by large-scale, high value projects to have large budget surpluses generated in some jurisdictions and large deficits in others because no effective means can be developed to transfer funds.

In the level one analysis, it is important that the mechanisms for facilitating or inhibiting such flows of funds be identified and applied in the impact discussion. In the level two analysis, several alternative forecasts may be made to examine the implications of these types of mechanisms and to identify the optimal strategy from the perspective of minimizing adverse effects. It should be noted carefully, however, that utilization of many of these mechanisms are political decisions that will be made within the local jurisdictions. This feature must not be lost in the assessment effort.

The absence or underestimation of tax revenue data from the proposed action(s) and failure to account for local flexibility in the management of revenues are frequent problems in facilities/services/ fiscal assessment. In general, such failure results in overstatement of the need for additional revenues -- usually translated into direct mitigation by the sponsor of the proposed action. Because project effects are uncertain (due to the options available for local response and the potential for change by the project sponsor) there is increasing interest in establishing contingency arrangements and monitoring programs to identify problems as they occur. Local jurisdictions are warranted in taking a highly risk averse position since they are frequently legally responsible for providing services and shouldering unexpected costs if no alternative arrangements can be made.

Forecast Demand for Facilities and Services

Consistent with the other assessment components, determination of the facilities, services, and fiscal effects of a proposed action requires analysis and forecasting of the baseline or "no-action" alternatives. In the level one assessment, only major capital requirements are identified, with no attempt made to address operation and maintenance costs that could have some long-term effects on local tax rates and/or service quality. However, the level one assessment does identify major staffing shortages. Together, these two aspects of facilities/services provision provide a fairly good indication of the degree of response required from the local jurisdictions and of their ability to respond.

The level two assessment provides detailed examination of all capital and operation and maintenance costs and yields an assessment of the net effect of the proposed action (over the baseline condition) in terms of capital requirements, operation and maintenance costs, and fiscal balances for each of the jurisdictions/agencies. This can be a tedious and complicated process. Although calculations can be done by hand, both the facilities/services and fiscal analysis are frequently done by computer.

Capital Requirements

For both the level one and level two analyses, it is necessary to determine the capital investments that will be required. To do this, a set of standards for the various capital facilities must be developed that is technically and politically appropriate for the communities under study. Developing these standards can be politically sensitive, and it is important that standards currently in use by the affected jurisdiction or mandated by the state be noted and utilized, if appropriate. However, experience has shown that many jurisdictions do not have operational standards, or are utilizing a standard which would be inappropriate under growth conditions (because of economies of scale, for example). A variety of secondary sources can be used to develop a set of standards for capital facilities. For convenience, Figure B-1 provides a set of standards that were developed in 1982 as part of a six-county study in western Colorado. It is felt that these standards would be appropriate for many rural communities in the West, but review of alternative sources and consultation with service providers in the study area to confirm appropriateness is highly recommended.

It should be noted that many agencies do not develop standards that are driven by population, the most useful type of standard for impact assessment. In addition, when dealing with specific facility design and planning, the detailed population characteristics (age/sex characteristics) may become important, but the intricacies of facilities/services program modification and mitigation are beyond the scope of this discussion.

The two main issues to be addressed in forecasting capital facilities requirements and expenditures for impact communities are timing and scaling. Communities which will experience a large temporary population influx that will last for less than ten years have a particular problem. A major strategy issue is how to provide adequate facilities for the peak population without burdening the community with excess capacity for many years after the temporary population has left.

To address this problem, an approach similar to that recommended in chapters 8 and 10 can be used. In this approach, the annual population estimates for the jurisdiction under consideration are graphed, as shown in Figure B-2, for both the baseline and with-project conditions. To determine the magnitude of the peak temporary population (and its resulting service demand), three points are identified on the graph: (1) the point at which the population reaches its temporary or construction phase peak (point A), (2) the point at which the population reaches its long-term permanent level

Figure B-1

Capital Requirements and Capital Costs

FACILITY	STANDARD	COST
City Administrative Space	800 sq. ft./1,000 population	$65/sq. ft.
Water Treatment Capacity	400 gpcd	$.45/gallon
Water Storage	400 gpcd	$.40/gallon
Water Waste Processing	100 gpcd—plant	$1.50/gallon
	1A/100—nonaerated lagoon	$12,000/acre
	1A/1,000—aerated lagoon	$120,000/acre
Streets	1.9 mi./1,000—local/residential	$250,000/mile
	0.9/1,000 collectors	$450,000/mile
	0.5/1,000 arterial	$600,000/mile
	3.3 total	$1,180,000/mile
Parks	6.2 acres/1,000	$24,000/acre
County Administration (not sheriff and jail)	1,000 sq. ft./1,000	$65/sq. ft.
Sheriff Department (includes jail)	400 sq. ft./1,000	$100/sq. ft.
County Shop	1,300 sq. ft./1,000	$40/sq. ft.
City Shop	1,600 sq. ft./1,000	$40/sq. ft.
Solid Waste	0.2/acres/1,000/yr.	$2,000/acre
Libraries	700 sq. ft./1,000	$50/sq. ft.
Fire Halls	1,000 sq. ft./1,000	$50/sq. ft.
Hospitals	3.3 beds/1,000	$65,000/bed

Schools:	sq. ft./student	Optimal Capacity	Site	Cost/sq. ft.
Elementary	80	400	10 acres	$48
Junior High	110	525	21 acres	$60
Senior High	125	650	33 acres	$60

Source: Mountain West Research, Inc., Colorado CITF, February 1982.

Figure B-2
Summary of Population Change

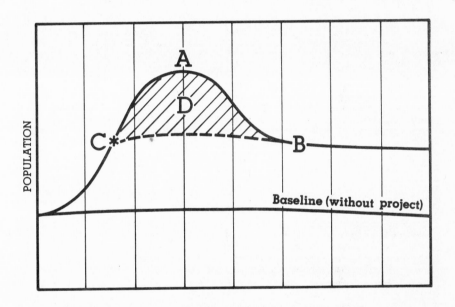

A Peak Temporary Population (with project)

B Long-term Permanent Population (with project)

C Point at which Population Reaches Long-term
Permanent Size

D Temporary Excess Population

(point B), and (3) the earliest point where the long-term permanent population level is reached (point C). By drawing a line between points C and B, it is possible to visually indicate the magnitude and duration of the excess temporary population (or demand) in a way which facilitates clearer assessment of capital facility requirements.

Using Figure B-2 as an example, it would make sense to consider providing permanent facilities adequate to the long-term permanent population, to try to have those facilities in place by the time point C is reached, and to provide temporary facilities to meet the excess temporary demand. By considering the difference in demand between the baseline and with-project conditions at times C, A, and B, the demand effects of the proposed action can be determined.

For level one analysis, the calculations are quite straightforward once existing facilities have been inventoried and standards have been established. They involve multiplying the total with-project population at each time period (for each alternative) by the standard to determine needed capacity, and then comparing that to the capacity required under baseline conditions to determine project-related demand. In order to evaluate the extent of overall demands placed on local decision makers and service providers, it is helpful to examine the timing and magnitude of change required to move from the existing condition to the baseline and with-project conditions. The cost of meeting any projected deficits can then be calculated, and a series of tables constructed for each jurisdiction.

Operation and Maintenance Costs

For the level one analysis, the total effect of the proposed action on area budgets will not be determined, but critical staffing requirements and minor capital outlays will be identified. As with the capital requirements analysis, a set of standards must be developed, either from local sources or from secondary sources. Once the standards have been determined and checked to verify local costs (and have been agreed upon by local officials), an approach similar to that described for capital expenditures is recommended. Utilizing this type of analysis will help facilitate efficient staffing during the temporary peak period, if one exists. Figures B-3 and B-4 provide some examples of standards and costs for staffing and minor capital outlays.

In level two analysis, the operation and maintenance ratios established during the inventory work are utilized, rather than staffing or minor capital outlay standards. These coefficients are applied to the population estimates to forecast total operation and maintenance requirements for each year of the study period for each alternative and for the baseline. Since the number of jurisdictions/agencies is frequently fairly large, it is increasingly common

Figure B-3

Staffing Requirements

MANPOWER GROUP	STANDARD
SWORN OFFICER	2.1/1,000 population
PHYSICIAN	1/1,200 population
DENTIST	1/1,200 population
PUBLIC HEALTH NURSES	1/3,500 population
TEACHERS	1/18 students

Source: Mountain West Research, Inc., Colorado CITF, February 1982.

Figure B-4

Minor Capital Outlays

UNIT	STANDARD	UNIT COST
PATROL CAR	0.7/1,000 population	$14,000
GARBAGE TRUCK	1/6,000 population	80,000
FIRE TRUCK	0.33/1,000 population	110,000
AMBULANCE	1/3,500 population	60,000

Source: Mountain West Research, Inc., Colorado CITF, February 1982.

for these calculations and tabulations to be done by computer, since hand calculation is tedious.[1]

Net Fiscal Balance

The forecasting of net fiscal balance under with-project conditions is central to the issue of facilities/services/fiscal assessment. The level one assessment does not provide comprehensive enough coverage to address fiscal balances, but can provide a good indication of the relative balance between service demands and revenue flows to flag problem areas and indicate which jurisdictions may have difficulty responding to project-related demands.

The level two assessment allows summation of total demand for expenditures (by year) for each jurisdiction -- capital requirements (which can be lagged to take lead time into account) and operation and maintenance expenses. Total expenditures can then be compared to the forecasts of total revenues to yield an annual forecast of the net fiscal balance. This process can be used to explore the consequences of different millage rates or taxing policies on net fiscal balance and to examine the effects of such strategies in terms of cost to residents versus lower service provision.[2]

Assess the Ability of Communities to Respond

Assessing the ability of a community to respond to the demands of a proposed action and identifying possible mitigative requirements constitutes the final step in the assessment process. Currently, this responsibility tends to fall upon the social assessor; unfortunately the facilities/services analysis often stops with the forecasting of service and facility requirements. When making this assessment, it is necessary to consider the following factors:

1) The magnitude of change demanded for any of the affected jurisdictions. If the change requires not only expansion of capacity but also modification in the nature of the organization or operation, the demands upon decision makers, service providers, and service users will be greater than if these types of qualitative changes are not necessary.

---

[1]For small communities (less than 2,500), it may be appropriate to conduct a cross-sectional analysis of communities of various sizes in the same state to develop a coefficient range that will capture the economies and diseconomies of scale which are likely to occur with population change.

[2]If large differences in property tax rates are a possibility, the distributional effects should be examined. Elderly residents on fixed incomes, for example, can be adversely affected by large property tax increases.

2) The cumulative change demanded of all jurisdictions/agencies serving a community. One of the problems created by large-scale development is leadership and administrative overload, accompanied by a crisis of community confidence. The more decisions and changes that are required of a community's facility and services providers over a short time period, the more difficult it is for decisions to be made well and in a timely fashion. Once the community's response begins to lag, uncertainty and anxiety can escalate rapidly, aggravating the response problems.

3) The complexity of the decision-making process regarding appropriate community response. Historically, a high proportion of agriculturally-based communities have experienced declining demand and resource bases, and are characterized by residents who favor conservative fiscal policy. When such communities are faced with complex problems such as those created by large, temporary population peaks, community response mechanisms can become paralyzed as leaders and residents debate the appropriate response. Communities appear to have less difficulty when response strategy is least uncertain.

4) The availability of resources, especially revenues. There is no doubt that communities with clearly adequate revenue flows have an easier time responding than communities where revenue flows are uncertain or inadequate. Inadequacy of revenues is a problem which has plagued many municipalities, limiting their ability to respond.

5) Leadership experience and the nature of existing mechanisms. One of the problems facing impacted communities is the need to mobilize response quickly, before conditions deteriorate, patterns of vested interest are established, and community residents lose confidence in leadership. Communities with experienced leaders (and an experienced populace) may be better prepared to act decisively than communities for which impact is a new experience. There is no question that communities with effective planning mechanisms already in place are at an advantage in marshalling their efforts to control growth and make community level decisions. The existence of clear, strong requirements for subdivisions and developers also facilitates response.

Taking the forecasts of demand for new facilities and services, the net fiscal balance, and these factors into consideration, the facilities/services/fiscal assessment should be summarized for each community. This summary should clarify the ability of the community to prevent service inadequacies, assessing the cost associated with preventing inadequacies and the potential consequences of those inadequacies. It is important that this final summary be made and that the assessment not stop with a description of the number of additional facilities required.

318

B.4 References

Burchell, R. W. and D. Listokin
   1978   The Fiscal Handbook. New Brunswik, N.J.:   Center for
          Urban Policy Research.

Argonne National Laboratories
   1976   A Framework for Projecting Employment and Population
          Changes Accompanying Energy Development: Phase II.
          Argonne, Ill.:   Argonne National Libraries.

Mountain West Research, Inc.
   1979   A Guide to Methods for Impact Assessment of Western
          Coal/Energy Development.   Reston, Va.:   U.S. Geological
          Survey (Missouri River Basin Commission).

Wolins, Martin and Yochanan Wozner
   1982   Revitalizing Residential Settings.   San Francisco:
          Jossey-Bass.

Index

320